Theoretical Scholarship and Applied Practice

Studies in Public and Applied Anthropology

General Editors: **Sarah Pink**, Monash University, Australia, and **Simone Abram**, Durham University

The value of anthropology to public policy, business and third sector initiatives is increasingly recognized, not least due to significant innovations in the discipline. The books published in this series offer important insight into these developments by examining the expanding role of anthropologists practicing their discipline outside academia as well as exploring the ethnographic, methodological and theoretical contribution of anthropology, within and outside academia, to issues of public concern.

Volume 1
Anthropology and Consultancy: Issues and Debates
Edited by Pamela Stewart and Andrew Strathern

Volume 2
Applications of Anthropology: Professional Anthropology in the Twenty-First Century
Edited by Sarah Pink

Volume 3
Fire in the Dark: Telling Gypsiness in North East England
Edited by Sarah Buckler

Volume 4
Visual Interventions: Applied Visual Anthropology
Edited by Sarah Pink

Volume 5
Ethnography and the Corporate Encounter: Reflections on Research in and of Corporations
Edited by Melissa Cefkin

Volume 6
Adventures in Aidland: The Anthropology of Professionals in International Development
Edited by David Mosse

Volume 7
Up, Down, and Sideways: Anthropologists Trace the Pathways of Power
Edited by Rachael Stryker and Roberto J. González

Volume 8
Public Anthropology in a Borderless World
Edited by Sam Beck and Carl A. Maida

Volume 9
Media, Anthropology and Public Engagement
Edited by Sarah Pink and Simone Abram

Volume 10
Witches and Demons: A Comparative Perspective on Witchcraft and Satanism
Jean La Fontaine

Volume 11
Theoretical Scholarship and Applied Practice
Edited by Sarah Pink, Vaike Fors and Tom O'Dell

Theoretical Scholarship and Applied Practice

Edited by

Sarah Pink, Vaike Fors and Tom O'Dell

berghahn
NEW YORK • OXFORD
www.berghahnbooks.com

First published in 2017 by
Berghahn Books
www.berghahnbooks.com

© 2017, 2019 Sarah Pink, Vaike Fors and Tom O'Dell
First paperback edition published in 2019

All rights reserved. Except for the quotation of short passages for the purposes of criticism and review, no part of this book may be reproduced in any form or by any means, electronic or mechanical, including photocopying, recording, or any information storage and retrieval system now known or to be invented, without written permission of the publisher.

Library of Congress Cataloging-in-Publication Data
Names: Pink, Sarah, editor.
Title: Theoretical scholarship and applied practice / edited by Sarah Pink, Vaike Fors, and Tom O'Dell.
Description: New York : Berghahn Books, 2017. | Series: Studies in public and applied anthropology ; volume 11 | Includes bibliographical references and index.
Identifiers: LCCN 2016053590 (print) | LCCN 2017009470 (ebook) | ISBN 9781785334160 (hardback : alk. paper) | ISBN 9781785334177 (ebook)
Subjects: LCSH: Applied anthropology. | Public anthropology.
Classification: LCC GN397.5 .T44 2017 (print) | LCC GN397.5 (ebook) | DDC 301--dc23
LC record available at https://lccn.loc.gov/2016053590

British Library Cataloguing in Publication Data

A catalogue record for this book is available from the British Library

ISBN 978-1-78533-416-0 hardback
ISBN 978-1-78920-528-2 paperback
ISBN 978-1-78533-417-7 ebook

CONTENTS

List of Illustrations   vii

Acknowledgements   viii

PART I. THEORETICAL SCHOLARSHIP AND APPLIED PRACTICE: OPPORTUNITIES, ETHICS AND ENTANGLEMENTS

Introduction: Theoretical Scholarship and Applied Practice: Opportunities and Challenges of Working in the In-between   3
Sarah Pink, Tom O'Dell and Vaike Fors

Chapter 1: Ethics in an Uncertain World: Between Theory and Practice   29
Sarah Pink

PART II. MAKING CONTACT AND MAKING SENSE

Chapter 2: Workshops as Nodes of Knowledge Co-production: Beyond Ideas of Automagical Synergies   53
Martin Berg and Vaike Fors

Chapter 3: The Conversation Analytic Role-play Method: Simulation, Endogenous Impact and Interactional Nudges   73
Elizabeth Stokoe and Rein Sikveland

Chapter 4: Making Theory, Making Interventions: Doing Applied Scholarship at the In-between in Safety Research   97
Sarah Pink, Jennie Morgan and Andrew Dainty

PART III. WORKING IN INTERDISCIPLINARY TEAMS

Chapter 5: From Emplaced Knowing to Interdisciplinary Knowledge: Sensory Ethnography in Energy Research 121
Kerstin Leder Mackley and Sarah Pink

Chapter 6: Working Across Disciplines: Using Visual Methods in Participatory Frameworks 142
Susan Hogan

PART IV. LETTING GO AND MOVING FORWARD

Chapter 7: How to Gain Traction? From Theoretical Scholarship to Applied Outcomes in Energy Demand and Housing Research 169
Yolande Strengers, Cecily Maller and Larissa Nicholls

Chapter 8: The Social Life of HOMAGO 189
Heather A. Horst

Chapter 9: Entanglements: Issues in Applied Research and Theoretical Scholarship 206
Tom O'Dell and Robert Willim

PART V. AFTERWORD

Chapter 10: Afterword: The Deep Dynamics of the In-between 227
Paul Stoller

Index 233

Illustrations

Illustration 2.1: One example of a method to bring together and 'build bridges between these [business and academia] to facilitate knowledge transfer' (Linton and Michanek 2012: 77).   57

Illustration 6.1: Midwife's art work from The Birth Project.   153

Illustration 6.2: Infographics. 5% of Domestic Workers by Matters of the Earth.   154

Illustration 6.3: Artwork from the art elicitation group. The Birth Project.   157

Table 7.1: Studying social life: epistemological and methodological assumptions.   175

Acknowledgements

This book is the outcome of discussions that have taken place across the world over the last years. Our work was generously supported by our project 'Ethnographic Innovations: Exploring Synergies between Applied and Theoretical Scholarship, Developing New Methods across Geographic and Disciplinary Boundaries', which was funded by the Swedish Foundation for International Cooperation in Research and Higher Education (STINT), between the universities of Halmstad, Lund (Sweden) and RMIT (Australia). We are grateful to STINT for this opportunity, as well as to the Swedish Centre for Applied Cultural Analysis at Halmstad University, the Digital Ethnography Research Centre at RMIT University and the Department of Ethnology at Lund University, for supporting our work.

We would also like to acknowledge the work of our contributors, without whom this book would have been impossible, and in particular to thank them all for joining us on this journey and quest to bring the relationship between theoretical scholarship and applied practice more explicitly into debate.

Part I

Theoretical Scholarship and Applied Practice

Opportunities, Ethics and Entanglements

Introduction

THEORETICAL SCHOLARSHIP AND APPLIED PRACTICE
Opportunities and Challenges of Working in the In-between

Sarah Pink, Tom O'Dell and Vaike Fors

Introduction

This book – *Theoretical Scholarship and Applied Practice* – addresses our contemporary context where applied research is increasingly taking centre stage as a core element of the work of academics. This advance of applied practice, however, does not mean that theoretical scholarship is receding. Instead, it signifies that many of us are now participating in a new research environment, where theoretical scholarship and applied practice need to be understood as evolving in relation to each other, not as distant and different fields of research activity. This, we argue, offers a series of opportunities and challenges that we need to address as academics in order to carve out a beneficial and ethical agenda for applied-theoretical research, which is driven by shared concerns of academics and those whom we encounter when we work across different settings and with diverse stakeholders. The particular focus of this book is to respond to this issue through a consideration of how theoretical scholarship and applied practice need to come together in order to develop this agenda as a viable future form of scholarship and practice, and as a way to *be* as an academic.

The bringing together of applied practice and theoretical scholarship might seem to some like an obvious way of working in a world where a range of organizations across corporate, policy and other sectors are already closely engaged with academics. Yet for others this very idea is challenging, and there remains a gulf between the theoretical and the applied. Indeed, some of the scholars whom we contacted during the conceptual stages of putting together a book proposal for this volume congratulated us on taking this initiative, and readily acknowledged the importance of it, but even took pause and wondered if we weren't biting off more than we could chew. Having worked for years in both applied and academic contexts, they were acutely aware of the manner in which these two contexts could (and quite often did) inform one another, but they also pointed out that the positions of applied researchers and their more theoretically oriented peers could be read as a battlefield map with more than its fair share of well-staked-out minefields and entrenched points of tension.

This, however, was not always the case; indeed, much academic research in anthropology, including that led by the academic stars of the history of the discipline – like Margaret Mead and Gregory Bateson (see Pink 2005, 2007 for discussions of this) – had an applied focus. Yet during the course of history since then, as the previous century progressed, a thought that remains disturbingly familiar in contemporary academia was hosted. Its proponents imagined a division between applied and theoretical forms of cultural and social research. It did not take long before this thought was transformed into something akin to conventional wisdom across some national academic cultures, and a morally charged landscape filled with villains, heroes, gatekeepers and heretics came into view. One of the prevalent vantage points from which we, as the editors to this volume, surveyed this landscape – first as students and later as professionals – was that of anthropology. Yet, however ingrained it has become, this view is now not sustainable and neither is it played out in our academic practice. As scholars and researchers whose careers have grown through routes that have included undertaking applied, critical and interventional research, we have never wanted or needed to separate theoretical scholarship and applied practice in our work. Indeed, it is unlikely that it would have occurred to us that these might be separated out, had academics of previous generations not sought to distinguish their ivory towers from what was imagined to be the less intellectual task of applied practice (see for example Mills 2005, Wright 2005).

We are not the only academics who take this view: there are many anthropologists across the globe who are actively practising applied-theoretical anthropology (e.g. see Cefkin 2009; Beck and Maida 2015; Malefyt and Morais 2012; Sunderland and Denny 2009, 2015). Nevertheless, we have found it difficult to find any existing open articulation of how an ethnographic-theoretical dialogue might be played out in applied anthropology: open a textbook on applied anthropology and the reader enters a world of issues that have been identified as highly relevant by scholars who identify themselves as applied anthropologists. These include: the general historical context of the development of applied anthropology, its methods, settings and roles of use, ethical considerations, and attempts to delineate its domains of engagement (e.g. Ervin 2004; Kedia and van Willigen 2005; Willigen 2002). Obviously, these are all issues that are of the utmost importance for the delineation of any academic field of study. Nonetheless, what is glaringly lacking is a larger and extensive discussion of how forms of applied, public and practised scholarship contribute to the development of cultural and social theory, and vice versa: how abstract theoretical insights can provide concrete proposals, insights or solutions and understandings in concrete contexts of daily life and work.

One explanation for this lacuna is the historical context we have referred to above. Another is simply that these are difficult questions to write about, and more so at an abstract level, since the dialogue between ethnography and theory inevitably, in anthropology at least, always emerges in practice. Likewise, in the wider literature about ethnographic methodology, methods and practice, there is a remarkable lack of advice about how to undertake an ethnographic 'analysis' (see for example texts ranging from Clifford and Marcus 1986; Harris 2007; Mitchell, Melhuus and Wulff 2009; Ingold 2008; O'Reilly 2005; Pink 2013, 2015). While reflexive accounts of ethnographic fieldwork experiences flow easily from the fingertips of many ethnographers, the stories of how they lived between theory and research materials during that time and the subsequent months are little exposed. It seems that it is simply not very conventional for most social and cultural researchers to describe these elements of their craft – or at least it is not something that is part of our training to do (see also O'Dell and Willim 2013; Leder Mackley and Pink 2013). This gap in the existing literature is one of the issues that this book, and the interdisciplinary group of scholars and researchers who have contributed to it, respond to.

Theoretical Scholarship and Applied Practice therefore approaches the relationship between applied and theoretical research from a fresh perspective. We argue for the carving out of a new route forward for applied social and cultural research, and for the ways in which students are educated in this field of research: one that both builds on the ethnographic-theoretical dialogue that lies at the centre of the ability of social anthropology to draw unexpected and fundamental insights about everyday worlds as they are lived *and* that acknowledges the interdisciplinary and multi-stakeholder environments in which applied social and cultural research are played out. Indeed, we propose that unless anthropologists are prepared to build bridges with other disciplines and practices, rather than critically separating and isolating their discipline from others, anthropology is unlikely to flourish as an active and influential discipline. We argue for an applied anthropology that moves forward into a world of diverse stakeholders, shared with designers, psychologists, sociologists and researchers from other cognate disciplines. This need not be an uncritical anthropology, but for it to emerge as an applied discipline that is active in the world does, we argue, require an acceptance of the value of other approaches that are effective in making critical and change-making interventions.

Among anthropologists' debates about the relationship between applied and theoretical research (Pink 2005; Roberts 2005), complaints about the inability of anthropologists to succeed as public intellectuals (unlike, for example, psychologists), particularly in some national contexts (Eriksen 2006) have been especially prevalent. For example, in the United Kingdom, proclamations that anthropology could not be a practical problem-solving discipline guided the discipline in the 1950s (see Mills 2005) and contributed to the rise of applied anthropology as a contested field in subsequent decades (Wright 2005), with distinctions between applied and theoretical anthropology as being respectively 'impure' and 'pure' still abounding in the early twenty-first century (Roberts 2005). As applied anthropology has become increasingly popular, over the last years much has been written about its history, sometimes seeking to explain how such a context has emerged (see for example Kedia and van Willigen 2005; O'Dell 2009; Partridge and Eddy 1987; Pink 2005; Wright 2005; Mills 2005). We do not repeat or rewrite that history here; instead we examine how the contemporary context constitutes a turn in its trajectory, and the possibilities and challenges that this might open up for the future. Indeed, some initiatives have sought to evade or go beyond the impasse created by the applied/theoretical distinction (Field and Fox 2007; Cefkin 2009; Beck and Maida 2015; Pink and Abram 2015). In fact, the Berghahn book series 'Studies in Public and Applied Anthropology', in which this book is published was established in 2003 specifically for the purpose of bringing applied research into an academic publishing context as a valid contribution to the theoretical and critical work of the discipline. The more recent 'turn' to applied research that we refer to advances this further. It is one in which, across various national contexts and for multiple reasons, academics from the social sciences and humanities are becoming increasingly involved in research that is implicated in catalysing processes of change, intervention or 'impact' in the world, or in evaluating these. This, we suggest, creates an opportunity that calls for a response that will both expand the scope of anthropology and its relationship to its cognate disciplines and demand that it casts off some of its prejudices.

In the remainder of this introduction we outline the contexts through which this exercise takes us, to reflect on interdisciplinary, institutional, national and pedagogical environments, and the opportunities and challenges these raise. We then consider the implications of this for the making of an ethical, responsible and open approach to interdisciplinary applied practice. Finally, we outline the book and its contents.

The Interdisciplinary Context

There has long since been an emphasis on the interdisciplinary nature of the settings that applied anthropologists might find themselves working in, and of their collaborations, for instance with agriculture, development, education, marketing, medical researchers and clinicians (e.g. Chalfen 2007; Kedia and van Willigen 2005; Lammer 2012; Malefyt and Morais 2012). Likewise, there is a history of discussion of the ways in which applied anthropologists work in collaboration (or conflict) with experts and professionals, particularly in international development and policy contexts (e.g. Green 2005; Sillitoe 2007). Indeed, this is demonstrated in several of the chapters of this book, where we see anthropologists working alongside academics from disciplines ranging from the arts and business administration (O'Dell and Willim) to designers and engineers (Leder Mackley and Pink), media studies and education studies (Horst) and organization studies (Pink, Dainty and Morgan).

In *Theoretical Scholarship and Applied Practice* we push this issue further. We go beyond the convention of showing how applied anthropology might get played out in interdisciplinary settings, to instead bringing examples of how applied theoretical-practical scholarship from other disciplines enters into a shared context with anthropology. Some of the most inspiring applied scholars we have encountered in considering how theoretical scholarship and applied practice are being brought together in effective ways are from beyond anthropology; their work has clearly demonstrable impact (a concept we explore below) in the world, and their ways of engaging beyond academia provide excellent examples for anthropology – a discipline which, as we have noted above, has so often bemoaned its inability to become such a sought-after public and applied discipline as, for instance, social psychology. Therefore, rather than simply repeating the tendency to voice anthropology's frustrated sense of entitlement against those disciplines that have traditionally dominated the space of applied and public research, we have invited leading scholars from those fields to contribute to this book. In doing so our intention is twofold: first, to demonstrate how applied anthropology is developing in the context of an ecology of related applied approaches in social science and humanities disciplines; and second, to examine some of the common elements that seem to contribute to the development of successful applied-theoretical combinations across disciplines.

For example, the U.K.-based social psychologist Elizabeth Stokoe has recently been spectacularly successful through her applications of conversation analysis to conflict resolution, through the CARM methodology discussed in Chapter 3. This has led Stokoe to a series of honours including a Ted Talk, a *Wired* magazine innovation fellowship, a Royal Institution talk and industry sponsorship, not to mention that she has also been honoured in the context of her own discipline. Stokoe's strategy of developing a theoretically informed practical method for understanding processes of conflict indeed mirrors some of the ways in which anthropology can be more successfully engaged as an applied methodology. That is, by developing a clearly defined approach that can be applied across a range of settings, in ways that are variable and flexible in terms of context. As Stokoe's work demonstrates this is a very effective way to establish the utility and relevance of an applied methodology. Other examples of successful academic branding of methods that can translate out of academia include Rob Kozinets' *Netnography* (2010), the technique described therein being one that does not necessarily need to be used in an academic context to be effective. As a much earlier example, Etienne Wenger's notion of *Communities of Practice* (1998) has likewise become an important and accessible theoretical concept both in academic research and in research that is able to cross applied-theoretical contexts.

Meanwhile in Sweden, the ethnologist Tom O'Dell has been undertaking an innovative form of applied and public scholarship, collaborating with organizations to develop projects focusing on spas, place marketing, urban planning and an array of destination and community development projects, while simultaneously playing a role as public scholar in the Swedish media. O'Dell has also, for the better part of the past decade, been educating a new generation of applied researchers through a master's programme in applied cultural analysis (MACA) run between Lund University, Sweden, where O'Dell is based, and the University of Copenhagen in Denmark. Such an education enables students to develop particular forms of expertise. Upon the completion of their degrees, MACA students have taken a wide variety of career paths. While some have chosen to work in the private sector for such corporations as Heinz, Capitol Impact, ReD Associates, the Healthy Marketing Team and Deutsche Bahn, others have moved into the public sector, working, for example, in positions that range from the Ontario Ministry of Government and Consumer Services (Toronto), Western Australian Museum (Perth) and the Department of Transportation in California (United States), to positions that give them the opportunity to help refugees in Vermont, or the unemployed in Sweden. The breadth of jobs that these students have been moving into reflects the diversity of the field of employment available to applied cultural analysts, but it also reflects the interdisciplinary approach that has been integrated into the MACA programme. This is a context in which students originating from widely different academic backgrounds are able to pursue and develop their own educational objectives as they come into contact with scholars and professionals from fields such as ethnology, anthropology, design and business administration.

In order to do this, however, students (as well as their teachers) have to navigate between a series of very different academic backgrounds and disciplines as well as occupational fields while simultaneously moving the cultural and social theories that they work with in highly diverse directions, deploying them in both public and private sector contexts. This forces them to perform a double analysis of the cultural phenomenon they are studying, on the one hand, and the manner in which they can communicate their findings to their clients, on the other. Traditionally much of this type of work has been left to students to figure out on their own, as a form of silent knowledge. The important point made by the experiences of MACA, and which is reiterated throughout this book, is the need to more explicitly explain the manner in which the relationship between ethnographic research practice and theory plays out for scholars coming from very different academic backgrounds.

Applied ethnographic research moves, in other words, betwixt and between academic fields, and the manner in which it does so is exemplified here by the work of non-anthropologist contributors presented and discussed in this volume. For instance, sociologist and STS (Science and Technology Studies) scholar Yolande Strengers in Australia has created – together with her Beyond Behaviour Change research group at RMIT University – an applied social practice theory approach. Working with this approach, she and her colleagues engage an agenda for understanding people's relationships to technologies, often in the context of environmental sustainability agendas. Significantly, Strenger's group's work responds critically and theoretically to the popular idea that 'Behaviour Change' programmes can be brought about in order to solve a range of the world's problems. Likewise, in the United Kingdom, Susan Hogan's work brings together art therapy practice and theory with social science methods and documentary practice, to create a novel configuration of applied, creative and academic disciplines that together are effective in revealing and addressing issues in both individual lives and in society. Art therapy is already an established practice outside academic contexts, and likewise art therapy research is an academic activity. Bringing art therapy together with other disciplines and approaches in an applied research domain creates an arena for change making through a theory-practice dialogue.

As is by now clear, we are not interested solely in the question of how anthropology can become more attractive to external research partners and wider publics. Rather, our agenda is to acknowledge the multiplicity of approaches that are emerging across disciplines (as well as in highly diverse occupational categories), and thus to argue for a situated anthropology that accounts for and could also learn from the strategies and approaches of its cognate disciplines of ethnology, social psychology and sociology. However, by no means do we wish to smooth over the differences between the cognate disciplines discussed in this book; it is often between closely aligned disciplines' interests and research practices that the most ferocious disagreements can come about. With this in mind, given that our focus in this book is on the relationship between theoretical scholarship and applied practice, a key difference between disciplines, and between different practitioners in the same discipline, is sometimes how and where theory becomes situated in the practices of research design, fieldwork, analysis and writing. For example, as we have noted above, in anthropology the ethnographic-theoretical dialogue is nearly always considered to be at the core of how anthropological knowledge, debate and critique is generated. Anthropologists have a habit of chipping away at the grand theories proposed by sociologists and others (as well as those of the few anthropologists who also produce grand theories). Indeed, it would be difficult to produce a general theory of society that could not be refuted by the ethnographic work of anthropologists from across the globe on a number of counts. This seems to us to be one of the reasons why so few anthropologists attempt to develop general or universal theories. Exceptions include anthropologists such as Tim Ingold, whose work has been remarkably influential across academic disciplines, yet nevertheless still criticized by some anthropologists (although not by us) precisely for working towards a general theory (see for example Ingold 2011). This tendency towards the specific is both one of the strengths and weaknesses of conventional anthropology. It enables anthropologists to explain difference and detail through an emphasis on in-depth investigations into how particular lives are lived and experienced in particular places. Yet it stands in the way of making more general 'branded' theoretical-methodological propositions, such as those discussed in the following sections. Some would of course be critical even of the idea that such a branding exercise would be a sensible thing for anthropologists to do. Yet the point is that translation of scholarship into applied research worlds tends to thrive on such forms of presentation. The trick then is to be able to achieve this without compromising one's disciplinary, theoretical or methodological principles.

Examples from this book demonstrate how researchers who develop rather different relationships to theory and research findings have been able to work across these boundaries. They show that it is possible to develop theoretically informed work, and indeed to continue to make contributions to academic scholarship, while nevertheless developing approaches that can be translated as externally relevant to industry and public sector partners. For instance, in Chapter 3 Stokoe and Sikveland discuss how they work up the categories they use in their analysis from their data, rather than using existing categories – such as gender or ethnicity – to guide the analysis. However, they also point out that their method is informed by a theory of language, which does guide their technique. Branded as CARM, this technique is translated into a message that can be understood by non-academics. Likewise, in Chapter 5, Leder Mackley and Pink write about research that was not theory-led, from the perspective that their ethnographic analysis was guided by particular categories, but they also sought to derive the categories they used from their research findings. As discussed elsewhere, the categories that emerged – of, for instance, movement, 'feeling right' and improvisation – were not predetermined (see www.energyanddigitalliving.com). Yet in this case, theoretical framings did form a key element of the research design in that the ethnographic practice was informed by a particular theory of the world as a processual and relational world, and on the imperative to learn about the unspoken and experiential elements of the everyday. This method is also presented as a technique that can be used in applied research projects, and is translated into an adaptable process on the website. In contrast, in Chapter 7 Strengers et al. write about research that is more explicitly theory-led, in that they discuss how they have engaged theories of social practice as a means through which to counter the 'positivist behavioural theories' that dominate the fields in which they undertake applied research, such as energy, housing and planning research. They are interested in the question of 'how to *gain traction* with any theoretical orientation that challenges accepted, dominant and inherently more highly valued ways of knowing' (Strengers et al., this volume). Thus in this example showing how theoretical debates can also be played out in the context of applied research agendas, and indeed that it is actually often important to do so precisely because some theoretical orientations tend to support particular political or policy agendas. Indeed, the work of Strengers and her colleagues in their Beyond Behaviour Change research group could be seen as a branding of their approach, and specifically employs social practice theory as a way to reframe research questions and problems as an alternative to existing paradigms that seek to develop 'behaviour change' initiatives.

As we have demonstrated in this section, the ways in which applied research and theoretical scholarship are combined can take a range of different forms, and similarly these can influence the ways in which such work can have impact within academic disciplines, in policy debate and in applied fields such as design and engineering.

Institutional and National Contexts

The work presented in this book, the book itself and the changes that have motivated us to develop it cannot be extricated from a wider set of institutional and national research contexts. As we have noted above, in a contemporary context academics across the globe are being urged by universities and research councils to do research that has impact in the world beyond academia. Because this urge towards applied research is an institutional agenda, it means that it is produced through institutional frameworks, which in turn constitute a whole new world for us to navigate, to seek careers in relation to and to endeavour to do good research within. While such agendas are developed differently in different countries, the national contexts that we have experience of – the United Kingdom, Sweden, Australia and the United States – and that we account for through the work of contributors, have in common an interest in academics undertaking applied research in collaboration with non-academic organizations, which is represented through funding initiatives that have supported the work discussed here.

This context is double-edged. On the one hand it is very welcome in that it supports and encourages scholars in the cultural and social sciences to do applied research, and as such it creates new possibilities, opportunities and forms of recognition for such endeavours. For example, Swedish sociologist Martin Berg (who has co-authored Chapter 2) has investigated the interface between academic research and consultancy in the creative industries as part of the large-scale project Flexit, funded by the Swedish Foundation for Humanities and Social Sciences. The Flexit programme is specifically designed to build bridges between research in social sciences/ humanities and stakeholders outside of academia by offering research positions within industry and other organizations. Through his participation in this programme, Berg had the opportunity to work within the creative industries for three years and to develop an approach that harnessed both academic sociological research on web-based social interaction and applied practice. This is part of a wider agenda. In Scandinavia, research councils now require applicants to clearly explain and legitimate the social and cultural impact of their work, and in a broader European context this is a basic prerequisite demanded of all research funding in the humanities and social sciences that is sponsored by EU research frameworks and programmes. There is also a growing body of government-funded research grants to apply for that demand clearly stated collaborations between academic scholars and industry partners from their applicants.

However, on the other hand this agenda can simultaneously create frameworks for impact that reproduce the very audit cultures that have been critiqued through the application of theoretical analysis to the structures that frame contemporary higher education institutions (see Strathern 2000; Shore and Wright 2015). A good example of this has been discussed through scholarship in the United Kingdom context. Here, as the anthropologist Jon Mitchell describes it:

> ... in the social sciences – among them anthropology – researchers are now to plan for economic and social impact. Scholars applying to the Economic and Social Research Council (ESRC – the member of RCUK that oversees social science funding) are required to develop a 'pathways to impact' statement that outlines their strategies for maximising potential impact. This might include public events, a website or weblog, policy briefing, publication of non-academic outputs (films, novels, comic strip etc.), liaison with governmental or non-governmental organisations etc. (2014: 276–7).

This on the surface would not appear to be a bad idea; yet when we look more deeply at what is required, as Mitchell points out there are mismatches between the RCUK conceptualization of impact and anthropological research. Just as for the 'audit culture' (Strathern 2000) of research ethics, discussed in Chapter 1 'The notion of planned impact poses a particular problem for anthropological research, which is normally based on ethnographic fieldwork that is by definition volatile, unpredictable and difficult to plan' (Mitchell 2014: 278). That is, if planned impact requires us to know in advance what our work will produce, it becomes difficult to reconcile with an understanding of knowing through research as being emergent from the encounter between researcher, participants and theoretical analysis. The conundrum of this situation has been eloquently summarized by anthropologists Daniel Miller and Jolynna Sinanan, who remind us that when it comes to the art of ethnography:

> the expertise lies not with the academic, but with the people they study. It is their creativity and inventiveness, their interpretations and accommodations, their insights and frustrations that we most share, and from them build a picture, a generalized image of what seems to be happening in their world (2014: 1f.)

If we use this insight as a point of departure for ethnographic research (and we in this volume do, as do most ethnographers) then defining the impact of one's work before conducting the research is the equivalent of placing the cart before the horse. Explaining that this order of developing knowledge (from the ground up and not vice versa) is the modus operandi for ethnographic work may be of little reassurance to research funders who want to hear promises of guaranteed results; and this is not helped by the fact that, as Orin Starn points out, 'fieldwork is always caught somewhere between all too predictable discoveries and moments of something like genuine learning and sometimes even revelation' (2015: 6f.). However, the strength of ethnography lies in an awareness that if everyday life looks mundane, it is far from simple. Finding answers to problems anchored in people's behaviours, values, routines and norms requires an appreciation of the complexity of the effort people expend to create a sense of order in their lives. Indeed, in the context of applied research, denying this complexity is even more problematic, since the research field is also likely to be inhabited by other stakeholders in the project who will likewise somehow shape the findings that emerge from a project and what might be done with them.

The drive for impact is therefore of course controversial, because it is part of the very neoliberal form of auditing (O'Dell and Willim 2013, 2015b; Strathern 2000; Shore and Wright 2015) and regulating good applied anthropology reveals itself as problematic. As the sociologists Caroline Knowles and Roger Burrows put it, in the United Kingdom context:

> In sociology and anthropology, research impact should not be problematic: the production and logics of social fabrics are our core business and it would be strange if we were not concerned with influencing them. It is hard to imagine a social issue or a set of circumstances that would not in some way benefit from the influence of sociological or anthropological investigation and analysis. But HEFCE's [the Higher Education Funding Council for England] impact agenda does not in any way embrace this intuitive version of impact (2014: 243).

Critique of such impact systems, what they stand for and awareness of how they frame our research agendas and the implications they have for our research practice are important. However, they should not diminish our enthusiasm for doing good applied-theoretical research, or our will to have a demonstrable impact on the world. What we believe they should do is to feed our awareness of the need to strive for effective applied research agendas across social sciences and humanities research. The chapters in this book offer something to build on in terms of examples of how such research can bring impact to both academic and societal contexts, without necessarily agreeing fully with the political and metric-based agenda that they have become entangled with.

The drive towards applied research, perhaps not funded by research councils but through collaborations with non-academic organizations, also brings a series of other complications and contradictions. These are not unsolvable – and perhaps part of the role of a growing generation of applied-theoretical researchers should be to work on such issues as members of institutions and in the context of actually doing research. We suggest this because some of the challenges faced are related to the ingrained division between applied and theoretical research, where theoretical scholarship in academia has been valued over applied practice. We need to shape a context in academia where the division between these two fields becomes redundant, and where the different configurations that are involved in each type of practice become context for reflection, rather than elements that define merit and prestige. If applied and theoretical research were to be considered and understood as part of the same research process, whereby each supports and informs the other, then the mapping of careers through applied scholarship would be more straightforward.

That said, many of the contemporary crossovers between academic and corporate anthropology are beginning to make the value of these connections evident. Some anthropologists working in corporate settings – especially in technology industries – are gaining increasing recognition as the stars of their fields.

Making Connections

Working as academic scholars in applied contexts also raises pedagogical questions surrounding how to approach external stakeholders, how to communicate both research questions and findings, and how to develop practices where the agendas of different partner organizations and researchers are shared and mutually constructive. Many universities, industries and public organizations today work with 'brokers' and 'facilitators' who are assigned to make contacts and create points of interaction in order to create opportunities for shared projects and the exchange of ideas. Even though this emerging group of professionals has a growing body of literature on methods for creativity and innovation to rely on (see for example Ries 2011; Thiel and Masters 2014), the understandings of the outcomes of these activities, the pedagogies that are generated through them and the reasons why they succeed or fail are scarcely found in academic literature.

Given the current expansion in the field of applied-theoretical research across the social sciences and humanities, there is a corresponding need for some degree of reflexivity regarding how these new configurations of roles and responsibilities are generative of particular outcomes. On a more practical level, there is also a need for an understanding of which models work well. Given that we are dealing here with questions about the human relationships and interactions that underpin the forming of research partnerships, it makes sense that social scientists should have some role in defining this. This lack of understanding leaves the very nexus, the social encounters, of collaborations between different stakeholders unproblematized and undertheorized. In Chapter 2, Martin Berg and Vaike Fors discuss what this entails through their interrogation of a workshop held in Sweden, designed precisely to bring together academics and industry representatives. They argue that in order to rethink applied research practice beyond dichotomies between the applied and theoretical, we need to use pedagogical frameworks to make the encounters between different practices (whether they be across or within the same groups of stakeholders) in applied research practice explicit, and to enable us to reflect upon and, where necessary, subsequently change the ways in which these processes are formulated. Chapter 2 therefore offers an example of a starting point for considering the issues that creating the relationships needed for applied research involves. Indeed, by providing an example of where academics felt there were obstacles to their ability to connect with industry representatives, this example brings to the fore and invites us to consider some of the key elements that should be part of the process through which academics assert their expertise as applied-theoretical researchers. All of the scholars contributing to this volume have experienced different processes of engagement with industrial and other external partners, as well as with research partners based in disciplinary fields other than their own, which have led to very productive and sometimes enduring research relationships. In some cases, these have been brokered by professionals whose role is specifically to create such contacts; in others, they have been made through professional networks, or as a result of public talks we have given. There is thus a growing field of expertise in this area, and as many of the contributions to this volume illuminate, there is a need among academics to further reflect upon where different models for encounters with industry and other external stakeholders might work best.

Through the different parts of the book there is a line of thinking about how to undertake applied research practice that moves beyond more easily accessed facilitators' method handbooks. The chapters of this book all offer different perspectives on how and what collaborators in applied research contexts can learn from working together in different stages of the process. By investigating and elaborating on these learning experiences, readers are invited to discuss and explore how to create engaging collaborative research practices.

The Ethics of Intervention

To conclude this introduction we fold back the discussion to a question that has been latently accumulating throughout the above: to reflect on the ethics and scales of intervention and impact in the world. These issues first emerged in the context of us discussing research that intervenes in the world at all – our very participation in applied research, and our use of theoretical scholarship for that purpose implies a certain sense of moral responsibility towards using our training and skills to play a role in social, economic or cultural change making. The discussion of the impact agenda, as it has been interpreted by scholars in the United Kingdom, also raises questions about *how* we might participate in political and metric-based agendas that both support and exist in tension with the very ways in which knowledge about society can be made and applied through the social sciences. What are the ethics of such participation? These questions are separate from the question of how to deal with the audit cultures of ethical conduct within applied research practice, which are discussed more fully by Sarah Pink in Chapter 1.

Instead, the question becomes one of how we might pursue an ethical research agenda that is informed by and also informs theoretical scholarship and theory building in the social sciences. The contributors to the different chapters of this book respond to this question implicitly in a number of ways. For instance, Strengers et al., associating their work with a theoretical approach that has already been pitched as an argument against a neoliberal behaviour change agenda, are able to show how by using a social practice theory approach they are supporting and furthering an argument against placing responsibility for individuals in, for instance the mitigation of climate change, through shifts in their own micro practices (see for example Shove 2010; Strengers 2013). Pink, Dainty and Morgan likewise attach an agenda to their work which seeks to bring new understandings to questions of how to acknowledge and encourage safety and health at work. In this example, claims about the high level of deaths resulting from accidents at work, for instance, in the construction industry (e.g. Pink et al. 2014) are meant to ensure that readers are aware that there is actually a life or death issue that such research seeks to address, or at least to contribute to if not to definitively solve. Like Strengers and her colleagues, Pink, Dainty and Morgan are also effectively arguing for attention to what people *do* and, in this case, how they already successfully stay safe, and arguing *against* a compliance model that seeks to change the 'bad' behaviour of workers who do not follow regulations. Both of these chapters offer responses to the points made by Mitchell, whose work invites us to contemplate 'the relationship between contemporary research agendas and the ethical programme of neoliberalism' (Mitchell 2014: 294). While Mitchell frames this relationship as problematic within the context of how impact planning 'requires researchers to recast the past and anticipate the future as points on a purposive and successful linear teleology' (2014: 294), when we combine this with the points made by Shove (2010) about the focus on the individual that is embedded in neoliberal approaches, then the point is reinforced. It invites us to ask what the ethics are of not participating, and the extent to which we should moralize about the implications of researchers *not* bringing the capability of their theoretical and applied research skills together to seek to offer alternative solutions to the perennial problems that endure in our cultures and societies.

Ultimately, however, it is not the purpose of this book to moralize about what researchers should or should not do, with whom they should collaborate or what kinds of impact they should seek to have. The work presented here is intended to provoke, to inspire and to suggest and demonstrate possible ways forward. It is not a set template for working between applied practice and theoretical scholarship, but an invitation to researchers at all stages of their careers, to engage in the practice, the theory and the debate, as participants in this emergent field as it develops.

The Chapters

Each chapter addresses a series of common key themes (outlined below) that are brought to life through the discussion of a central example of actual empirical applied-theoretical research, through which the themes will be developed. In addition to this, all the contributors to this volume have been invited to contribute because they are involved in developing significant projects that combine theoretical and applied research, and include world leaders in their fields, who are equally widely known for their methodological work and achievements as well as their success in applied research in different but related disciplines. For example, Sarah Pink and Heather Horst's interdisciplinary applied work is rooted in anthropology, and Tom O'Dell's work is likewise interdisciplinary but rooted in ethnology, with close links to anthropology. However, many of the scholars participating in this volume have backgrounds in subjects other than anthropology. Elizabeth Stokoe, for example, engages the realm between applied and theoretical from her position as a professor in social interaction with a background in social psychology and an ongoing methodological specialization in conversation analysis. Vaike Fors's academic background is in pedagogy, but her applied work is heavily informed by the fields of anthropology and cultural sociology with a methodological emphasis on sensory ethnography, and Susan Hogan works at the intersection of art therapy and visual anthropology methods. Yolande Strengers, Cecily Maller and Larissa Nicholls work mainly in the discipline of sociology, as does that of Martin Berg. The issues that they describe encountering and facing appear rather similar, even if the precise ways in which they bring together the applied and the theoretical differ to some extent, as outlined above. Thus, while anthropology constitutes the predominant base from which this book views the applied/theoretical nexus, often the individual chapters included in this volume work to widen the scope of our understanding of how practice and theory can be understood to not only inform one another, but to be tightly integrated.

This book is divided into five parts. The first part is shared by this introduction and, in Chapter 1, Sarah Pink's discussion of ethics in a contemporary field of applied-theoretical research. Here, following on from some of the core themes identified in the introduction, Pink puts at the core of her discussion what she refers to as a 'deep irony', although not one that leaves us without hope. This, she argues, suggests that we need to rethink ethics in the context of a new demand for research that has interventional and change-making consequences in the world. Building on the discussion of how applied research has been co-opted by initiatives such as the U.K. impact agenda, which we have referred to in this introduction, in Chapter 1 Pink shows how doing ethics for applied research is framed by similar institutional initiatives. These, by seeking to constitute ethics in advance of the uncertain research and intervention scenarios in which ethical conduct will actually play out, leave little scope for the dialogues between practice and theory through which research emerges. Here, she suggests the possibility that 'the institutional governance of research ethics has the (perhaps unintended) consequence of limiting the potential of research, design and intervention to enter into the improvisatory open-ended collaborations that enable successful, participatory and ethical change making'. She argues that ethics need to be thought out in ways that account for the processual nature of applied-theoretical research and intervention, to account for change making and to welcome generative forms of uncertainty.

Having framed as such the issues and debates in which a contemporary turn towards applied-theoretical dialogue is emerging, Part II of this book – Making Contact and Making Sense – focuses on the role of applied-theoretical research in 'making contact' and 'making sense'. That is, it looks at questions around understanding, and making communication between different groups of people work in new ways. The role of the applied anthropologist has often been referred to as that of 'cultural broker'. This part of the book shows how this conceptualization is actually common across other applied-theoretical disciplines and approaches, in that it draws on examples developed by researchers in social psychology, sociology, education studies and anthropology. It examines and establishes the potential of research that develops a strong applied-theoretical relationship in contexts of mediation, communication and regulatory frameworks. It also engages with different methods (which are of relevance to researchers across disciplines), workshops (which are becoming an increasingly important part of the way that social researchers and non-academic stakeholders engage with each other), ethnography (used across anthropology, sociology and human geography) and conversation analysis (used across social psychology, sociology and some parts of human geography).

In Chapter 2 Martin Berg and Vaike Fors critically review academic-industry collaborations in so-called idea-generating workshop models, and how academic scholars experience these. Instead of a more conventional critique of intellectual stagnation and loss of critical stance, the authors focus on how such workshops – described in widely used method handbooks within the creative industries – are played out, both in terms of advantages and pitfalls (see also Strengers et al., this volume). With a starting point in common descriptions of how these encounters provide 'automagical' synergies just by putting together people with different backgrounds according to workshop methods, this chapter moves beyond these black-boxed descriptions and analyses what happens in these rich social and cultural encounters between professional practices. The fieldwork presented in this chapter is done at a so-called 'innovation camp', where academic scholars and people from small companies were brought together at a workshop facilitated by workshop experts in order to bring about creativity and innovation. The analysis of the fieldwork unveils how these strict workshop protocols can in practice become counterproductive, and in fact have the converse effect, of constraining social learning. By contrasting innovation with cultural improvisation (with reference to Hallam and Ingold 2007), the authors open up new routes for further explorations of how to both understand and develop workshop encounters as material and intellectual door-openers between different stakeholders.

In Chapter 3, Elizabeth Stokoe and Rein Sikveland provide an important but different contribution to this volume. Rather than being grounded in ethnography, as most of the chapters to this book are, their work is anchored in conversation analysis. More specifically, their chapter illustrates the manner in which a very particular form of conversation analysis, Conversation Analytic Role-play Method (CARM), that has been developed by Stokoe, can provide invaluable insights leading to direct interventions in a wide array of occupational fields. Their chapter in this volume explains how CARM, building upon ethnomethodology, can contribute to communication training, helping to change the manner in which the individuals they work with (in this case a mediation service geared to resolve conflicts between neighbours or partners) engage and connect communicatively with the clients to whom they are trying to provide services. One of the important points about theory and practice that their chapter illuminates concerns the risks that top-down theory-driven engagements with actors in daily life social contexts present for producing egregious conclusions that can be avoided when the study of what people actually do and say is foregrounded over theory.

Next, in Chapter 4, Sarah Pink, Jennie Morgan and Andrew Dainty focus on another aspect of the making sense process, in their demonstration of what might be seen as a rather typically anthropological approach, whereby 'the ethnographic-theoretical dialogue can produce alternative ways of understanding the realities of the everyday worlds that applied research focuses on'. However, it is their aim not simply to use this technique conventionally to understand and make theoretical arguments about the findings of their research, but instead to consider its purpose for 'generating new ways of creating innovative applied interventions that advance both theory and practice for change' (Pink et al., this volume). The field they refer to, occupational safety and health (OSH), has been virtually unaccounted for by anthropologists. Yet as they point out, the statistics for accidents and fatalities at work in the industries they have researched in – particularly in the case of the construction industry – are alarming, thus making this a field which it might be considered 'urgent' for anthropologists to become involved in, in an applied capacity. They argue that by interweaving their ethnographic findings with theoretical explorations, they have been able to produce a series of applied insights that were generated through the ethnographic-theoretical dialogue. In this way, by situating theory building as part of the generative process of applied research, they seek to move debates in this field on.

Part III of the book – Working in Interdisciplinary Teams – focuses on the nature of interdisciplinary working that forms part of how applied-theoretical scholarship is conducted. In this part contributors explore how communications work across disciplines within project teams, the ways in which people from different disciplines work together and the implications of this, and the possibilities that interdisciplinary working offers for applied research.

Chapter 5, by Kerstin Leder Mackley and Sarah Pink, considers the development of applied-theoretical sensory video ethnography research in the context of an interdisciplinary team. Ethnographic description usually focuses on the fieldwork experiences (see Pink 2015), rather than those through which materials are made sense of and shared, yet as is shown here (see also O'Dell and Willim 2013) there is much to learn from a reflection on how theoretical and ethnographic findings and ideas emerge and are communicated to research partners from other disciplines. In such interdisciplinary environments the theoretical and ethnographic principles we work with might need to be compromised so that they can connect to the work of other disciplines.

In Chapter 6, Susan Hogan pushes the discussion of the impact scholarship can have in relation to the everyday life experiences of people beyond academia by problematizing the difficulties that arise in various forms of interdisciplinary or multidisciplinary work. Above all else, she focuses on the fields of tension that arise between the arts, visual methods and scholarship in the social sciences. As Hogan points out, moving between forms of artistic representation and scholarly genres of academic writing brings with it many difficulties. In her case, Hogan worked with video documentation in conjunction with 'The Birth Project'. This project aimed at helping both care providers and birthing women to better understand the ways in which experiences of compassion fatigue, stress, birth suffering and post-natal readjustments can impact upon the mental health of all those involved in the birthing process. From the very beginning, questions of authenticity had to be addressed. What did it mean to place people in front of a camera? Is this a radically different endeavour from placing people in front of an audio recording device? If so, in what way? How does the scholar handle issues of validity when moving between the genres of documentary filming and scientific scholarship? As Hogan points out, it was one thing for her as a scholar to identify key quotes in the video footage she captured, but editing such material into a coherent film sequence is a very different challenge. In addressing these types of issues Hogan's contribution to this volume illuminates the challenges that interdisciplinary work can encounter, particularly when spanning the juncture between the realm of the arts, visual methods and scholarship in the social sciences. However, it also points to the advantages that such interdisciplinary work can have in connecting with and helping to improve the daily lives of people beyond academia – in this case, in relation to issues of mental health for birthing mothers and health care providers alike.

Part IV explores the afterlife of applied-theoretical research. In this context research can both be published by (possibly multi-team) academics and move on as applied findings to be implemented in ways that go beyond the control of the researchers involved. These are again issues that impact on researchers across applied disciplines. The contributors to this part work in sociology, ethnology and anthropology. The chapters in this part explore the question of how to gain 'traction' – that is how to convince and have influence in the contexts where we work as applied-theoretical researchers; what meaning theory can have in such contexts; and the implications of 'letting go' of the research.

The point that Hogan emphasizes is that working at the juncture between disciplines can take many different forms, and in fact, it has to if it is to succeed in delivering concrete results to the diverse groups of people (and problems) we want to help and engage. However, this is a politically complex endeavour in which the interests of many different actors, and hierarchical relations of power, are ever in play, and the playing field is far from symmetrically ordered. It is the asymmetry of this playing field that forms the point of departure for Strengers, Maller and Nicholls's contribution in Part IV of this book. In their chapter they problematize what it means to work with an interpretive 'people perspective' in fields of work dominated by very strong positivist traditions and agendas. How can a cultural theorist make a difference here? How can one make one's voice heard? How, indeed, does one 'gain traction'? One way in which Strengers, Maller and Nicholls have chosen to do this is by assuming the role of the agitator or facilitator, 'in which', they write, 'we seek to disrupt normal practice by introducing different theoretical and methodological orientations' than their more positivist-oriented peers in the environmental and housing fields. It is a way of working that affords them a degree of manoeuvrability away from their partners' presumptions about the 'nature' of their work. But it does so, one could argue, by opening a 'third space' between the dominant positivist view of the engineers they work with, and the daily lives of the people they want to have an impact upon. That is, they use the dominant language of their peers (a language of numbers and quantification) and apply it to their own qualitative research to provide their results with a slightly different profile than many scholars in the cultural sciences are comfortable with, but nonetheless, a profile that is recognizable and understandable to colleagues coming from more positivistic academic traditions. The choices that Strengers, Maller and Nicholls make to meet their scholarly peers on their own terms (at times), are not without problems, as the authors acknowledge, but the intention of their contribution to this volume is to call attention to the compromises that working in between can bear with it. In so doing, it helps us further to open a discussion about what is required for scholars in the cultural and social sciences to 'gain traction' for the ideas their knowledge generates in order to have an impact beyond academia.

Where Strengers, Maller and Nicholls's chapter (and to a certain extent even Hogan's chapter in Part III) work to primarily problematize the 'in-between' in interdisciplinary work and the question of how scholars with different academic backgrounds can make their voices heard, the final two chapters in this volume shift perspective: from considering what happens to ideas and concepts as they move between disciplinary fields, to the question of what happens to them when they leave academia altogether (permanently or temporarily). Central to these two final chapters is the issue that Heather Horst presents: that of 'understanding how ... concepts are exchanged and revalued for different ends or purposes'.

Horst's work takes its point of departure in a large research project based in the United States that aims to understand the connection between American youths and modes of informal learning in connection with digital media and learning theory. The work that Horst was engaged with led to the identification of different (if at times overlapping) ways in which youths learn and work with digital media: Hanging Out, Messing Around, and Geeking Out (or HOMAGO for short). Findings from this research project were published on an open website, written up in a report published in a White Paper, and summarized in a two-page executive summary. They gained mass media attention, not least of which was from large daily newspapers, which in turn led to the further development of the project, in which research results were given life in the reorganization of parts of the Chicago Public Library. And the proverbial carousel proceeded to turn, but it did so in ways that were increasingly beyond the control of any one scholar (or limited group of scholars). As the HOMAGO project developed, jumped fields and came to expression in ever shifting forms (from printed texts, to digital media, to refurbished public spaces) the significance attributed to the concept shifted. As it moved from theory to practice, and back again, it continuously shifted between very different regimes of value, and it did so not because HOMAGO was designed as a top-down project, but because the scholars involved were accustomed to directing their work towards specific groups of practitioners (educators and pedagogues). The project had, in other words, a bifurcated target, leading to the production of scholarly papers, but also direct engagement with educators. In this way, Horst's work raises questions about how we as academics might be able to reframe and rethink our work as being aimed at a receiving audience of not only academic peers, but also one of practitioners and policy makers.

This is the theme that O'Dell and Willim focus upon in the concluding chapter to Part IV of this book. They argue for the development of a deeper appreciation of the academic endeavour as a multi-targeted effort, that does not simply lead to the production of a final report, journal article or monograph, but one that increasingly has to be geared to meet the expectations and goals of very different publics (from those existing in academia to those of very different groups beyond the ivory towers). As part of their argument, they strive to further diminish the strength of the theory/practice dialectic by questioning the degree to which activities beyond academia can truly be understood as 'atheoretical'. O'Dell and Willim's contribution reminds us that many scholarly concepts and theories (from notions concerning culture, identity, flow, the knowledge society and the creative class to multi-culturalism, diversity and branding) do find their way from the halls of academia and gain a new life of their own in society at large. The case is not that the people we work with lack theoretical bases for their work or understandings of the social and cultural world, but more in lines with Horst's argument in this volume, that the significance and meaning of these concepts and theories transform as they move. As a consequence of this insight, O'Dell and Willim argue for the development of new forms of multi-targeted ethnography that are not only sensitive to and engage with the theoretical predispositions of the groups we collaborate with beyond academia, but that even dare to relinquish control of our findings and entrust them (with the expectation that they will be further transformed) to those collaborators. They then go on to ask what we might learn by following the manner in which our research results change and develop in conjunction with the work of our collaborators.

Part V is composed of a short afterword from Paul Stoller (United States), a senior international scholar who has made an important contribution to this field.

Sarah Pink is Professor of Design and Emerging Technologies, and Director of the Emerging Technologies Research Lab, at Monash University, Australia. Her work is interdisciplinary and brings together academic scholarship and applied practice. Her recent publications include the books *Digital Ethnography: Principles and Practice* (2016) and *Digital Materialities: Anthropology and Design* (2016).

Tom O'Dell is a Professor of Ethnology at Lund University, Sweden. He is Guest Professor of Ethnology at Halmstad University, and Stockholm University, Sweden. Among his previous publications are *Spas and the Cultural Economy of Hospitality*, *Magic and the Senses*, and *Culture Unbound: Americanization and Everyday Life in Sweden*.

Vaike Fors is Associate Professor of Pedagogy in the School of Information Technology at Halmstad University, Sweden. She formerly led SCACA (the Swedish Centre for Applied Social and Cultural Analysis) and her applied work includes collaborative projects with both the museum sector and industry. Her area of expertise lies in the fields of visual and sensory ethnography in relation to research on learning and digital technologies. Recent publications include *Visuella metoder* (2015).

References

Beck, S. and C.A. Maida (eds). 2015. *Public Anthropology in a Borderless World*. Oxford/New York: Berghahn Books.
Cefkin, M. 2009. 'Introduction: Business, Anthropology, and the Growth of Corporate Ethnography', in M. Cefkin (ed.), *Ethnography and the Corporate Encounter: Reflections on Research in and of Corporations*. Oxford/New York: Berghahn Books, pp. 1–37.
Chalfen, R. and Rich M. 2007. 'Combining the Applied. The Visual and the Medical: Patients Teaching Physicians with Visual Narratives', in S. Pink (ed.), *Visual Interventions*. Oxford/New York: Berghahn Books, pp. 53–70.
Clifford, J. and G. Marcus. 1986. *Writing Culture*. Berkeley, CA: University of California Press.
Eriksen, T.H. 2006. *Engaging Anthropology: The Case for a Public Presence*. Oxford: Berg.
Ervin, A. 2004. *Applied Anthropology: Tools and Perspectives for Contemporary Practice*. Boston, MA: Pearson/Allyn & Bacon.
Field, L. and Fox, R. 2007. *Anthropology put to Work*, Oxford: Berg.
Fischer, M. 2003. *Emergent Forms of Life and the Anthropological Voice*. Durham, NC: Duke University Press.
Green, M. 2005. 'International Development, Social Analysis, … and Anthropology?: Applying Anthropology in and to Development', in S. Pink (ed.), *Applications of Anthropology: Professional Anthropology in the Twenty-first Century*. Oxford/New York: Berghahn Books.

Hallam, E. and T. Ingold. 2007. 'Creativity and Cultural Improvisation: An Introduction', in E. Hallam and T. Ingold (eds), *Creativity and Cultural Improvisation*. Oxford: Berg.
Harris, M. 2007. 'Introduction: Ways of Knowing', in M. Harris (ed.), *Ways of Knowing: New Approaches in the Anthropology of Experience and Learning*. Oxford/New York: Berghahn Books.
Ingold, T. 2008. 'Anthropology is *not* Ethnography', *Proceedings of the British Academy* 154(11): 69–92.
Ingold, T. 2011. 'Worlds of sense and sensing the world: Reply to David Howes'. *Social Anthropology*, vol 19, no. 3, pp. 313–317, 323–327.
Kedia, S. and J. van Willigen. 2005. 'Applied Anthropology: Context for Domains of Application', in S. Kedia and J. Willigen (eds), *Applied Anthropology*. London: Praeger Publishers, pp. 1–32.
Knowles, C. and R. Burrows. 2014. 'The Impact of Impact', *Etnográfica* 18(2). Available online at http://etnografica.revues.org/3652.
Kozinets, R. 2010. *Netnography*. London: Sage.
Lammer, C. 2012. 'Healing Mirrors: Body Arts and Ethnographic Methodologies', in S. Pink (ed.), *Advances in Visual Methodology*. London: Sage.
Leder Mackley, K. and S. Pink 2013. 'From Emplaced Knowing to Interdisciplinary Knowledge: Sensory Ethnography in Energy Research', *Senses and Society* 8(3): 335–53.
Malefyt, D.V.T. and R. Morais. 2012. *Advertising and Anthropology: Ethnographic Practice and Cultural Perspectives*. London: Bloomsbury.
Miller, D. and J. Sinanan. 2014. *Webcam*. Cambridge: Polity Press.
Mills. D. 2005. 'Dinner at Claridges? Anthropology and the "Captains of Industry", 1947–1955', in S. Pink (ed.), *Applications of Anthropology: Professional Anthropology in the Twenty-first Century*. Oxford/New York: Berghahn Books.
Mitchell, J.P. 2014. 'Anthropologists Behaving Badly? Impact and the Politics of Evaluation in an Era of Accountability', *Etnográfica* 18(2): 275–97.
Mitchell, J.P., M. Melhuus and H. Wulff (eds). 2009. *Ethnographic Practice in the Present*. Oxford/New York: Berghahn Books.
Morean, B. 2007. *Ethnography at Work*. Oxford: Berg.
O'Dell, T. 2009. 'What's the Use of Culture?', *Culture Unbound*. 1(1): 15–29.
O'Dell, T. and R. Willim. 2013. 'Transcription and the Senses: Cultural Analysis When It Entails More Than Words', *Senses and Society* 8(3): 314–34.
O'Dell, T. and R. Willim. 2015a. 'Rendering Culture and Multi-Targeted Ethnography', *Ethnologia Scandinavica* 45: 89–102.
O'Dell, T. and R. Willim. 2015b. 'Applied Cultural Analysis and the Compositional Practices of Rendering Ethnography', in P. Sunderland and R. Denny (eds), *Handbook of Anthropology in Business*. Walnut Creek, CA: Left Coast Press.
O'Reilly, K. 2005. *Ethnographic Methods*. London: Routledge.
Partridge, W.L. and E.M. Eddy. 1987. 'The Development of Applied Anthropology in America', in E. Eddy and W. Partridge (eds), *Applied Anthropology in America*. New York, NY: Colombia University Press, pp. 3–58.
Pink, S. 2005. *Applications of Anthropology: Professional Anthropology in the Twenty-first Century*. Oxford/New York: Berghahn Books.
Pink, S. 2007. *Visual Interventions*. Oxford/New York: Berghahn Books.
Pink, S. 2013. *Doing Visual Ethnography*. London: Sage.
Pink, S. 2015. *Doing Sensory Ethnography*. London: Sage.
Pink, S. and S. Abram (eds). 2015. *Media, Anthropology and Public Engagement*. Oxford/New York: Berghahn Books.

Pink, S., J. Morgan and A. Dainty. 2014. 'Safety in Movement: mobile workers, mobile media', *Mobile Media and Communication* 2(3): 335–351.

Ries, E. 2011. *The Lean Startup: How Today's Entrepreneurs Use Continuous Innovation to Create Radically Successful Businesses.* New York, NY: Crown Business.

Roberts, S. 2005. 'The Pure and the Impure? Reflections on Applying Anthropology and Doing Ethnography' in S. Pink (ed) *Applications of Anthropology.* Oxford/New York: Berghahn Books.

Shore, C. and S. Wright. 2015. 'Governing by Numbers: Audit Culture, Rankings and the New World Order', *Social Anthropology* 23(1): 22–28.

Shove, E. 2010. 'Beyond the ABC: Climate Change Policy and Theories of Social Change', *Environment and Planning A* 42(6): 1273–85.

Sillitoe, P. 2007. 'Anthropologists Only Need Apply: Challenges of Applied Anthropology', *Journal of the Royal Anthropological Institute* 13(1): 147–65.

Starn, O. 2015. 'Introduction', in O. Starn (ed.), *Writing Culture and the Life of Anthropology.* Durham, NC: Duke University Press.

Strathern, M. 2000. 'Afterword: Accountability … and Ethnography', in M. Strathern (ed.), *Audit Cultures: Anthropological Studies in Accountability.* London: Routledge.

Strathern, M. 2006. 'A Community of Critics? Thoughts on New Knowledge', *The Journal of the Royal Anthropological Institute* 12(1): 191–209.

Strengers, Y. 2013. *Smart Energy Technologies in Everyday Life: Smart Utopia?* London: Palgrave Macmillan.

Sunderland, P. and R. Denny. 2009. *Doing Anthropology in Consumer Research.* Walnut Creek, CA: Left Coast Press.

Sunderland, P. and R. Denny. 2015. *Handbook of Anthropology in Business.* Walnut Creek, CA: Left Coast Press.

Thiel, T. and B. Masters. 2014. *Zero to One: Notes on Startups, or How to Build the Future.* New York, NY: Crown Business.

Van Willigen, J. 2002. *Applied Anthropology: An Introduction.* Westport, CT: Bergin & Garvey.

Wenger, E. 1998. *Communities of Practice: Learning, Meaning, and Identity.* Cambridge: Cambridge University Press.

Wright, S. 2005. 'Machetes into a Jungle? A History of Anthropology in Policy and Practice, 1981–2000', in S. Pink (ed.), *Applications of Anthropology: Professional Anthropology in the Twenty-first Century.* Oxford/New York: Berghahn Books, pp. 27–54.

Chapter 1

ETHICS IN AN UNCERTAIN WORLD
Between Theory and Practice

Sarah Pink

Introduction

The ethics of applied scholarly research are, like those of all academic research projects, increasingly regulated by institutionally driven ethical approval processes. While the precise extents and ways in which this is done vary across different national contexts, ethics are definitely on the agenda in new ways – for institutions, critical scholars and applied researchers. There are undeniably some positive and constructive aspects associated with these moves. Yet there is one deep irony: in an era where applied scholarship and the need for research to have impact and make positive change in the world are emphasized, the institutional governance of research ethics has the (perhaps unintended) consequence of limiting the potential of research, design and intervention to enter into the improvisatory open-ended collaborations that enable successful, participatory and ethical change making. While research that is intended to have an impact and to lead to interventions in the world necessarily has to embrace the unknown and the uncertainty of the future, ethical regulation seeks (like other regulatory and audit frameworks discussed below and in the Introduction and 5 of this book) to create forms of certainty.

The involvement of research institutions such as universities in the ethical practice of researchers is not always a bad thing. When developed in a responsible way that is sensitive to disciplinary practice, and which acknowledges that (most) researchers already take on board ethical responsibilities, even bureaucratically framed discussions of ethics can be helpful. The very process of going through an ethical approval application can invite reflection on aspects of the research process and the ethical consequences of particular methods that we would not otherwise have engaged with. Yet there are some issues concerning the institutional governance of ethical practice that need to be problematized because they cannot map onto the theoretical understandings of the world that underpin improvisatory future-oriented research and intervention practice. This does not mean that such practice is unethical. On the contrary; it reveals that there are theoretical understandings of the world that ethical approval processes appear not to account for and that this failure could potentially impede groundbreaking ethical ways of undertaking research and intervention. In this chapter I discuss some of these issues, arguing that we need to be mindful of them (but not paranoid) and work towards new forms of awareness about how ethical research practice embraces uncertainty. In doing so, I discuss some examples of how ethics have been played out in the context of projects that recognize that we live, research in and are (with research and intervention participants) part of a processual, continually emergent and uncertain world.

Ethics and Uncertainty

Questions of certainty and uncertainty are at the core of institutional ethical approval processes. Put simply, by creating the certainty that research will be ethical if approved, ethical approval processes can dispel uncertainty and relieve anxieties around the use of a range of innovative and traditional methods in research. Yet when our research is motivated through an understanding that we live in an uncertain world whose future is unknown, this creates an impasse. Research that seeks to make change, to co-design new ways of doing and being and to share responsibility with participants cannot be based on certainties about what will be encountered and what will happen when it is. Intervention and change-making research, whether through applied social sciences or at the interface between social and design research disciplines, needs precisely to harness the improvisatory potential of humans to deal with uncertainty as they keep moving on into the unknown of the future. As such, it deals in uncertainties, and not in the expectation that we know what we will find in the world, or that we could ever produce a predetermined framework through which to accommodate it. This viewpoint is well established in anthropology; as Vered Amit put it, 'To overdetermine fieldwork practices is … to undermine the very strength of ethnography, the way in which it deliberately leaves openings for unanticipated discoveries and directions' (2000: 17). The same would apply to any academic discipline for which research is about encountering the not yet known. Yet it is not necessarily a comfortable scenario for ethical approval committees, for whom preventative risk mitigation is preferable to leaving the doors wide open for the unanticipated to happen.

Amit was writing in the context of a discussion of shifts in academic ethnographic research locales and mobilities at the turn of the century; as noted above, this has some strong parallels with the ethical conundrums faced by applied researchers in the second decade of the twenty-first century. However, since then three things have complicated this issue further: a new focus on doing applied research and working across disciplines and with external stakeholders, with its concomitant concentration on research impact; the related new connections between anthropology, ethnography and design; and the digital context in which most applied research is now implicated, even if indirectly. We now generally work in ethnographic worlds that are simultaneously digital and material, where new forms of visuality and mobility are emerging through camera phone and social media use (Hjorth and Pink 2014), and where these elements, along with others, are entangled in the everyday environments in which we research, work and live (Pink et al. 2016). I discuss these issues further on.

Applied research, design and digital mobility, moreover, all call – even if in different ways – for a revised understanding of the temporality of research. While the push towards research with impact and the new connections being forged between the social sciences and design are giving applied scholarship and practice an increasing future orientation, the context Amit discussed was part of an anthropology that was, for ethical reasons, written into the past. In anthropology writing into the past has its roots in critiques of the use of the 'ethnographic present' developed by Johannes Fabian (1983). The ethnographic present, as James Clifford put it, created 'a synchronic suspension' that 'effectively textualizes the other and gives a sense of a reality not in temporal flux, not in the same ambiguous, moving *historical* present that includes and situates the other, the ethnographer and the reader' (Clifford 1986: 111). Writing into the past as such also enabled ethnographers to write in such a way that meant we could – even when facing uncertainty about the question of 'truth', and of what others would do with our accounts – be loyal to our subjects in some way, in that 'if we are condemned to tell stories we cannot control, may we not, at least, tell stories we believe to be true' (Clifford 1986: 121). The current context creates new challenges. Clifford acknowledged the uncertainty of the future and the issues it raised in his mention of the fact that we cannot control what will happen to our writings and accounts of other people's (and by implication our own) lives and experiences. The same has been expressed in the context of ethnographic filmmaking (see Pink 2013 for a discussion of this). However, research that is intended to intervene in the world and to participate in future making raises a new challenge. This is because we can no longer relegate our research to the ethnographic past and take ethical refuge there; instead we need to expand the temporality of our work into the ethnographic future. This simultaneously creates a new temporality for ethical research practice; we are not only responsible for representing what has happened already, but also for participating in what will happen but is not yet known, and indeed with a certain intentionality. This is akin to the design research process advocated by designers Yoko Akama and Alison Prendiville who, drawing on the phenomenological anthropology of Ingold, describe co-designing as a process whereby 'we are engaged in designing ourselves, people and the world around us in an on-going process' (2013: 38). The design anthropologists Gunn and Clausen have also noted that the future orientation of this subdiscipline is something that distinguishes it from traditional anthropology. They draw on Ingold's concept of 'foresight' (Ingold 2012: 27), which they suggest 'as a way of prophesizing about rather than predicting the future, that can welcome how "uncertainty and continuous reframing are keys to innovation" ([Gunn and Clausen] 2013: 174)' (Pink and Leder Mackley 2015). These points are equally relevant to the kind of interventions made in applied and public anthropology practice.

Uncertainty is therefore not new for ethnographic practitioners. However, the temporalities through which we are engaging with it in an applied and impact-focused research context create new issues for us to confront. Whether we are connecting our work to recent developments in design anthropology or considering other ways in which to work with stakeholders towards future change, the implications are similar. We need to ask how we can ethically engage with the unknown as we step forward into the uncertainty of a future in which we seek to intervene with research/design project participants, partners or other stakeholders. This involves considering our roles as researchers working in future temporalities beyond the 'traditional' past-oriented ways of writing up social research that informed the development of earlier ethics frameworks, guidance and protocols (and that also informed our own training).

When participating in interdisciplinary projects that seek to bring about change, the question of how the future might be understood and situated theoretically in such work comes into view. There is a growing literature in the social sciences around how futures are imagined, anticipated and aspired to, and about expectations. Works in this field cover, for instance, the forecasting of economic futures, the place of science fiction in how designers imagine futures, the future scenarios of governmental risk mitigation strategies and more (e.g. Adam and Groves 2007; Anderson 2010; Kinsley 2011; Brown and Michael 2003; Samimian-Darash and Rabinow 2015). I do not go into these debates in detail here, but mention them where relevant in the discussion. However, attending to contemporary ways of conceptualizing the future is also relevant to the ways in which applied research is conceptualized more broadly, because it alerts our attention to the need to comprehend the ways in which the future is perceived by our research partners, stakeholders, clients or other collaborators in applied interdisciplinary work. It is specifically relevant for the study and practical implementation of research ethics because, as I outline below, ethical regulation processes are governed by an anticipatory and preventative logic that seeks to control the future, while ethnography, design and other disciplines might be guided by other ways of conceptualizing and situating the future. When analyses of the ways in which such future-oriented ways of thinking, planning and acting are also used to understand ethics guidelines and frameworks and the work of ethical approval committees, they also offer us a new perspective on how research (and its design) are (ethically) framed by certain ways of comprehending, anticipating and making future worlds in the present.

In the next section I outline a set of historical and contextual issues around the development of ethics in contemporary research and the anticipatory regimes they constitute, and then relate these to the specific context of applied research. Then in the following sections I discuss how ethics scenarios might be played out in applied research that spans the written, visual, digital, sensory and participatory approaches that are becoming increasingly popular when working with external stakeholders.

Audit Cultures and Anticipatory Logics: Two Critical Approaches for Understanding Ethics

Anthropologists have acknowledged and interrogated the impact of what have been called 'audit cultures', which signified the emergence, around the end of the twentieth century, of new forms of accountability in the institutional lives of academics (Strathern 2000; Shore and Wright 2015). This, it has been argued, has led to a context whereby 'Our lives are increasingly governed by – and *through* – numbers, indicators, algorithms and audits and the ever-present concerns with the management of risk' (Shore and Wright 2015: 23). I briefly outline this context and the debates and critical commentaries that were initiated in anthropologists' interrogations, since these offer a starting point for some of the issues I raise and also identify a historical landmark in the making of the contemporary ethics context I discuss below. The rise of ethical approval committees in some national academic contexts in the 1990s was part of this process. According to Peter Pels, traditionally anthropological approaches tended to understand ethics as a form of 'specific technology of the (professional) self', that it was not necessary to discuss in any detail, which 'changed under the influence of the new technologies of domination that characterize the spread of neoliberal market models and auditing techniques' (2000: 136). One of the outcomes of this was that 'codes of ethical conduct are increasingly voluntary means to publically reduce the anxieties that research sponsors and employers might have about research performance' (Pels 2000: 142), and as Amit discusses in relation to the Canadian context, 'an elaborate system of monitoring and surveillance that leaves much to the interpretive discretion of ethics review boards' (2000: 227). Marilyn Strathern summed up that this rendering of people who participate in research as 'human subjects' 'pushes the exploratory, indeterminate and unpredictable nature of human relations (between ethnographer and her or his third party) back onto a "point of production", with the ethnographer as initiator'. The implication, as she put it, was that 'However much talk there is of collaboration or of conserving the autonomy of subjects or recognizing their input into the research or taking power into account, this aspect of *ethics in advance*, of anticipated negotiations, belittles the creative power of social relations' (Strathern 2000: 295, emphasis added). These models reflect what Limor Samimian-Darash and Paul Rabinow have more recently called 'attribution scenarios', which are a 'preparedness technology' that 'create[s] a possible event before one has come about and then treat the proxy event as if it were real and needs to be prepared for' (2015: 6). If we then contrast such approaches to ethics as *'ethics in advance'* with the idea of *ethics as ongoing*, the latter offers more possibilities for empowering research participants to actually participate.

These ethics regimes have thus constituted a context where institutional ethical approval processes tend to focus on a set of core possible 'ills' or problems to be avoided. It is not my intention to document these here, since they vary between contexts, and also tend to be reiterated in ethics guidance and methods books. As I have discussed elsewhere, they cover issues such as informed consent, covert research (and the conditions under which this is considered permissible), anonymity and confidentiality, harm to participants, data management and storage, ownership and timescales for eventual destruction of research materials (Pink 2013), and the ways in which these kinds of issues will be articulated through the use of research methods. They infrequently, however, make provision for harm to researchers, although this is increasingly covered under a different form of regulation, which follows similar anticipatory logics of researcher safety evaluations. These kinds of framework are not completely coherent with traditional anthropological ethnography, whereby the self of the researcher is at the centre of the ethical status of research, as demonstrated in the work of Pels, Amit and Strathern as outlined above. They are moreover complicated by what have been called innovative or creative research methods, and particularly those that make use of the potential of digital technologies. For example, visual research methods challenge the notion of anonymity, because they reveal precisely who participants are, and give them the opportunity to represent themselves through film or photography if they wish (Pink 2013). Likewise, as Markham and Buchanan (2014) have argued, internet research challenges the categories set up by ethical review procedures. For instance, the emphasis on 'human subjects' is problematized in big data contexts, where the humanness of human subjects can sometimes be obscured. Likewise, the participatory possibilities of using online platforms for collaboration make the outcomes of digital methods unpredictable. Moreover, while traditional forms of data can easily be stored in locked cabinets, participant-generated videos of their own lives, which are uploaded to YouTube *with their agreement*, cannot be regulated as such.

Recent discussions (some emerging from visual methods literature) have sought to open up the possibilities of ethical practice through critical but conciliatory approaches to ethical regulation. For instance, the concept of 'situated ethics' (Clarke 2012) suggests that ethical processes that emerge from the research context are useful. I have focused on the ways that collaboration in visual research, working with participants and 'layered' approaches to ongoing consent can be effective in developing ethical approaches (Pink 2013). Additionally, the possible ethical qualities of research that focuses on our embodied experience, sensory perception of the world and empathetic capacities have been commented on by a number of sensory scholars who have indeed suggested that there is a certain moral quality and form of ethical practice attached to research approaches that focus on unspoken and felt empathetic understandings of others (Pink 2015). For instance, Paul Stoller has suggested that 'If we allow humility to work its wonders it can bring sensuousness to our practices and expression. It can enable us to live well in the world' (1997: 137). Indeed, this focus on the embodied and the researcher's experience resonates with Pels' suggestion that the ethics of anthropological ethnography might be seen as 'technologies of the self' (Pels 2000). Yet these approaches go beyond anthropology, and are also rooted in more historical and contemporary uses of sensory approaches and methods in human geography (Pink 2015) and ethical design (Akama 2012).

In a way that is typical of regulatory codes, the ethical approval processes discussed above seek to create certainties. By creating rules around research practices, the uncertainties that they generate can be reassuringly soothed. Such systems create a sense of ethical certainty by framing practice with a set of specific rules. Therefore, following this argument, we could suggest that by creating the certainty that research will be ethical if approved, ethical approval processes can relieve particular sets of anxieties, which might indeed themselves actually be constituted through ethical approval processes. The anxieties might be institutional anxieties, in terms of the need to ensure that researchers do not do anything that would lead an institution to be blamed for their conduct. Yet there is another forgotten element here, since such processes might also create researcher anxieties. Within this context, being 'ethical' becomes less to do with the ethical self, and more to do with responding to the anxieties created through an ethical approval process that seeks to create certainties in what is in fact an uncertain world. Indeed, for the ethnographer – for whom the research process is always a personal experience, and an embodied and reflexive encounter – this is a particularly difficult situation. This is because any concerns that we might experience as ethnographers about ethics – be they in relation to our responsibilities to participants, or our responsibilities to ethics committees – are inevitably also personal. They are not experienced as process, but as human issues that go to the core of our ethical selves. If we see ethical approval processes as a way to deal with uncertainty, this raises a question. Research is for many of us precisely about encountering uncertainty; it brings to the fore the previously unknown, unseen and unexpected. As ethnographers we embrace the uncertain, we follow the new paths that our research invites us along. For instance, video ethnographers often record life as it happens, that is as we continually step with our participants from the present into the future, into what we do not yet know, and cannot yet know. As the future unfolds, we ongoingly confront uncertainties; we improvise around something that has never happened before on the basis of what we have already experienced. If as applied researchers we are to accompany people as they move forward in and through the uncertain world, and seek to accompany them in future making, then how can we guarantee that we will follow the rules of ethical conduct that have been set out for a world of certainties? The harm here then might not be to participants, but to the researcher as an individual who is put in the impossible bind of being responsible both for a research process that is inevitably uncertain and for an institutional ethics process that seeks certainties. While this is written as an abstract scenario, and takes the issue to an extreme, it is nevertheless a possibility that we should be attentive to and mindful of.

The logics of such ethics processes have a future orientation that has its parallels in other regulatory or future-making processes. Indeed, the ideas discussed in this chapter have not emerged because I was specifically interested in analyzing ethics for applied scholarship, but rather because two key themes in my work – both of which involve critically understanding how future scenarios are implemented in professional practice – provided the tools through which to reflect back on ethics. The first is through design research and the second safety research. While these might at first glance sound like unlikely candidates for a comparison with ethics frameworks, both are in fact very relevant. Design practice as outlined above is concerned, in a way that most traditional scholarship is not, with the future. However, in contrast to the open approaches advocated by Akama and Prendiville (2013), Gunn and Clausen (2013) and others writing at the design anthropology interface, other design traditions follow a process that seeks to construct something about the future that *is* or at least *seems* knowable, so that there can be a future scenario to design for. This might involve constructing future scenarios, using ethnographic methods along with economic and other future forecasting data to predict what life will be like and what types of people will live it. In this practice, 'personas' – which are models of future people – are made, based on thematic analyses of sets of real research participants, who are then coalesced into types. Personas have certain characteristics and are expected to act in particular ways. My point here is not to critique the use of personas in design. Interestingly they can be used in and created through participatory design processes, and can potentially play a number of roles in how we imagine the future. Here, however, I note that because they are constructed as points or moments in the future that can be designed towards, their use constitutes a very different logic to that of the ongoingness in designing towards the unknown represented in the work of Akama and Prendiville (2013). While the former approach creates forms of certainty, the latter does not.

The work of human geographers is particular pertinent for understanding future-oriented logics. In relation to design, the work of Kinsley is particularly interesting in discussing how HCI (human-computer interaction) designers' visions of the future tend to be informed by science fiction narratives (Kinsley 2011). However, other work in this discipline offers a way in which to further situate ethics in relation to the progression of anticipatory modes that have emerged in a world where risk mitigation is increasingly important in some domains. For example, work on national security focuses on the concept of prevention, which is also core to occupational safety and health (OSH) regulation (Pink et al. 2015). For instance, for Massumi prevention is 'derivative', and as such he comments that 'preventive measures ... will be regulated by the specialist logics proper to those fields' (Massumi 2007: 6). This can be seen in the case of the work of Adey and Anderson on UK Civil Contingencies (2011), as well as in Pink et al.'s work on OSH (Pink et al. 2015). The discussion of Civil Contingencies shows that it, 'in common with OSH has an anticipatory focus in preparing for emergencies including "industrial accidents" (as well as terrorism and weather) (Adey and Anderson 2011: 2879)' (Pink et al. 2015). Safety practitioners, for instance in occupational safety and health, also work in regulatory contexts where creating certainties, or as near as one can get, is important for the development of processes that will avoid accidents at work. Guidelines are developed with the implication that if they are followed the certainty of safety can be achieved. Yet the problem is that the environments in which safe 'behaviours' or 'practices' are meant to be performed are often uncertain and changing. For instance, writing with Jennie Morgan and Andrew Dainty (see Chapter 4, this volume) from a research project that brings together theoretical scholarship and ethnography to develop applied insights into occupational safety and health, we have discussed how safety is enacted among workers who have to visit other people's homes as part of their jobs. As we have shown there, the home is a site of multiple uncertainties which require improvisatory and contingent solutions that safety guidance regulatory frameworks are ill-equipped to tackle (Pink et al. 2015). Therefore, both Civil Contingencies and OSH both deal similarly with uncertainties through procedures, whereby potentially unpredictable events are already planned for. They are part of a similarly risk-averse preventative logic that is designed to avert scenarios of unethical conduct before they happen. They begin with the premise that harm *could* be caused by potential scenarios and seek to ensure that, through the provision of a series of safeguards, this will not happen. This might seem like a diversion from the issues of ethics, yet institutional ethics procedures are similar in many ways.

In the next section I reflect on a series of examples of how ethical issues have played out in my own experience of future-oriented applied research. I do not pretend to cover all facets of this question, but by approaching it through examples that connect to three key themes my aim is to illustrate how ethics might be encountered in particular ways in such work. These themes are: interdisciplinarity and working with non-academic partners; visual methods – which have generated a significant literature around ethics and are commonly used in applied and impact-focused research and indeed in the work of a number of the contributors to this volume

(Hogan, Stokoe, Leder Mackley and Pink, and Pink, Morgan and Dainty) – and digital methods, which are never far from contemporary research; and sensory methods.

Anticipating Ethics across Disciplines and with External Partners

Several of the chapters in this book deal with interdisciplinarity directly, and all of the chapters, because they are concerned with applied research, inevitably reflect on projects that involve engagements across disciplinary boundaries and/or with external stakeholders. The ethics of social science research – that is, accounting for the social dimensions of research with human subjects when completing ethical approval applications for review by ethics committees – is not always a simple process. It involves interpretation and knowing the meaning of the questions. Doing ethical approval applications across disciplines therefore also needs to be an interdisciplinary endeavour. Furthermore, elements of social research ethics (like those involved in anthropological ethnography, discussed above) that are not accounted for through ethical approval processes are continually negotiated throughout the research process. One outcome of this is that within an interdisciplinary project the terms of engagement between researchers, external stakeholders, participants, the data produced and how this can be published might continually shift throughout the lifetime of the project. This need not impact on original ethical approvals. However, it does create an constantly changing ground in terms of the ways in which team members might be able to work together with research materials or data, what can be revealed and how materials can be used when shared. In this section I comment briefly on some of my experiences of such contexts, with specific reference to chapters in this book, and other existing work.

For example, in Chapter 5 Kerstin Leder Mackley and I discuss the way in which we worked across disciplines with engineers and designers, in the Low Effort Energy Demand Reduction (LEEDR) project in the U.K., and the methods through which we sought to communicate sensory ways of knowing (about) participants in our research in this context. As we note there, our ethical process involved follow-up meetings with participants, so that we could review video recordings with them, and give them the option to edit out any parts of our recordings that they were not happy with. The ethics procedure that we developed for the social science part of this project was 'layered' in that we continually asked participants to review video materials, if and when they wished to, to edit or comment on them, and to give us permission for the publication of written and video materials, if they wished to, on a case by case basis, once they had had an opportunity to check that they were happy with them. In this scenario we could not necessarily know in advance or explain to other members of the LEEDR team what the possibilities would be for our use of any one set of materials, until the arrangements and permissions for those materials had been agreed, after they had been produced. Using the materials within our team – as outlined in Chapter 5 – was indeed possible. One of our reasons for using this careful layered ethics procedure was because I had found it successful in earlier projects to involve participants in consent processes.

In the project discussed in Chapter 4, where I worked with Jennie Morgan and Andrew Dainty in a team developing the ethnographic part of an occupational safety and health project, we used a similar process. Here our ethnographic work was also a strand in a larger interdisciplinary project, and likewise we asked research participants to approve their interview transcripts as well as the uses of visual and written materials relating to them in our publications. Such processes can be time-consuming, but at the same time both ensure that participants who wish to remain engaged in the research can be, and that they are aware of how their materials are being used.

Indeed, research that involves working with industry or other research partners can involve sharing materials with those partners, as well as disseminating them to academic publics and beyond. For example in 2014, with colleagues John Postill (an anthropologist), Yolande Strengers (a sociologist), and Nadia Astari (a documentary filmmaker), I developed the Complex, Clever and Cool (CCC) project in partnership with Unilever in the U.K. Our participants in this video ethnography project, all based in Indonesia, were, like the LEEDR participants, offered a range of options regarding how they would allow their materials to be used in research publications, mainly focusing on questions of which media they would be happy to be published in and whether they would like to be identifiable or not. As for other similar projects I have developed, the agreements that we make with participants also apply when the materials are shared with industry partners. Some such organizations have their own ethical approval processes for research with human subjects. However, as with the international distribution of ethics governance, this tends to be patchy, and often ethics is left to the research institution involved. Whatever the case, when working with shared research materials, gaining insight into the ethical procedures of partner organizations is important, as is working in ways that are ethical and respectful in relation to research partners. Once we had delivered our reports to Unilever in 2014, Nadia Astari and I began to develop the documentary film *Laundry Lives* (2015) based on the Complex,

Clever and Cool project. The film sought to represent a context where with the emergence of the new middle class in an economically vibrant Indonesia, new uses of domestic technologies and configurations for doing domestic work might be implicated in environmental sustainability agendas. In developing this film, we were responsible for ethically representing and consulting with participants, Unilever and their sustainability agenda, and indeed to consider whether the arguments we were making in the film were themselves responsible perspectives on environmental sustainability in domestic life. It was also our intention that the film should be oriented towards the future, in suggesting that the realities and aspirations of the participants we represented in it could be a starting point for considering how to move towards sustainable domestic configurations.

Therefore, in most of my projects, ongoing ethics are also important because our small ethnography teams are not the only researchers or stakeholders involved. In LEEDR, the video and written texts were not the only materials that participants offered to the project. Indeed, the wider project gathered and produced considerably more data about the participants than our ethnographic strand did alone. However, it was through the ethnographic strand that participants were potentially identifiable, due to our use of visual methods and the options we gave them to have their real names used in publications. Therefore we needed to think beyond our own ethical perspectives, or our own knowledge of what we knew about participants, to instead view the ethics of our own work in the context of the participants situated within the project in ways that went far beyond the ethnography. In the IOSH project we did not share participants with other research teams in the project, but our participants all worked in organizations; we did not know whether, if during our research their situations in these workplaces were to change, this would impact on their willingness for us to publish the research materials produced through our research encounters with them or not. Above I have noted the concept of 'situated ethics' (Clarke 2012). In applied social or ethnographic research in the context of large-scale projects the situating of ethics goes much further, and it is up to us to consider, with participants, the meaning of this situatedness. Indeed, this is not a fixed way of thinking about ethics within research, because if we are dealing with our own data about participants while colleagues working in other teams are dealing with theirs in different ways (which we might not even have the tools to understand), the situatedness of participants in projects and the ways in which we deal ethically with the materials they are implicated in likewise shift. Such layering of ethics goes beyond the layers that we create within our own work, and therefore also needs to account for the additional layers that are created by other disciplines or by other stakeholders in research projects. Essentially these are fields of uncertainty, in that we do not know precisely how these ethics entanglements will pan out, or how they will impact on how participants feel themselves to be situated and how this might change during the research process. The outcome is that we need ethical processes to be flexible, ongoing and renegotiable in collaboration with participants as projects of this complexity progress – specifically so that ethical conduct can be achieved. This does not mean more detailed auditing, but rather needs openness to work within sets of relevant principles.

Approaches and Ethics in Applied Research

In this section I continue the discussion of how ethics are implicated in applied research from a different angle, by focusing on methods and approaches. In doing so I again draw from my own work to examine how the ethics of visual (Pink 2013), sensory (Pink 2015) and digital (Pink et al. 2016) methods are situated within the temporalities of applied and impact-focused research.

Visual methods are increasingly used in applied research, and have particularly been associated with applied consumer ethnography, some fields of design and user experience ethnography, health research and applied anthropological filmmaking (see Pink 2007 for a history of this). In the last decade, with the growing international interest in and practical application of visual methods, questions of visual research ethics have engendered an increasingly large field of study, occupying visual methods conferences with great popularity, and generating a significant literature – notwithstanding national and legal differences (Rowe 2012). In English-language research communities, the UK National Centre for Research Methods developed a series of publications emerging from research into how visual ethics were articulated and experienced by researchers (e.g. Prosser et al. 2008; Wiles et al. 2011; Wiles et al. 2012; Clarke 2012) and there is an entry on visual methods in the online ethics guidebook at http://www.ethicsguidebook.ac.uk/Visual-methods-296. Likewise in Australia, a growing interest in visual methods and in the ethical implications that they create is demonstrated in the work of the Visual Research Collaboratory (University of Melbourne), which has produced a set of guidelines for visual ethics in research, online at http://vrc.org.au/guidelines-for-ethical-visual-research-methods. Other discipline-specific guides include the International Visual Sociology Association's ethical guidelines, online at http://visualsociology.org/about/ethics-and-guidelines.html. These discussions have, among other things, attended to the different ways in which ethics is conceptualized across different 'visual' disciplines, to the need for 'situated ethics' (Clarke 2012), and to questions around ensuring that the ethics of visual research is properly understood and acknowledged by ethical approval committees.

Visual research materials (photography and video) have often been associated with the temporality of the past, seen as 'capturing' what has happened, and being appropriately used in ethnographic works in ways that do not pretend that the people photographed 'do this', but that they 'were doing this in the specific moment when they were photographed'. However, if we depart from the idea that video and photography only bring a representation of the past into the present, we open up the possibility of considering how they might help us in future-oriented research. For example, I have argued elsewhere (Pink and Leder Mackley 2012) that we might understand video not as 'taking us back' but as something that we move forward with when we view it, in order to think with it anew. This enables us to consider the meaning of video recordings not as fixed in the past where they were made, but as emergent through the experience of moving into the future with them as they are viewed. For example, in the FabPod Futures research project undertaken with Yoko Akama and Annie Ferguson at RMIT University, we used video in ways that transgress the past-present-future distinction (Pink et al. 2017). We asked participants to be recorded on video as they reconstructed their first encounter with the architectural object we were researching with them, to show or discuss with us what it had felt like to inhabit or use it, and to consider speculative encounters with its future. While the recording of the videos was obviously done in the past, the temporalities in the encounters were more complex; they brought both past and future into the present, and acknowledged that there was a future encounter in store when the video would be viewed again. Our expectation is therefore that these videos, as well as those made in other projects discussed in this chapter (such as the *Laundry Lives* film mentioned above and the LEEDR website below) will continue to somehow 'act' in the world. Yet we are not exactly sure how they will do this.

The emergence of digital research methods, including internet methods (Markham and Baym 2008), online methods (e.g. Boellstorff et al. 2014), virtual methods (e.g. Hine 2015), netnography (Kozinets 2010) and digital ethnography (Pink et al. 2016) has, like visual methods, generated a significant amount of discussion about ethics. This has, as with visual methods, become a concern for professional associations, and Annette Markham and Elizabeth A. Buchanan's guidelines for internet research published on the website of the Association of Internet Researchers (AOIR) at http://aoir.org/ethics/ are a good example of how they have been thoughtfully developed. The digital context, likewise, impacts on the ways in which applied research is developed, discussed, undertaken, disseminated and shared. It brings to applied research environments new possibilities for collaborative and participatory research, including online sharing, and co-working. Digital collaborations, and the visual, textual and audio possibilities that they generate in applied research offer both new possibilities for working together with participants and stakeholders and new ethical challenges. Online methods open up new uncertainties in that we cannot predict all the outcomes of online collaborations and sharing. Equally, just as Clifford (1986) pointed out, we cannot tell what will happen to our ethnographic writing, and we cannot predict how videos, photographs or other materials we post online will be appropriated. At the same time, the digital environment creates new ethical issues relating to the use of big data, how to understand participation in projects, and potential harm to human subjects, among other things. As the work of Markham and Buchanan demonstrates, the issues relating to ethics in internet research are not straightforward; they are just as messy as they would be in traditional contexts. After a thorough review of the key issues that internet researchers might consider, they suggest two principles that should be kept in mind: 'Ethical dilemmas are less visible from a distance, and harm or vulnerability can never be fully understood in advance' (Markham and Buchanan 2014). These points also emphasize the uncertainty of ethics online – that is the impossibility of knowing what we cannot yet see, or of predicting what will happen next.

Above I have noted both how human geographers have suggested that there is a certain ethical or moral mode to research that focuses on the sensory, embodied and unspoken (see Pink 2015 for a summary of this). Moreover, the anthropologist Paul Stoller has argued that what he calls a sensuous scholarship is characterized by a form of humility (Stoller 1997), which in itself, through the respect it generates, creates an ethical stance towards participants in research. In contemporary applied research the sensory dimension might also involve seeking to learn from participants, to understand how they 'feel' or aspire to feel in a sensory and embodied as well as emotional way in particular circumstances. Indeed, if applied scholarship and practice seek to somehow make better the worlds that we live in, the question of how social researchers can participate in making future worlds feel better should take centre stage in our investigations.

To demonstrate some of these issues I discuss the Energy and Digital Living website (see http://energyanddigitalliving.com/) and more generally the principles of working online in a Web 2.0 context. When we started the LEEDR (Low Effort Energy Demand Reduction) project of which our ethnographic work was part, we didn't know if all our participants would be happy to work with video or for us to show the videos in seminars, use still images in articles, or put video clips of them online. Because we were doing ethnographic research about things that participants didn't usually speak or think about, neither we nor they knew in advance exactly what we would find in their homes or how we would feel about it. Above I have explained the process of ongoing consent developed in the ethnographic strand of this project. The outcome of this process was that most of our participants agreed for us to include certain clips from the research undertaken with them, and which they approved in advance, on the project dissemination website, Energy and Digital Living.

The Energy and Digital Living website is not simply a record of our project; it is an experiment in applied and public research dissemination. Its intentions are various: to show our participants how the research has led to the development of design interventions; to disseminate the findings of our research in an accessible way to an interested general public, designers, policy makers, businesses and to academics from disciplines beyond the social sciences; to disseminate our applied sensory ethnography and design methodologies, which I hope other researchers will find useful to adopt or adapt; there is also a pedagogy to the website and its presentation and I hope that it will be used in teaching; and finally, the project also serves as a showcase for our method and the possibilities that it affords, and can be used as a demonstrator in discussions with potential research partners or stakeholders in future projects.

The Energy and Digital Living website involved the collaboration and agreement of participants in relation to the materials it included, but not in terms of its actual development. Web 2.0 contexts – with the participatory, collaborative ways of being and creating online in a Web 2.0 world – invite us into another ethical domain where much is possible and much that is visual can be felt to be unethical. The possibilities of this for applied and public anthropology research are being explored in a number of ways online – a good example is Matthew Durington and Samuel Collins' Anthropology by the Wire project, online at http://anthropologybythewire.com/ (and also see Durington and Collins 2015 for a discussion of this work as a form of public engagement). Although in-depth discussion on and reflection about ethics in such work remains latent, it is likely to generate further discussion in the future.

Conclusion: A Processual Ethics?

Future-oriented disciplines such as design have no single ethical orientation but maintain a critical debate over questions around ethics and the different ideas of what ethics is in this context. For instance, in her review of *Ethical Design*, the designer Yoko Akama (2012) joins others in critiquing rationalistic, market-driven and 'ethical' approaches to making improvements in relation to the 'poor' or the 'environment'. Akama instead builds on Western and Japanese philosophy to call for:

> ... an embodied re-orientation to design through the practice of reflection could have transformative agency. We can become 'ready' to being open to new encounters and being self-aware in the world in a situated and embodied way, forging a different kind of connection with others. This awareness brings forth an openness, mindfulness, compassion, empathy, reverence, acceptance and a sense of belonging with others and to our being in the world (Akama 2012).

Akama's approach to design resonates with the acknowledgement of the involvement of the ethnographer as an embodied, sensory and empathetic practitioner of ethics – or as Pels put it, as 'technologies of the self' (2000). It offers us a coherent way in which to begin thinking about the relationship between an ethical future-oriented research practice and its relationship to intervention.

In future-oriented applied research the past-present-future configuration shifts, as it has done for the anthropology in design anthropology. When we work in this new ethnographic temporality we need to account for how and where the future is situated – that is for questions of how the future is made in the present, and what our roles are in participating in this process. By the very joining of people in their present and accompanying them as we all slip over in the future, we are in some ways participating in the making of their (our shared) futures. When you add to this the intentionality of research projects that deliberately seek to have impact in the world, the ethical configuration is also different to when we write ethnography into the past. While institutional ethics already has a future-oriented logic, this logic does not accommodate the ways in which researchers are already ethical because these emerge from the processual realities in which we research. As the examples I have outlined above have shown, a processual ethics is possible, and can indeed be navigated in relation to the needs of ethical approval frameworks, and in relation to non-social science disciplines and external stakeholders. To put it into place, we need to think of ethics as including but also going beyond simple compliance with ethical approval committees and their demands/needs, and return to the essential questions of how we as researchers can best deal with researching in uncertain worlds.

In this chapter I have shown that an approach to ethical research in contemporary applied research involves thinking about ethics as not simply a practical issue, and not simply an auditable process. It does involve practical tasks and commitments. It is also subject to the regulations of national or institutional ethical approval committees. Yet at the same time, as I have shown, like the very conduct of applied research, the ethics of applied research which seeks to make interventions, impact on the world and to participate in change or future making, needs to be developed at the intersection between theoretical scholarship and practical work.

Acknowledgements

Part of this chapter was inspired by a keynote lecture I gave in 2014 at the symposium Exploring Ethical Frontiers of Visual Methods, which can be viewed online at http://vrc.org.au/visual-research-ethics-symposium-videos. There the initial ideas are developed from which the discussion above emerged. This chapter, however, expands the issues further and in relation to the wider question of applied research.

Sarah Pink is Professor of Design and Emerging Technologies, and Director of the Emerging Technologies Research Lab, at Monash University, Australia. Her work is interdisciplinary and brings together academic scholarship and applied practice. Her recent publications include the books *Digital Ethnography: Principles and Practice* (2016) and *Digital Materialities: Anthropology and Design* (2016).

References

Adam, B. and C. Groves. 2007. *Future Matters: Action, Knowledge, Ethics*. Leiden: Brill Academic Publishing.

Adey, P. and B. Anderson. 2011. 'Event and Anticipation: UK Civil Contingencies and the Space-times of Decision', *Environment and Planning A* 43(12): 2878–99.

Akama, Y. 2012. 'A "Way of Being" in Design Practice: Zen and the Art of Being a Human-centred Practitioner', *Design Philosophy Papers*, no. 1, pp. 1–10.

Akama, Y. and A. Prendiville. 2013. 'A Phenomenological View to Co-designing Services', *Swedish Design Research Journal* 1(13): 29–40.

Amit, V. 2000. 'The University as Panopticon: Moral Claims and Attacks on Academic Freedom', in M. Strathern (ed.), *Audit Cultures: Anthropological Studies in Accountability*. London: Routledge.

Anderson, B. 2010. 'Preemption, Precaution, Preparedness: Anticipatory Action and Future Geographies', *Progress in Human Geography* 34(6): 777–98.

Boellstorff, T., B. Nardi, C. Pearce and T.L. Taylor. 2012. *Ethnography and Virtual Worlds: A Handbook of Method*. Princeton, NJ: Princeton University Press.

Brown, N. and M. Michael. 2003. 'A Sociology of Expectations: Retrospecting Prospects and Prospecting Retrospects', *Technology Analysis & Strategic Management* 15(1): 3–18.

Clarke, A. 2012. 'Visual Ethics in a Contemporary Landscape', in S. Pink (ed.), *Advances in Visual Methodology*. London: Sage.

Clifford, J. 1986. 'On Ethnographic Allegory' in J. Clifford and G. Marcus. (eds). *Writing Culture*. Berkeley, CA: University of California Press.

Clifford, J. and G. Marcus. 1986. *Writing Culture*. Berkeley, CA: University of California Press.

Durington, M. and S.G. Collins. 2015. 'Anthropology by the Wire', in S. Pink and S. Abram (eds), *Media, Anthropology and Public Engagement*. Oxford/New York: Berghahn Books.

Fabian, J. 1983. *Time and the Other: How Anthropology Makes its Object*. New York, NY: Columbia University Press.

Gunn, W. and C. Clausen. 2013. 'Conceptions of Innovation and Practice(s) of Inhabiting Indoor Climate', in W. Gunn, T. Otto and R.C. Smith (eds), *Design Anthropology: Theory and Practice*. London: Bloomsbury.

Hjorth, L. and S. Pink. 2014. 'New Visualities and the Digital Wayfarer: Reconceptualizing Camera Phone Photography and Locative Media', *Mobile Media and Communication* 2: 40–57.

Hine, C. 2015. *Ethnography for the Internet: Embedded, Embodied and Everyday*. London: Bloomsbury.

Ingold, T. 2012. 'Introduction: The Perception of the User–Producer', in W. Gunn and J. Donovan (eds), *Design and Anthropology*. Farnham: Ashgate.

Kinsley, S. 2011. 'Anticipating Ubiquitous Computing: Logics to Forecast Technological Futures', *Geoforum* 42(2): 231–40.

Kozinets, R.V. 2010. *Netnography: Doing Ethnographic Research Online*. London: Sage.

Markham, A. and N. Baym. 2008. *Internet Inquiry: Conversations About Method*. Thousand Oaks, CA: Sage.

Markham, A.N. and E. Buchanan. 2014. 'Ethical Considerations in Digital Research Contexts', in J. Wright (ed.), *Encyclopedia for Social and Behavioural Sciences*. Oxford: Elsevier.

Massumi B. 2007. 'Potential Politics and the Primacy of Preemption', *Theory & Event* 10:2.

Pels, P. 2000. 'The Trickster's Dilemma: Ethics and the Technologies of the Anthropological Self', in M. Strathern (ed.), *Audit Cultures: Anthropological Studies in Accountability*. London: Routledge.

Pink, S. (ed.) 2007. *Visual Interventions*. Oxford/New York: Berghahn Books.

Pink, S. 2013. *Doing Visual Ethnography*, 3rd edition. London: Sage.

Pink, S. 2015. *Doing Sensory Ethnography*, 2nd edition. London: Sage.

Pink, S., H. Horst, J. Postill, L. Hjorth, T. Lewis and J. Tacchi. 2016. *Digital Ethnography: Principles and Practice*. London: Sage.

Pink, S. and K. Leder Mackley. 2015. 'Social Science, Design and Everyday Life: Refiguring Showering through Anthropological Ethnography', *Journal of Design Research* 13(3): 278–92.

Pink, S., J. Morgan and A. Dainty. 2015. 'Other People's Homes as Sites of Uncertainty: Ways of Knowing and Being Safe' *Environment and Planning A*. volume 47(2): 450–464.

Prosser, J., A. Clark and R. Wiles. 2008. 'Visual Research Ethics at the Crossroads'. NCRM Working Paper. Realities, Morgan Centre, Manchester, UK. Available online at http://eprints.ncrm.ac.uk/535/.

Rowe, J. 2012. 'Legal Issues of Using Images in Research', in E. Margolis and L. Pauwels (eds) *The SAGE Handbook of Visual Research Methods*. London: Sage.

Samimian-Darash, L. and P. Rabinow. 2015. *Modes of Uncertainty: Anthropological Cases*. Chicago: University of Chicago Press.

Shore, C. and S. Wright. 2015. 'Governing by Numbers: Audit Culture, Rankings and the New World Order', *Social Anthropology* 23(1): 22–28.

Stoller, P. 1997. *Sensuous Scholarship*. Philadelphia, PA: University of Pennsylvania Press.

Strathern, M. 2000. 'Afterword: Accountability ... and Ethnography', in M. Strathern (ed.), *Audit Cultures: Anthropological Studies in Accountability*. London: Routledge.

Wiles, R., A. Clark and J. Prosser. 2011. 'Visual Research Ethics at the Crossroads', in E. Margolis and L. Pauwels (eds), *The SAGE Handbook of Visual Research Methods*. London: Sage.

Wiles, R., A. Coffey, J. Robison and J. Prosser. 2012. 'Ethical Regulation and Visual Methods: Making Visual Research Impossible or Developing Good Practice?' *Sociological Research Online* 7(1): 8. Available online at http://www.socresonline.org.uk/17/1/8.html.

Part II

Making Contact and Making Sense

Chapter 2

WORKSHOPS AS NODES OF KNOWLEDGE CO-PRODUCTION
Beyond Ideas of Automagical Synergies

Martin Berg and Vaike Fors

Introduction

Academics are increasingly expected to collaborate with partners outside of academia and to strive to make an impact at various societal levels. Yet the methods through which this might be achieved are not often interrogated, and the worth of such exercises is still questioned. As we show here, often approaches to bringing academics and industry together can be seen to depend on what we call *automagic*. This term is derived from programming jargon and refers to a process that is automatic but with a certain touch of magic, resulting in things that inexplicably *just work* (OED Online 2015). Simultaneously in the social sciences and humanities, it is often argued by academics that such collaborative efforts put intellectual standards at risk due to an assumed lack of rigour and methodological transparency in the processes of collaborative knowledge production (Roberts 2005). In this chapter we argue that greater attention needs to be paid to the means through which such partnerships might be initiated and nurtured, and that to achieve this we need to find appropriate ways to shape environments and processes where academic expertise can be usefully put to work. In so doing, we approach the question of why and how innovation does not always happen and point out how barriers to collaborations between academia and industry can be created by the very mechanisms put in place to make them happen.

To achieve this, we critically review one illuminating example of how academic-industry collaborations are commonly organized through workshop models and how academic scholars experience these. Our example is set in the Swedish context where the field that we work in – applied social and cultural analysis – is still nascent, thus also offering an example of a situation where it is particularly important for academic reflection to play a role in the shaping of such partnership building. Engaging with a Swedish context, we outline a set of key insights calling for a move beyond more conventional critique of intellectual stagnation and loss of critical stance (Roberts 2005; Ehn and Löfgren 2009). Instead we constructively engage in questions of how to avoid potential pitfalls when staging collaborative workshops (see also Strengers et al. in this volume). We concentrate on an example of how structured attempts at creating innovation between academia and the creative industries in fact appeared to obstruct possible ways in which academics and potential industry partners might collaborate and creatively improvise together. In doing so we identify barriers to improvisation, which we suggest are constituted by clashes in professional expectations, and which took the form of tensions in workshops that are staged by expert brokers. These, we argue, were conditioned by the underlying ideas of a pedagogy generated through loosely connected activities as the foundation of innovation and creativity. However, the full potential of an activity-based pedagogy was not developed during the workshop, since it did not afford or acknowledge the development of practices and processes through connectivity between, and negotiation of meanings within, activities in the pursuit of a joint enterprise. Instead, the featured pedagogy appeared to be closed to negotiations and unanticipated processes, which leads us to propose a more open approach with a basis in ideas of collaborative improvisation to improve the co-productive potential in these kinds of workshops.

We do not claim to be able to generalize the results from this research across the myriad ways in which encounters between academia and industry are played out. However, since the workshop method we analyse here can be found in method handbooks within the creative industries, the analysis of this specific setting could be argued to be transferable to other similar settings, too. In short, we would like to contribute to an academic exploration of 'automagical' processes as not magical at all, but instead as rich social and cultural encounters between professional practices with potential. Yet, we will argue that this potential can remain underestimated and hidden precisely because of the strict workshop methods that tend to frame such encounters. Ironically, while such methods have the explicit objective of producing creativity, they can in fact have the inverse effect, of constraining social learning.

Contextualizing the Co-productive Workshop

In the early 1990s the Swedish Council for Research and Planning (FRN) commissioned a research project aiming to get a view on the future of universities. A group of international scholars in the field of science studies were summoned and the outcome was presented in a now widely cited book, *The New Production of Knowledge* (Gibbons et al. 1994). In this book it was claimed that science systems are in transformation, from scientific knowledge production that is located primarily in scientific institutions and structured by scientific disciplines, toward much more heterogeneous locations, practices and principles.

Theoretically, this chapter takes a perspective on knowledge co-production that does not assume science as a unitary social institution, or that scientific knowledge production can be a process structured entirely according to policy and political reform. Instead, we explore a specific knowledge-producing encounter as a local and social learning activity. Subsequently, in contrast to the vast body of knowledge within the field of knowledge co-production that emanates from science studies (Gibbons et al. 1994), we here start by scrutinizing what happens on a social level in the concrete situations where knowledge co-production is supposed to take place. In this way we add to the picture of 'scientific knowledge production' in applied and experimental contexts as not only part of a political reformist agenda, but also a process of scientific inquiry and learning situated (and therefore conditioned) differently from conventional research within social sciences and humanities.

While certain disciplines within academia are well equipped by tradition to cooperate in workshops of this kind, other academic fields are not. For instance, in Scandinavia, the field of applied cultural analytic research is relatively nascent. Moreover, the debate has partially been circulating around complaints of what an accelerating commercialization and market adaptation of these scientific fields might lead to in terms of loss of a critical stance in research (Ehn and Löfgren 2009). However, in this chapter, we will not dwell on these alleged conflicts. Instead, we regard them as background to the motivation for drilling deeper into what happens in the actual meeting between academic scholars within these fields and industry, during a collaborative workshop. Since workshops like these are part of a relatively common and well-used collaboration format, both in industry and the public sector, we find it interesting to analyse the relationship between theoretical scholarship and applied research through precisely this interface between academic scholars and professionals.

The Automagic of Idea-generating Workshops

We base our analysis on fieldwork that involved both our own participation, and research into other academics' experiences of participating in a particular collaborative endeavour that is sometimes used in order to create encounters between academia, industry and public stakeholders: namely *idea-generating workshops*. These workshops in collaborative settings are conceptualized in method handbooks as a method that functions as a 'catalyst' when producing knowledge, new ideas, networks and inspiration (Linton and Michanek 2012). However, in social scientific research literature, little or no attention is given to how these workshops work or what they do. In handbooks of the above-mentioned kind, activity-based idea-generating workshops are said to be viable routes to provide collaborations between academia, industry and the public sector with places for experimentation and refuelling of inspiration in order to create good ideas for business. The basic idea is that being brought together with different perspectives during organized activities creates new ideas and facilitates knowledge co-production. The ideas behind these workshops can be found in workshop method handbooks (see for example Linton and Michanek 2012; Michanek and Breiler 2013) (see Illustration 2.1 below) as well as in government-funded reports on methods for increasing collaboration between academia, industry, institutes and society (Algotson and Daal 2007). In the latter format, efforts within this area are grounded in ambitions to create competitive research environments and societal growth.

Illustration 2.1 shows an example of a workshop handbook description of how to undertake a workshop to bridge the distance between academia and industry, with a particular focus on the number of participants and the various professional roles required. The ambitions of these workshops are grounded in the belief that things will happen as long as you bring people with different backgrounds together in staged settings; however, where these ideas actually originate is not explicitly explained. The authors of the handbook admit that much can be said about these matters 'on an abstract, theoretical level' but they 'leave the theoretical polished play to others' and instead focus on doing 'things', 'acting' and getting 'dirt' under their fingernails. We argue that such understandings of encounters between academia and industry as automagical sites of knowledge production should be nuanced and deepened. Rather than referring to these practices as something that 'just works' if they are staged according to particular methods, we suggest that the practices through which knowledge co-production is assumed to take place are conditioned

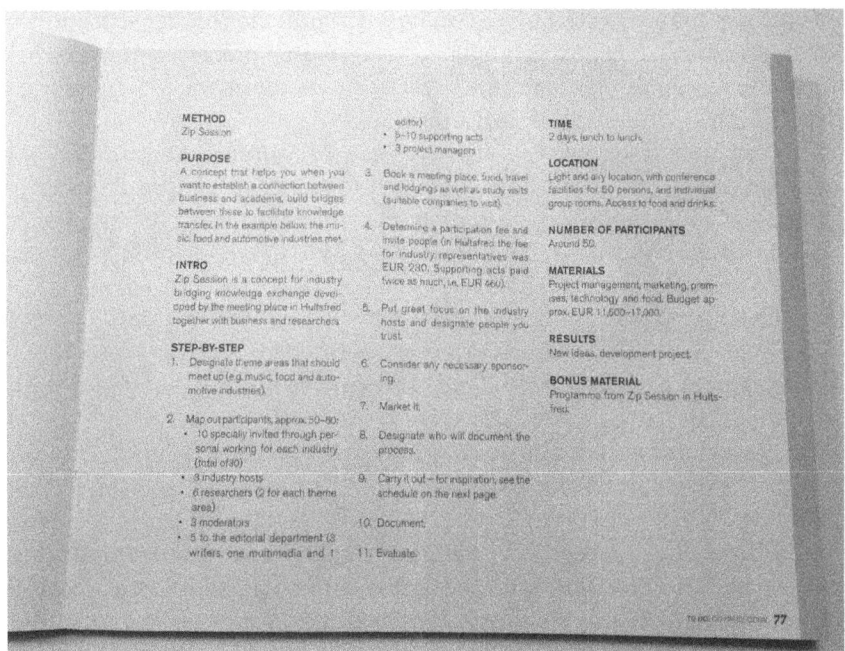

Illustration 2.1: One example of a method to bring together and 'build bridges between these [business and academia] to facilitate knowledge transfer' (Linton and Michanek 2012: 77). Published with permission from author.

and rendered possible by an array of negotiations of expertise, professional expectations and ideas of learning that need to be further explored.

We will demonstrate our arguments through our research at and prior to a particular encounter called 'innovation camp'. The innovation camp was organized by a project funded by a municipality in Sweden with the specific objective of strengthening their region as a good environment for live in, an area with thriving entrepreneurship and an appealing cultural scene. Selected local companies were invited to bring in their specific issues, such as how to create an attractive spa culture, that were processed together with artists and researchers, facilitated by the organizers according to a preset protocol. The innovation camp was part of a process that would eventually lead to a 'prototype lab', where the organizers and the invited companies (but surprisingly, not the researchers) would activate the ideas generated at the innovation camp. This case study provides insights into how we can understand these collaborative workshops as part of organizational and discursive tendencies within the creative industries, as well as providing insights into how academia-based researchers may take part in such events. In sum, the chapter will address the overarching question of what kind of dynamic processes unfold when encounters between researchers and industry partners are framed by expectations of automagical outcomes.

In the next section we will explore the context and underlying assumptions about workshops in order to sketch a picture of them as situated sites for knowledge production with a particular history. We do this through a critical reading of handbooks for arranging innovative and creative workshops.

Workshops as Sites for 'Cool' Encounters

The creative industries constitute a rapidly expanding field that is often assumed to go hand in hand with economic growth and societal change (Fleming 2007; Pratt 2000; Florida 2002). This field of cultural, economic and technological activities is part of – or perhaps even leading – the transformations of working life towards being what some have argued is liquid and indeed individualized, with a particular emphasis on flexibility and creativity (Deuze 2007, 2011). Knowledge in these industries is often understood as instantaneously produced, ephemeral and somehow bound up with aesthetics and lifestyle markers rather than formal degrees and positions within the organizational scheme. With such an approach to knowledge, it follows that workshops are often preferred sites for collaboration since they are assumed to put the participants on equal ground and facilitate moving beyond the specificities of academic as well as marketing jargon. This is not a coincidence, since workshops are often understood as sites for sharing and creating knowledge under conditions that embrace multiplicity and spark creativity without depending on traditional hierarchies or forms of knowledge.

Working life within the creative industries often revolves around a certain notion of freedom, informality and individuality, and is supported by a cool, creative and egalitarian self-image (Gill 2002, 2011; McRobbie 2003; Gregg 2011; Banks and Milestone 2011; Taylor and Littleton 2012). The perceived coolness of creativity is an important factor in understanding what is going on within the creative industries, and how spontaneity, curiosity and various lifestyle markers become favoured in place of traditional forms of knowledge production. This notion comes to life in workshops that could easily be understood as sites where the bringing together of people is celebrated with reference to the broader culture within the creative industries. Workshops of the kind that are studied in this chapter often serve as display windows for the prevailing understandings of knowledge and forms of collaboration within the creative industries. One illuminating example of such a putting on display is the numerous publications and handbooks that are published on the topic of how to arrange creative workshops that support innovation and creative ideas (Kelley and Littman 2005; Ries 2011; Thiel and Masters 2014). The instructions in these handbooks often point towards a process with various clearly defined steps as a means to unfold new ideas through bringing together people with different backgrounds. It is not uncommon that they take the form of a recipe for social interaction that relies on an obscure formula that is somehow assumed to enable certain automagical outcomes.

Here we will look closer at one publication in this trajectory of handbooks, which is also said to be inspired by advocates for so-called 'cultural planning' (see Ghilardi 2001; Landry and Bianchini 1995), and that is produced and published by the very organization that arranged the innovative camp that this chapter focuses on. It is a stylish publication indeed, with a cover image that sums up the above-mentioned coolness of the creative industries. With a darkish colour scheme and matte paper, it depicts two feet dressed in striped socks and well-polished brogues, one of which is balancing on a skateboard. The potential reader is invited to read a book that is not only cool but also gives the impression of being on the move. The manifesto style title, *To Do: Development of Cultural and Creative Industries in Practice* (Linton and Michanek 2012), accentuates the impression of being 'on the move' and somehow in constant flux (see an example from the book in Illustration 2.1).

The book proffers itself as a companion to help overcome the difficulties associated with cooperation within the creative industries and across disciplines by providing 'practical approaches' to create good, new and exciting *meetings*. It is said that such meetings lead to the formation of new relationships, which in turn lead to innovation and growth. The idea seems fairly attractive in its simplicity: if we find the proper forms of interaction, the outcome will automagically not only follow but also be more or less awesome. The building of relationships is thus at the centre of this workshop model, but it is clear that the 'how' is far more interesting than the 'why' and the 'whom' in these workshops. It is explicitly said that 'methods, processes and activities' are needed in the form of 'recipes for what creative and constructive meetings for developing movements with creativity in mind might look like' (Linton and Michanek 2012: 14–17).

Clearly, the workshop descriptions and the social learning processes they rely on are of a theoretical nature, but in their effort to provide practical suggestions and step-by-step guides, the theoretical underpinnings are left out – perhaps even forgotten – but of course present in their absence. In the next section we contrast the structure and the expected outcomes of workshops as they are described in handbooks with experiences of participating in a workshop as expressed by the academic participants. The empirical findings we describe below are based on our own fieldwork from participating in the innovation camp, as well as a series of interviews and evaluations with the other researchers who took part in the workshop. Subsequently, the research material consisted of our own field notes, together with one group and two individual interviews with six researchers after the workshop, and the written evaluations that were sent to the workshop organizers after the workshop.

Automagical Structures

In the workshop models presented in the handbook there is a strong emphasis on understanding innovation as carrying out activities and coming up with new ideas, rather than planning or analysing. In contrast to a traditional understanding of incremental innovation (as outlined by Schumpeter 1912) as a process where available resources are transformed in new and perhaps even unexpected ways, this workshop model tends to lean towards an understanding of innovation as merely resulting from an encounter between people with different experiences. Although such an encounter might be important, little is said about how the multitude of experiences should feed into the dynamics of the workshop and thereby add to the knowledge production and processes of idea generation. In most cases the workshop instructions make clear how many people should participate in the workshop, how much time should be spent on each step and if there is a need for equipment, such as pens, sticky notes, chairs, tables and so forth (see Illustration 2.1 above).

Although precise in terms of what equipment is required in the various steps of the process, the workshop itself seemed to be thought of as automagically structured; that is, we were expected to 'trust the process'. In the field notes, the experience of entering such a process was further reflected on:

> Each company was presented to us as a case. Interestingly, all cases were described with the word 'how'. How should they do this, and how should they become that. It wasn't really clear why those questions had been posed or how the various competencies in the room were supposed to collaborate with and strengthen each other. Isn't a question always directed to someone? Doesn't it need to be framed in a certain way depending on whom one is asking? Later on we chose a case and got to briefly explain why we had chosen it. The company representatives (here labelled 'case owners')

presented their specific challenges and we were then allowed to ask questions during a very tight time frame (I think it was around five plus five minutes). This exercise was followed by the team members discussing and providing feedback on the case and jotting down their thoughts on Post-it notes. During roughly ten minutes, the case owner was supposed to stay at the back, just listening. It felt weird. It was not until later that the case owner was allowed to partake in the discussion. During the different steps (I think there were about fourteen in total) of the workshop, the process leaders walked from table to table, listening to the discussions and somehow checking (at least, that's how it felt) that the participants did what they were supposed (!) to do. Interestingly it seemed as if the process itself was more important than the dynamics that unfolded around the different tables. Sometimes it felt as if we were simply players in a game in which the rules were the only thing that mattered, not the players. It was slightly provoking to think of knowledge as bound up with a predefined obscure process through which ideas should simply pop up by jotting down words, sentences and figures on colourful sticky notes. What is the methodology of this method? How is it possible to approach the future without even knowing about the past? (Excerpt from field notes)

As the above quote shows, the workshop in which we participated was of a very structured kind, and it left us with as many questions as there were steps in the process. As an illuminating example of how processes of this kind are described, Illustration 2.1 shows a page from a rather common way of describing and teaching the methods used in idea-generating workshops in these contexts. Workshops of this kind often tend to assume that 'meetings' are unproblematic and conditioned mainly by the structure; a good structure creates constructive meetings. In the workshops it is often said that themes should be discussed and perhaps even jointly analysed, but what happens in such a situation and in the complexity of interactional patterns that are involved is rarely acknowledged. Clearly, the pedagogy generated through these prescribed methods is activity-based; however, to simplify activity and doing as separate from social practice and collective knowing may have practical consequences in the outcome of the workshop. As the last quote exemplifies, the non-contextualized approach of the method brought questions of professional expectations to the fore, and worries about how the different professional competencies and roles, together with the unfolding content of the discussion in the smaller group, would be enabled to develop through the staged process. In other words, the process was clearly based in different concrete *activities*; however, the doing of these activities seemed to be disconnected from the resources that were brought in by the participants in terms of knowing, both in terms of what we knew and how and why we might do things. Paradoxically, while the method was designed to bring together people with different backgrounds to create creativity, it simultaneously neglected the fact that bringing together people also creates opportunities for different practices to unfold, since we were all expected to *do the same things*. However, if we all do the same things in the same way during the same conditions, it is hard to create spaces for different outcomes in social settings. This way of controlling different variables (like time, activity, constellation and number of people) may be constructive in a laboratory setting, but in a social context, this control leads to a neglect of the potential that a multitude of competencies and knowledge bring with them.

Activity and Practice – Differences and Implications

From a theoretical point of view, the above mentioned neglect can be understood through the concept of *social practice* as it has been developed in the context of research about learning and knowledge. Practice is inherently social, since it is influenced by how activity is received by others, and this reciprocal relationship between activity and the social environment constitutes how these activities can be carried out. The implications of this for learning and collaboration have been elaborated on within the social sciences during the last decades. For instance, scientists at the Center for Collective Intelligence (CCI) at MIT have mapped out that the performance of a group is not primarily based on individual factors like intelligence and so forth, but in the group members' average social sensitivity (see the CCI web page: http://cci.mit.edu/). Another perspective of the sociality of practice is that 'any episode of human action must occur in a specific, cultural, historical, and institutional context, and this influences how such action is carried out' (Wertsch 2000: 18). Thus, social practice connotes doing, but not doing in and of itself: 'It is doing in a historical and social context that gives structure and meaning to what we do' (Wenger 1998: 47). From this social perspective on activity, learning is not an individual endeavour and knowledge is not something that you simply carry with you. As scholars like John Dewey (1966) and Jean Lave and Etienne Wenger (Lave and Wenger 1991; Wenger 1998) insist, learning is an inevitable part of participation in social practices, and happens in the pursuit of joint enterprises. Subsequently, knowledge is not primarily something you can obtain and then bring with you in a cognitive sense, but is based and developed in the social practices in which it is situated. From this particular perspective, the famous quote 'learning by doing', which is often dedicated to John Dewey but hard to find in his actual writing, invites us to think about doing as always doing *in* a specific practice, and about knowledge as something you become *part of* by participating in this practice. In our particular case many activities were staged, but the potential practices that could unfold through these activities were not acknowledged by the workshop method. Instead, the processes that could lead up to emerging joint practices, or in Wenger's (1998) words, *communities of practice*, lingered through the programme of the workshop, unnoticed and sometimes, as is exemplified through the excerpt below, even discouraged by the facilitators:

> We sat down around a small table; we were two researchers who knew each other and two people who wanted to develop their small business in new directions. We were given the task of writing down all the things we could think of that related to their business, both in terms of activities and products. We started writing everything we could think of on sticky notes and placed them on the table in different formations. One thing led to another, and when the business owners got to talk (they were not allowed to talk in the beginning) they started to touch upon deep philosophical ideas about what their work was about. I suggested that they could organize a public seminar series to help them develop both their thinking and a public awareness about their craft. I wrote 'public seminar' on one sticky note, and 'deep thinking' on another and finally 'dialogue' on a third. One of the facilitators came by and looked at the sticky notes on the table and started to rearrange them together with us. She reminded us of our task and the number of sticky notes we were supposed to end up with. She took my last three sticky notes and put them aside saying: 'these are interesting, but they are not really relevant to the task in hand'. I said that it came naturally to me as a researcher to analytically drill deeper into what was literally on the table when looking for unanticipated takes on the business. The facilitator answered that I should try to think 'outside' of academia and sort of 'go with the flow'. Later on, at the coffee break, one of the business owners approached me and wanted to continue our conversation about how to analytically conceptualize his thoughts about his business. (Excerpt from field notes)

An innovation camp might – from a first glance at a method book – look like it is based in social learning theories. However, through the talk of taking a 'mental leap into the future', 'knowledge transfer' and 'how to bring our different knowledge into the discussions', it seems to be more focused on cognitive/rational ideas of the mental and the mind as the primary source of knowledge to be released from the situations through which it has emerged. With an experimental rigour that brings scientific experiments to mind, the workshop is meant to make the conditions perfect for creating new ideas. The problem is that the idea of automatic generation of ideas and 'knowledge transfer' by simply bringing people together in situations framed by activity-based methods does not account for the perspective of knowledge as situated in social practice. Seemingly, the workshop as a site of knowledge production did not primarily acknowledge that it is also a site where social interaction takes place, and that such an interaction (and indeed what it leads up to) in turn is also situated. Good ideas are not only crafted with strict schedules, coloured pens and sticky notes, but are rather crafted from interpersonal processes where ideas, emotions and knowledge have a history that stretches far beyond the actual workshop situation. This example from our field notes shows a built-in ambiguity in the way the methods are framed in the method books and how they are carried out in relation to the activity-based methodology they are said to embrace.

We suggest that by articulating what seems to underpin these workshops in terms of the cultural and historical practices through which they have emerged, this helps to uncover why the social learning processes that actually take place are not acknowledged. In turn, recognizing these social processes might lead to interesting ways of developing these workshops. The process descriptions do to some extent point out that ideas and innovation stem from relationship building, and if relationships are important then it must necessarily be equally important to understand the human components of these workshops. In the next section we will elaborate further on these processes and their implications for how participation in these workshops can be experienced.

Experiences of Being Secret Researchers

Our participation in the innovation camp was already marked from the beginning by an uncertainty about what to expect and how to feed into the collaborative processes that were about to take place. Despite having been part of several workshops over the years, it was not long until we experienced an awkward sensation of being out of place during this particular workshop. In the field notes one of us reflected upon the first encounter in this setting:

> On our way to Varberg, we were all a bit confused and didn't really know what to expect from the day. Innovation camp. The word does remind me of a boot camp. I opened the web browser in my iPhone to see if any further information had been posted about the workshop. The organizer's web page explained that 'a mobile and temporary research and development unit' were coming to the city of Varberg and that four secret companies from the Halland region would work with a number of equally secret and internationally recognized researchers from Lund, Halmstad and Melbourne.

> It felt weird but exciting. Why did we have to stay secret? Of course, there's nothing wrong with (for once) feeling like a secret agent, but what was the reason for doing so? We were all very confused and started talking about our possible roles and why we weren't able to actually do some research on the companies that we were supposed to work with. We arrived in Varberg, and found our way to the place of the workshop. After a while we were seated and the organizers welcomed us. They informed us that they would soon reveal (!) the schedule and the process that should guide us through the day. First, they said, some house rules needed to be explained. One of them was that we should all be there on an equal basis and no professional titles should be used. We were asked to write our names on a nametag without any information about our affiliation, professional role or similar. Instead, we should all trust the process as such. The feeling of being a secret researcher was intensified further, and I looked at the people in the room, trying to figure out who they were and why we had come there. (Excerpt from field notes)

This feeling of being literally forced away from expertise and instead instructed to rely on a process designed with an experiment-like approach of which we knew little, gave us all a slightly Kafkaesque feeling. Why were we invited as researchers and scholars if we were not supposed to make use of our expertise? Why were the industry representatives not supposed to make use of their extensive knowledge of the fields from which they had come?

As a follow-up to the innovation camp we gathered the researchers for a group interview where our experiences could be discussed. This interview quickly transformed into a workshop in itself, where we tried to address the questions that were somehow omitted from the innovation camp. We all shared the feeling of not knowing what had actually 'happened', and as one of the participants put it, 'I felt a little bit out of body'. This experienced distance between what we were trained to do and what we were now supposed to do caused a great deal of uncertainty among us. As one of us admitted during the interview: 'I was this sort of this figure sitting there. Saying things, but not really being able to say exactly what I wanted because that would be too difficult.' This feeling of not *knowing* or *being able* to engage properly in the ongoing processes was partly due to a lack of knowledge about what the organizers had in mind when inviting us *as* researchers. They clearly had some idea of us being equipped with a particular embodied knowledge and creative potential, but there were no opportunities to actually render the use of this potential possible with support from the facilitated workshop method. If we understand knowledge not as encapsulated in our minds and extracted at appropriate moments, but rather as coming to life through social practices that can adapt to the dynamics of the surrounding setting, then it is in these emerging practices that we can find keys to develop the workshop method. Through the analysis of the interviews and evaluations in relation to our conceptualization of the workshops as sites for 'cool' encounters according to 'automagical structures', we identify a tension that relates to ideas of improvisation in connection to professional expectations. Here we understand improvisation as a central aspect of the making of social and cultural life, thus being at the core of the social fabric in which we become enmeshed through practice (Hallam and Ingold 2007). Two core dimensions of this tension are a counterproductive *loss of improvisation* and a feeling of *being out of practice*. However, implicit in this tension we have also identified routes for development of the workshop method that support the *development of social practices*. These dimensions point at an inherent difficulty in running workshops across disciplinary boundaries and simply relying on process structures to make ideas unfold and innovation take place, and call for a development of workshop methods that acknowledge the social processes that emerge when bringing people together in a less strict manner when it comes to planned activities. We will elaborate further on these dimensions below.

Loss of Improvisation

During, as well as after the workshop, we wondered why a workshop like this needed to be so heavily structured, merely in order to draw out ideas. It appeared to us that not only was the relationship between the various phases of the workshop structured, but also the possible forms of interaction within these phases. Such a structure implies that the participants are not fully allowed to approach the problem or the question from different angles, nor are they allowed to experience the unfolding of a common experience and perhaps even language. During the workshop the facilitators sometimes told us explicitly to stop talking or to move in another (correct) direction, thus trying to control different variables, as if we were situated in a laboratory setting. Ironically, this variable control was done as a means to encourage improvisation and the mutual exchange of ideas, but it felt restricting and we could only follow certain threads or develop certain ideas in a situation where we were tied to a structure with sticky notes everywhere. As one of the research team members said during the interview: 'We started to get somewhere with that [a specific exercise] and then we had to drop everything and move to another room and leave all the sticky notes behind.'

It seemed to us that the workshop was so heavily structured that it did not allow us to reformulate the conditions for its various steps, and in consequence it was nearly impossible for the continuously generated thoughts to 'kick back' and alter the process or the direction of the flow in the workshop. By having a fixed schedule and predefined deliverables for each and every step, it soon became clear that neither could we improvise and thus make use of the social dynamics in the group for a creative outcome, nor could we find new routes for engaging in knowledge-producing activities with alternate outcomes, creating new practices as we moved on. Instead, the workshop structure forced us to leave behind unfinished work simply in order to move on to the next step. This predefined route and pace was further commented on by another member of the research group:

> Finally, one thing that really struck me about the event was how it did not enable us to do any thinking that was joined up or connected; instead it made us move from one thing to another, through different tasks and filters. This I think prevents innovation or novel things from happening, because in academic work it is precisely when we put together ideas in new ways, and make them do new work, that we improvise and advance our fields. Here in contrast we were being asked to produce small bytes of ideas, inspirations, abstractions (personas) and to then mix them around with other people's. This encouraged segmented thought and not connected and coherent thought. By the end of it I was not sure I would be able to bring things together and I was surprised that I was able to create a coherent narrative about the prototype we had made. (Excerpt from interviews)

The experience of losing the ability to improvise is thus a matter of losing potential routes to knowledge, and indeed also ways to access the embodied experience of the participants. The highly valued social dynamics of the workshop are not fully used as a resource, since they are mediated by predefined processes and deliverables where sticky notes and the process description turn into a general language that we are all supposed to speak fluently. That way the workshop structure does not seem to take advantage of what makes a social practice flow, namely creating joint enterprises through negotiating what makes it meaningful, and creating situated language, knowledge and activities as we go (Wenger 1998). If we agree on a method that brings knowledge to life through social practices, one needs to embrace the development of specificity – not a general knowledge transfer – and the feeling of belonging in a project, not a 'hit-and-run' method where competence is seen as a commodity that can easily be separated from the person and the practice through which it emerged.

Being Out of Practice

The facilitators wanted us to be very clear in our reflections, and told us not to use overly academic jargon. But in our experience the clients actually enjoyed us tuning in to a more philosophical state of mind, posing questions of the kind that they would not normally hear. At some occasions during the workshops, when some of us intellectually drifted away (during the above-mentioned crafting experience), we were kindly told to stick to the subject. This way it felt as if the actual idea-generating interactions between participants were not valued as much as they could have been. But there were two dimensions to that experience. On the one hand, they wanted our field-specific expertise to feed into the process, but on the other hand we were not allowed to provide any feedback or actually change the structure of the process; and perhaps that is where our knowledge would have actually added to the workshop: to provide new routes for knowledge production, to reconceptualize the ideas being crafted and to find new terrain to explore a particular phenomenon.

During the workshop we often encountered situations where there was an obvious need to engage in research activities in order to, just to take one example, find out how potential customers could possibly be described and what would actually matter in their lives. At several times, we found themes and questions in need of clarification and further exploration that could indeed have added significantly to the knowledge being produced, but the workshop structure did not allow for any such activities to take place. As one of the researchers said during the interviews 'Why involve researchers if we shouldn't do any research?' Instead of letting the generation of ideas be based on 'real' data of some kind, imaginary constructs, personal ideas and perhaps even dreams of the perfect customers and so forth were used as a point of reference in the discussions. This might be rooted in an understanding of research as something overly complex and incompatible with the desired workshop structure, but it was provoking and even counterproductive in many ways. The use of imaginary data might fit the workshop process, but does not add significantly to the process of collaboratively producing knowledge. Although the use of imaginary data to some extent did push the discussions forward, it was also confusing, and provoked one of the team members to rightfully ask: 'Why would they have people not knowing anything about their business to help them to develop their business? Isn't that a really bad idea?' This notion of us working with *imaginary* data to solve *real* problems was further commented on in the follow-up, where one of the participants reflected on whether it actually works:

Some of it worked, there were some good moments where I did get some inspiration, but much of the time I was frustrated because we were being asked to create certainties (e.g. personas) and close off routes through the filtering process whereby we lost our less 'relevant' Post-its. We were asked to ignore rather than reveal the vulnerability of admitting what we do not know (i.e. needing research), which is the very thing that in fact enables us to move on and to create something that is new and ultimately hopefully more useful. ... So I don't want to say it was all negative; some of it did work well, but I sometimes ... got the feeling that the people leading the camp were using a set of techniques that are really conventional in that area but that they had not really reflected on how they worked. (Excerpt from interviews)

Acknowledging the Social Dynamics: A Route to Developing Workshop Methods

Through both these dimensions of experiencing a loss of improvisation and feeling out of practice runs an implicit yet noticeable process of forming social and dynamic bonds around the joint goal of investigating and elaborating on the different businesses. These processes seem to be partly constrained by the workshop method, but at the same time, partly afforded by it. Both empirical examples above show how the workshop method used constrained the moments of forming improvisational social practices (Hallam and Ingold 2007) by proposing rules for time limits, use of Post-its and content of discussions that did not account for the relational social processes that took place in the smaller work groups. But at the same time, due to the inherent social aspect of bringing people together with a specific task (discussing and developing the different companies' ideas for business), 'good moments' came out of it. With this in mind, we would suggest that one way of developing these workshop methods would be to order the meeting as a social event that connects the dots between the different activities during the workshop from a perspective of supporting situated, contextualized social practices, instead of trying to standardize and keep the different time and place variables fixed across different working groups, independent of the group members and the ideas and flows that these members create together.

The experience of loss of improvisation and being out of practice is a direct consequence of the desire to have a workshop model that fits multiple contexts with various constellations of participants. However, in many social scientific research contexts there is a professional expectation of improvisation that contradicts the idea of one-method-fits-all and the rhetoric surrounding business agendas on innovation, ideas and expectations that is embedded in theories of social learning. As Hallam and Ingold (2007) argue, there is an apparent tension between innovation and improvisation, since the former is oriented towards results whereas the latter emphasizes the processes that eventually lead up to those results. This tension is crucial when it comes to understanding the social dynamics of workshops and the possibility of allowing for a collaborative improvisation that is not constrained by scripts or the necessity to stick to a protocol.

Conclusion

In this chapter we have approached the question of why and how innovation does not always happen in collaborations between academia and the creative industries, and have pointed out some key barriers to collaborations between academia and industry that are created specifically by the very mechanisms put in place to make this happen. Workshops of the kind where people come together across disciplines and from both academic and commercial sectors imply not only an encounter between people but also between different sets of situated knowledge, social practices and professional expectations related to improvisation and creativity. As we have seen, these workshops are often heavily structured and rely on predefined (and slightly mystifying) processes, rather than the expertise of the participants and the social practices that unfold in such situations. We have seen that workshop methods exhibit an instrumental view on innovation in place of improvisation: ideas and knowledge are supposed to materialize as a product of the various steps of the process. While on the other hand, as Hallam and Ingold (2007) suggest, improvisation relies on the processes as such rather than their outcome:

> The difference between improvisation and innovation, then, is not that the one works within established convention while the other breaks it, but that the former characterizes creativity by way of its processes, the latter by way of its products (Hallam and Ingold 2007: 2).

The implications of this encounter between differing ideas and expectations on innovation and improvisation can be seen in how the innovation camp did not sufficiently engage the participants in practices (as understood theoretically as a place for developing situated learning and knowledge; see Wenger 1998; Lave and Wenger 1991) and how this lack of recognition of social processes caused confusion and, to some degree, frustration among the academic participants. Through such a restricted process, the 'automagical synergies' that are sought simply cannot be realized. We are thus in a situation where the possible outcomes of the workshop can never extend beyond the way in which the workshop itself is structured.

As an alternative to the product-focused workshops, we suggest that creative processes take place in situations marked by social learning that is irregular and iterative rather than linear. What clearly needs to be facilitated is thus the intertwinement of these forms of knowledge along with their different ways of producing knowledge. The workshop as a structured process involves various, and indeed, far-reaching simplifications of complex matters like *activity*, *doing* and *practice*, but in so doing, something crucial is lost, namely the ever so important encounter between people and their different experiences and expertise. The very ideas that emerge in and through the social learning encounters in a workshop must be able to alter the routes of the workshop and to some extent allow the process to be sensitive to the outcomes of each and every step or phase.

Martin Berg is Associate Professor of Sociology and Media Technology at Malmö University, Sweden. Berg is currently engaged in an international research project on self-tracking and life-logging technologies. Previously he was an industrial post-doctoral researcher within the creative industries, with financial support from the Swedish Foundation for Humanities and Social Sciences.

Vaike Fors is Associate Professor of Pedagogy in the School of Information Technology at Halmstad University, Sweden. She was formerly the director of SCACA (Swedish Centre for Applied Social and Cultural Analysis) and her applied work includes collaborative projects with both the museum sector and industry. Her area of expertise lies in the fields of visual and sensory ethnography in relation to research on learning and digital technologies. Recent publications include *Visuella metoder* (2015).

References

Algotson, S. and C. Daal. 2007. *Mötesplatser för upplevelseindustrin: metoder för samproduktion av kunskaps- och kompetensutveckling*. Stockholm: The Knowledge Foundation.
Banks, M. and K. Milestone. 2011. 'Individualization, Gender and Cultural Work', *Gender, Work and Organization* 18(1): 73–89.
Deuze, M. 2007. *Media Work*. Cambridge: Polity.
Deuze, M. (ed.). 2011. *Managing Media Work*. London: Sage.

Dewey, J. 1966. *Democracy and Education*. New York, NY: The Free Press.
Ehn, B. and O. Löfgren. 2009. 'Ethnography in the Marketplace', *Culture Unbound* 1: 31–49.
Fleming, T. 2007. *A Creative Economy Green Paper for the Nordic Region*. Oslo: Nordic Innovation Centre.
Florida, R. 2002. *The Rise of the Creative Class: And How It's Transforming Work, Leisure, Community and Everyday Life*. New York, NY: Basic Books.
Ghilardi, L. 2001. *Cultural Planning and Cultural Diversity*. London: Noema Research and Planning Ltd.
Gibbons, M., C. Limoges, H. Nowotny, S. Schwartzman, P. Scott and M. Trow. 1994. *The New Production of Knowledge: The Dynamics of Science and Research in Contemporary Societies*. London: Sage.
Gill, R. 2002. 'Cool, Creative and Egalitarian? Exploring Gender in Project-Based New Media Work in Europe', *Information, Communication and Society* 5(1): 70–89.
Gill, R. 2011. 'Life Is a Pitch: Managing the Self in New Media Work', in M. Deuze (ed.), *Managing Media Work*. London: Sage, pp. 249–262.
Gregg, M. 2011. *Work's Intimacy*. Cambridge: Polity Press.
Hallam, E. and T. Ingold. 2007. 'Creativity and Cultural Improvisation: An Introduction', in E. Hallam and T. Ingold (eds), *Creativity and Cultural Improvisation*. Oxford and New York: Berg, pp. 1–24.
Kelley, T and J. Littman. 2005. *The Ten Faces of Innovation: IDEO's Strategies for Defeating the Devil's Advocate and Driving Creativity Throughout Your Organization*. New York, NY: Doubleday.
Landry, C. and F. Bianchini. 1995. *The Creative City*. London: Demos.
Lave, J. and E. Wenger. 1991. *Situated Learning. Legitimate Peripheral Participation*. Cambridge, MA: Cambridge University Press.
Linton, A. and J. Michanek. 2012. *To Do: Development of Cultural Creative Industries in Practice*. Varberg: The Alexanderson Institute.
McRobbie, A. 2003. 'Clubs to Companies: Notes on the Decline of Political Culture in Speeded up Creative Worlds', *Cultural Studies* 16(4): 516–31.
Michanek, J. and A. Breiler. 2013. *The Idea Agent: The Handbook on Creative Processes*, 2nd edition. New York and London: Routledge.
OED Online. 2015. Oxford: Oxford University Press. Available online at http://www.oed.com/view/Entry/249985?redirectedFrom=automagicallyand.
Pratt, A. 2000. 'New Media, the New Economy and New Spaces', *Geoforum* 31(4): 425–36.
Ries, E. 2011. *The Lean Startup: How Today's Entrepreneurs Use Continuous Innovation to Create Radically Successful Businesses*. New York, NY: Crown Business.
Roberts, S. 2005. 'The Pure and the Impure? Reflections on Applied Anthropology and Doing Ethnography', in S. Pink (ed.), *Applications of Anthropology: Professional Anthropology in the Twenty-first Century*. Oxford/New York: Berghahn Books, pp. 72–89.
Schumpeter, J.A. 1912. *The Theory of Economic Development*. Piscataway, NJ: Transaction Publishers.
Taylor, S. and K. Littleton. 2012. *Contemporary Identities of Creativity and Creative Work*. Farnham: Ashgate.
Thiel, T and B. Masters. 2014. *Zero to One: Notes on Startups, or How to Build the Future*. New York, NY: Crown Business.
Wenger, E. 1998. *Communities of Practice: Learning, Meaning and Identity*. Cambridge, MA: Cambridge University Press.
Wertsch, J.V. 2000. 'Intersubjectivity and Alterity in Human Communication', in N. Budwig, I. Uzgiris and J.V. Wertsch (eds), *Communication: An Area of Development*. Stamford, CT: Ablex Publishing, pp. 17–32.

Chapter 3

THE CONVERSATION ANALYTIC ROLE-PLAY METHOD
Simulation, Endogenous Impact and Interactional Nudges

Elizabeth Stokoe and Rein Sikveland

This chapter will show how ethnomethodological theory, and its related conversation analytic method, can be used in innovative and effective ways to develop change-making applied research and intervention. It is located in debates about application in ethnomethodology, broadly, and conversation analysis, more specifically. Ethnomethodologists and conversation analysts aim to reveal the order and organization of social interaction – talk and embodied conduct – in both domestic and workplace or organizational settings. In so doing, they reveal the tacit knowledge that people display as they progress through courses of action. Ethnomethodologists and conversation analysts can identify, by examining the different ways people design social actions (e.g. requests, questions, offers, explanations), the endogenous impact of those different designs on the trajectory and outcome of the complete encounter (e.g. whether or not a patient agreed to take medication; whether or not a caller to a service became a client). They can, therefore, establish what works and what is less effective in communicative encounters, akin to identifying an interactional 'nudge'.

We start by charting the development and theoretical underpinnings of conversation analysis, before moving on to discuss application and intervention. We describe traditional forms of communication training and their basis in simulation, and show how these forms may be fundamentally challenged by conversation analysis. The chapter's applied example is the Conversation Analytic Role-play Method (CARM), a method for turning research findings into communication training. We will explore how, in developing and delivering CARM training, the academic acts as a 'cultural broker' between academic conversation analysts and practitioners; between those who produce knowledge about a setting and those whose setting it is. A key question within such debates is whether or not using the methods and empirical findings of conversation analytic research can be used to deliver practitioner and user interventions 'without compromise'.

Conversation Analysis and Theory

Conversation analysis (CA) emerged in the 1960s and 1970s in the work of the American sociologist, Sacks, and his colleagues Schegloff and Jefferson. Sacks's aim was to develop an alternative to mainstream sociology: an observational science of society that could be grounded in the 'details of actual events' (Sacks 1984a: 26). CA involves the study of technical transcripts of recordings of everyday (e.g. domestic telephone calls, face-to-face talk between friends) and institutional (e.g. workplace and organizational settings) talk, focusing on the turn-by-turn organization of interaction and studying 'social life as it happens' (Boden 1990). It has developed into an influential programme of work with many findings about how conversation works.

Sacks (1984b: 413) describes the basic aim of CA thus:

> to see how finely the details of actual, naturally occurring conversation can be subjected to analysis that will yield the technology of conversation. The idea is to take singular sequences of conversation and tear them apart in such a way as to find rules, techniques, procedures, methods, maxims (a collection of terms that more or less relate to each other and that I use somewhat interchangeably) that can be used to generate the orderly features we find in the conversations we examine. The point is, then, to come back to the singular things we observe in a singular sequence, with some rules that handle those singular features, and also, necessarily, handle lots of other events.

This quote is suggestive of CA's roots in ethnomethodology (EM: literally, 'the study of people's methods'), a programme developed by another sociologist, Garfinkel (1967), which was in turn influenced by the phenomenological philosophy of Schütz (e.g. 1962) and Goffman's (e.g. 1959) work on the interaction order. Garfinkel's basic idea was that people in society, or members, continuously engage in making sense of the world and, in so doing, methodically display their understandings of it: making their activities 'visibly-rational-and-reportable-for-all-practical-purposes' (Garfinkel 1967: vii). Language is central to the EM project of explicating members' methods for producing orderly and accountable social activities. For Schegloff (1996: 4), talk is 'the primordial scene of social life ... through which the work of the constitutive institutions of societies gets done'. And so EM's most thoroughgoing empirical translation was through conversation analytic studies of every kind of social setting, studying 'the world as it happens' (Boden 1990).

Within its home discipline of sociology, EM 'did not find a ready or fullhearted acceptance' (Heritage 1984: 224), often being trivialized as 'a method without substance' (Coser 1975). Later, CA and EM became increasingly contrasted with other theorized, explicitly political and 'interested' forms of qualitative analysis (e.g. Billig 1999; Schegloff 1997; Wetherell 1998). It is relatively common, then, outside of the empirical work itself, to find CA and EM 'accused' of being atheoretical in their approaches and methods, for their 'pointless' empiricism, their dangerous adoption of relativism, their focus on 'nothing but the text', and their failure to deal with subjectivity (for examples of such criticism, see Frosh 1999; Parker 2005: 91–92; for replies, see Edwards, Ashmore and Potter 1995; Edwards 2006, 2007). Furthermore, CA's preference for recordings of actual interaction, as opposed to retrospective interviews, has been criticized by those researchers who take as their primary data what people say in interviews and focus groups (e.g. Griffin 2007) – often under the aegis of 'psychosocial' and, particularly, 'thematic' or 'interpretative phenomenological' analysis (see Benwell and Stokoe 2006). As Lynch (2001) writes, 'Ethnomethodology has been criticized for its apparent lack of epistemological foundation and normative commitment, but proponents of the approach argue that their understandings and judgments have an ordinary basis in communal life rather than an epistemological foundation furnished by an academic school, theory, or method.'

CA/EM also reject a traditional social science approach to the relevance of a society's categories to understanding social life. Rather than start with, say, gender, class, ethnicity, culture, personality, and so on, to develop claims about how such categories are related to varying accounts, behaviour, or codified variables of some kind, CA starts with how participants themselves make relevant such categories in particular courses of social action (see Benwell and Stokoe 2006). For example, speakers invoke gender categories in specific ways to accomplish particular interactional goals, such as complaints, denials or accusations (see Stokoe 2009, 2010). In the body of CA work on gender, sexuality and ethnicity that has emerged in the last twenty years, many of the findings both upend what we think we know about the impact of gender on, say, interruption (see Kitzinger 2008), while at the same time demonstrating the import of such categories to everyday social life.

Much of the criticism of CA/EM is caricatured. Interestingly, it fails to engage in (or challenge) the details of the actual empirical work and its findings about social interaction. Instead, critics make sweeping, and erroneous, claims about CA/EM's (lack of) underlying theory (see Stokoe et al. 2012). For us, CA/EM is grounded in *ethnomethodological* theory, of course; a theory of social order and social organization. But it is also embedded in a theory of *language*. Grounded in Wittgenstein's (1963) ordinary language philosophy, and perhaps best articulated in the psychological manifestation of ethnomethodology, discursive psychology, CA/EM reject the communication or transmission view of language. In other words, they reject the theory that language is simply a tool to access the minds, cognitions, attitudes, experience, emotions, and so on, which 'lie beneath' (Edwards and Potter 1992). In that sense, CA/EM are akin to approaches that align themselves with the now well-trodden path of performativity, constructionism, and so on, treating language as constitutive and action-oriented (Stokoe 2008).

Conversation Analysis and Application

While conversation analysts pay a great deal of attention to the 'primordial' settings of everyday or 'ordinary' life (Schegloff 1996), CA's roots lie in Sacks's study of an institutional or 'applied' setting: telephone calls to a Los Angeles Suicide Prevention Centre. Since then, they have studied workplaces of all kinds, alongside domestic settings (see Llewellyn and Hindmarsh 2010 for an overview). Regarding the ordinary/institutional distinction, ordinary talk has been defined as 'forms of interaction that are not confined to specialized settings or to the execution of particular tasks' (Heritage 2005: 104). The organization of ordinary talk has been found to contrast systematically with institutional talk. For example, in institutional settings, participants have institution-specific goals to accomplish, and the kinds of contributions that can be made are constrained. The practices of ordinary conversation (as 'master institution') are therefore used and adapted in more 'specialized and restricted' contexts (Heritage 2005: 104).

Doing 'applied' or 'institutional' conversation analysis, in contrast to 'pure' or 'ordinary' CA, has been the subject of discussion across the discipline, with much of the focus being on the distinguishability between institutional and ordinary settings, the location of institutionality in talk or setting, and the empirical value of studies of talk applied settings over conducting 'basic' groundwork with 'ordinary' data (e.g. Benwell and Stokoe 2006; Drew and Sorjonen 1997; Have 1999; Heritage 2005; Hester and Francis 2001).

Furthermore, in a broader academic context where interventions are simultaneously prized by governments and funding bodies, yet often treated as less 'intellectually satisfying' and esteemed by academics themselves (e.g. von Prondzynski 2009), this chapter (and this book) raises questions about 'blue skies' versus 'interventionist' research and the inevitable hierarchical ordering of this dichotomy.

Despite these debates, conversation analysts have been making interventions in institutional practice for some years (see chapters in Antaki 2011). Application is possible because of a central insight of CA: that talk is highly routinized and systematic, with 'order at all points' (Sacks 1992: 484). In contrast to Chomsky's (e.g. 1965) assumption that, because real talk is too disorderly to study, linguists should study invented or idealized talk, the cumulative body of CA research has shown that it is 'repetitive, uniform, typical and cohort-independent' practices that comprise social life (Heap 1990: 46).

It is this systematicity in social interaction, as revealed through analysis, which permits the kinds of interventions made by conversation analysts. Writing about medical settings in particular, Heritage (2009) argues that 'the examination of real data using CA is found by many to be a potent experience capable of triggering changes in attitudes and clinic practices that are beneficial for patient care'. For example, Booth and Swabey (1999) developed a communication skills programme for carers of people with aphasia, using CA to produce individually tailored advice, with an assessment technique called the 'Conversation Analysis Profile for People with Aphasia' (Whitworth, Perkins and Lesser 1997). Pre- and post-intervention measures included whether or not carers understood more accurately their relatives' aphasia, whether or not the severity of the aphasia decreased, and whether or not trouble sources could be repaired more quickly, with some positive results.

In that conversation analysis is grounded in exposing the rules or maxims that *ordinary people use* to interact with one another – from turn taking to turn design – there is less of a conceptual, theoretical or epistemic 'gap' between theorist and practitioner, or between academic and user, than in more theoretical approaches to qualitative analysis. In institutional settings, practitioners' expertise is in doing their job. CA expertise is in exposing systematic patterns in practitioners' interaction, including what works and does not work. We move on to consider the relationship between conversation analyst, practitioner and communication training in the next section.

Communication Training, Simulation and Guidance

Communication training and assessment is dominated by simulation or 'role-play'. These are ubiquitous methods for training people in workplace settings of all kinds to better interact with other colleagues and members of the public. Van Hasselt, Romano and Vecchi (2008) define role-play as 'simulations of real-world interpersonal encounters, communications, or events' (p. 251). Typically, role-play methods involve the people being trained or assessed interacting with actors or other simulated interlocutors, using 'narrative adaptations' of hypothetical or actual scenarios as the basis for the simulated encounter (Van Hasselt et al. 2008: 254; see also Rosenbaum and Ferguson 2006). In addition to its training function, role-play is used to assess 'communication skills' across numerous workplace settings. It is also used more generally as a pedagogical tool in educational contexts (e.g. Andresen 2005), and to assess other sorts of psychological competences (e.g. Leising, Rehbein and Sporberg 2007).

The guiding assumption of simulated encounters is that they sufficiently mimic 'real life' interactional events to be effective in two ways: to practise the conversational moves that would comprise an actual encounter, and to assess what participants do in an actual encounter. However, as we have discussed elsewhere (Stokoe 2011; 2014), the authenticity of role-played interaction is assumed and asserted, but largely untested. Indeed, we have shown that there are some striking differences between simulated and actual encounters (cf. Leder Mackley and Pink, this volume, on *re-enactments* of domestic activities such as doing the laundry for the purposes of video ethnography research versus the natural occurrence without the researcher presence). For instance, in a study comparing police officers interviewing real suspects with officers in training interviewing actors playing the part of suspects, Stokoe (2013a) found that officers in training did things that they did not do in actual encounters. A number of differences emerged between the two sets of recorded interviews, in terms of the way in which actions such as eliciting suspects' names or explaining rights to legal representation were accomplished. In simulations, such actions were unpacked more elaborately, exaggeratedly, or explicitly, ensuring that particular features of their talk were made interactionally visible. A useful analogy might be taking a driving test and showing the examiner that 'I am looking in the rear-view mirror' by gesturing one's head unambiguously towards it.

This comparative analysis has a number of implications, including the importance of doing such comparative work in other settings, particularly in medical and healthcare interactions where role-play is used pervasively, to challenge the stasis of simulation as the only way to train professionals.

Conversation analysis reveals what is often referred to as 'tacit knowledge' – that is, the 'routine practices and ordinary language' – that people use to progress through any encounter (Lynch 2001: 136). Tacit knowledge of conversation, as opposed to 'explicit knowledge', may include things that speakers do to ask effective questions, respond well to requests, or explain services in an appealing way. But this knowledge is difficult to articulate post-hoc. While practitioners may be effective in their real-time encounters, they are rarely able to specify what worked, when positive outcomes turn on a particular word, intonation, or question format. As Kelly (2009: 245) notes,

> there are oral communication competencies that workers have developed and use to effect in their everyday practices but which have not been articulated and thus are not recognised in assessment measures related to training packages. The analysis of recordings of the talk used in authentic tasks, through which such competencies are made visible, can offer one way to ensure that such competencies become not only available for assessment but also available for formal recognition and credit for trainee employees.

Yet training for, and assessment of, communicative encounters, is often built from people's attempts to make explicit their tacit knowledge and build that into guidance and recommendations. We argue that this leads to failures in identifying the right 'trainables' or 'assessables', because people's 'memories' of their communicative encounters are shaped by stereotypes and normative assumptions (a classic psychological insight into the way memory works: Neisser 1962). This argument is shown empirically when one compares, say, guidance for police officers to pose effective initial questions to suspects with what works in actual encounters. The guidance states that:

> Best-practice interview protocols advise that interviewers elicit a 'free-narrative' account of offences through adherence to non-leading open-ended questions where possible, i.e., questions that encourage an elaborate response without dictating what specific information is required (Powell et al. 2010).

Consider the following extract, from an interview between a police officer and a suspect. The data are transcribed using Jefferson's (2004) system for conversation analysis, and the transcript includes information about timed gaps and pauses (numbers in brackets) and other markings relevant to intonation and pacing. We will explain these symbols when it becomes relevant to the analytic point we are making. The code 'RP1' is a corpus-identifier and is standard practice when referring to particular recordings in a large collection. P is the officer; S is the suspect.

Extract 1: RP1, police interview
```
 1  P: ↑FIRstly um: (.) I'd like y't'tell me about (0.8) your day: (.)
 2      from: when you woke up this mornin' until the point that we ↓met.
 3             (1.8)
 4  S: *Uh:: got up,h* (0.6) *went t'th'toilet:* (1.4) 'ad breakfast:
 5      (0.3) wen' t'Tesco, (1.4) got ju:mped on.
 6             (1.1)
 7  P: Okay, .hhh um: (.) would y'care t're- to: (0.4) expand on tha'
 8      an' give me some more detail.=t'describe: (0.6) your day.
 9             (0.3)
10  S: *Uhm::* (1.1) *got up,* (1.2) wen' toilet, h (2.5) uh:: (1.4)
11      wen' for a poo, (0.5) £.shih£ (0.4) uh: (.) wen' downstairs:
12      (1.8) uh: put toast in: toaster, […]
```

A basic observation about this extract is that P's question at line 1 adheres to the ideal question format as described in Powell et al. (2010). Indeed, Powell et al.'s description of best practice will be familiar to any social scientist who has read guidance for semi-structured or narrative interviewing of research participants. Yet, in the interview above, it generates an account from S that is not what was sought from P; our evidence for this is that P redesigns the question and asks it again (lines 7–9). Compare this to another example, from another interview:

Extract 2: PN-8, police interview
```
1  P: Could you tell me (0.3) uh the circumstances that le:d (0.4)
2      t'[you bein' arrested.
3  S:    [Uh- basically, (0.8) me an' Bob 'ad a little (0.6) ding-dong
4      we're fallin' ou:t, (0.7) 'e chucked me ou:t an' I just fli:pped
5      an' I went- (0.7) I jus' (0.4) 'it his doo:r with me golf club
6      basically, (0.5) that was it,
```

In extract 2, P's question is markedly (or subtly, depending on one's preferred level of engagement with conversational data) different to what happens in extract 1. The turns are grammatically different ('could you tell me' is a yes/no interrogative formatted question; 'I'd like you to tell me' is an imperative); they include different noun phrases ('your day'; 'the circumstances' and verbs ('met'; 'arrested'); and focus broadly (extract 1) or more narrowly (extract 2). They also produce quite different kinds of responses from suspects; in extract 2, S produces an account of his actions that orient to the relevant part of the day and his actions in a different way to S in extract 1.

Here, then, we can see that the 'guidance' question does not produce the kind of account that is valued by officers. Another type of question does that and, one might argue, should therefore feature in guidance. It is also relevant to point out that extract 1 comes from a simulation, in which the officer translates the guidance into an 'ideal' question and the suspect, an actor, subverts the process by doing things that real suspects do not. More generally, we found that paid actors playing the part of suspects often did things that real suspects did not – because they could; because the consequences for them were not as they would be for a real suspect in a real interview (Stokoe 2013a).

In another research project (see Shaw et al. 2016), we analysed neonatologists interacting with parents of extremely premature babies. We focused on episodes of talk in which critical care decisions were being initiated and progressed between the parties. We found that two distinct communicative approaches to decision making were used by doctors: 'making recommendations' and 'providing options'. Different trajectories for parental involvement in decision making were afforded by each design, as well as differences in terms of the alignments, or conflicts, between doctors and parents. 'Making recommendations', which included direct invocation of the 'best interests of the baby', led to misalignment and reduced opportunities for questions and collaboration; 'providing options' led to an aligned approach with opportunities for questions and fuller participation in the decision-making process. However, we also found that published guidance for such conversations recommends that doctors invoke 'best interest' (e.g. Royal College of Paediatrics and Child Health 2004).

Guidance for communication, then, is, at best, normative and ineffective or, at worst, counterproductive to professional and other communicative goals. It is generally driven top-down by a theory of communication, rather than bottom-up, from practice to guidance (e.g. Rogan, Hammer and Van Zandt 1997; Vecchi, Van Hasselt and Romano 2005). In contrast to these traditional ways of evolving guidance, and using role-playing techniques to enact that guidance, the Conversation Analytic Role-play Method (CARM) is an evidence-based, bottom-up approach that aims to identify 'trainables' and produce guidance and training on the basis of conversation analytic research about the sorts of problems that can occur in interaction, as well as the techniques and strategies that best resolve these problems. These are identified by analysing people's endogenous practices as they do their communicative work. CARM uses animated audio and video recordings of real-time, actual encounters as the basis of its training technique, and thus provides a unique opportunity to discuss and evaluate, in slow motion, actual talk as people do their jobs. It also provides an evidence base for making decisions about effective practice and communication policy in organizations. Emmison (2013: 5) has recently commented that, 'in the context of the need for CA to make its findings more relevant for lay practitioners, Stokoe's development of CARM – the Conversation Analysis Role-Play Method – is perhaps the most significant of these developments'. We turn to the development of CARM in the next section.

The Conversation Analytic Role-play Method

CARM is, first and foremost, an approach based on conversation analytic evidence about the sorts of problems and roadblocks that can occur in interaction, as well as the techniques and strategies that best resolve and overcome them. The research findings that were to underpin CARM workshops were generated in a UK Research Council-funded study of neighbour disputes (e.g. Stokoe and Edwards 2009). The project was designed around collecting naturally occurring data from contexts in which neighbours might talk to one another and engage in defining what counted as a 'good neighbour relationship'. In addition to investigative police-suspect interviews in cases of neighbour crime, and calls into various local authority council offices, we approached community mediation services to ask if they might record encounters between mediators and clients. Towards the end of the project, the focus turned away from analysing the design of neighbour complaints and towards the organization of initial inquiries themselves, and, in particular, whether or not callers became clients of community mediation organizations by the end of their encounter with a mediator. Given that the services are generally free, it was surprising that many callers were not 'converted' into clients.

As conversation analysts, we know that our data provides the basis for 'naturally occurring experiments' which can, because of the 'next turn proof procedure', generate evidence about the effectiveness or otherwise of communicative practices. In analysing initial inquiries to mediation services, we found that certain types of mediator activities were more likely than others to result in a positive outcome. For example, as we will illustrate in the next section, we identified ways of explaining mediation that were more or less effective, demonstrated by callers' responses (Stokoe 2013b). By collecting such endogenous measurements, CA provides evidence of the outcomes achieved with 'interactional nudges', from uncovering how customers are encouraged to pay 'Gift Aid' on their entrance fee in an art gallery (Llewellyn 2015) to the difference one word can make to reduce patients' unmet concerns in consultations with GPs (Heritage et al. 2007). By identifying practices that led to successful and unsuccessful outcomes, we generated research-based information for mediators to better engage callers and convert them into clients: a bottom-line issue for services (e.g. Edwards and Stokoe 2007; Stokoe 2013b; Sikveland and Stokoe 2016).

This research fed into the development, with further research council funding for knowledge exchange, of CARM. CARM workshops, using anonymized recordings presented in real time with technical transcripts, take trainees through the live unfolding of actual service encounters, stopping to discuss, then explain, the practices that work, or do not work (Stokoe 2011). A workshop is developed by selecting extracts from research findings about a particular practice (e.g. explaining a service). In workshops, animation software is used to play the audio and transcript synchronously. This means that workshop participants live through conversations without knowing what is coming next, and then 'role-play' what they might do next to handle the situation. If party A makes a particular comment, how might party B respond most appropriately? Participants discuss likely responses in small groups and report to the whole group. At that point party B's actual response is played. Participants evaluate what party B did, and report back to the whole group. Participants see and evaluate different responses, identifying effective practice on the basis of what actually happens in real interaction. CARM provides participants with a unique opportunity to examine communicative practices in forensic detail, and to understand what works from a rigorous empirical basis. Examining the anonymized talk of people doing the work that participants do is often instantly compelling; there is also a ready fit between CA research (in which analysts make explicit members' own analyses of each turn as an interaction unfolds), and showing conversational data to non-CA audiences, because the conceptual gap between research and practice is small.

From Caller to Client

One set of workshops has been built from studies of the initial inquiries, or intake calls, that people make to mediation services. As we have shown elsewhere (Stokoe 2013b), callers to mediation services typically do not know anything about mediation and have often been given the number by another organization. It is a challenge, then, for call takers to sell an unknown service to someone who did not know they wanted that service in the first place. But describing and selling mediation to potential clients is something that can be done in different ways. Some ways work, others do not. This matters, because if mediators only manage to convert a small number of callers into clients, then the service will struggle to survive. Indeed, several of the services from whom we originally collected data no longer exist.

When people call a mediation service, their first substantive project is to explain the problem they are having with their neighbour, partner, or whomever they are having a dispute with. After the caller has explained their problem, mediators explain what mediation involves. Analysis reveals that this information can be packaged in different ways, particularly with regards to the way mediators explain 'impartiality'. Inside the 'naturally occurring experiments' of conversational data, we can see the effectiveness of different explanations by examining how callers respond to them. The effectiveness of the explanation is in the next turn. The extract below is typical of one way that mediators explain the impartiality of the process. Before seeing this explanation, we often ask mediators to produce an explanation of impartiality that they might use on their organization's website.

Extract 3a: HC-7
1   M: We wouldn't take si:des, we wouldn't- (0.7) try an' decide who's right
2   or wrong but would- .hh would try to help you both um:: (0.8)
3   sort out uh: the differences between: (0.2) between you.

Across the data we found explanations like this one, which include phrases like 'we don't take sides', 'we don't decide who's right or wrong', as well as other things like 'we don't have any authority' or 'we don't offer solutions'. These phrases co-occurred with the caller saying 'no' to mediation. However, these sorts of phrases are regularly used by mediators to explain the process, including on their websites. After discussing M's explanation, the caller's response is revealed.

Extract 3b: HC-7
1   M: We wouldn't take si:des, we wouldn't- (0.7) try an' decide who's right
2   or wrong but would- .hh would try to help you both um:: (0.8)
3   sort out uh: the differences between: (0.2) between you.
4   (2.5)
5   C: Well I-hh (1.2) to be qui:te honest I don't think she'd cooperate.

Because callers have phoned up with a one-sided problem – it is the other party's fault – the offer of a *two-sided* solution is generally unattractive. As noted earlier, callers take the opportunity to negatively characterize the other party, and this kind of account, that the other party is 'the kind of person who won't mediate', was commonly used in callers' rejections of mediation as a course of action. Explanations of mediation that focused on process and procedure, and did not include phrases like 'we don't take sides', were more effective in keeping callers engaged and more likely to make them agree to mediate.

By this point in workshops, participants have learned a lot about CA's technical transcription, and know that the silence at line 4, when it is played, is indicative of upcoming bad news. What they see is that, at line 4, what does *not* happen is an enthusiastic response to M's explanation. Again, they discuss what they might do in response to line 5.

Extract 3c: HC-7
1 M: We wouldn't take si:des, we wouldn't- (0.7) try an' decide who's
2   right or wrong but would- .hh would try to help you both um::
3   (0.8) sort out uh: the differences between: (0.2) between you.
4   (2.5)
5 C: Well I-hh (1.2) to be qui:te honest I don't think she'd cooperate.
6   (0.4)
7 M: N:o:.

We found that some mediators have effective ways to handle this most common route out of mediation: that the other person is unlikely to mediate. However, M does not. He does not know that this way of formulating mediation is likely to generate such a response, and does not have a strategy for handling it. In CARM workshops, we present a number of explanations that do not work, and a number that do. Here is an example of a different type of explanation.

Extract 4: EC-37
1 M: We're a mediation projec- (0.4) project in the:: (.) Stockham area,
2 C: Ye[h.
3 M: [.hhh and what - (0.2) we try t'help neighbours that are in dispute::,
4   [.hhh What we do first um: .pt send a letter out to your neighbour straight=
5 C: [Uhuh.
6 M: = away .hh t'say that: y- we've been in touch with you, .h[hh and hm- =
7 C: [Yeh,
8 M: = ask 'em (0.2) whether they would (0.4) .hhh get in touch with us so that
9   we can discuss it with them? Hh=
10 C: =Yeh,
11 M: If they sa:::y- if they phone up an' say yes then we make an arrangement
12   t'come an' see you both separately, .hhhhh [but with (0.3) but with the =
13 C: [Yes.
14 M: =aim of: (0.2) <eventually,> gettin' (0.3) round a table an' discussing
15   matters with you all,
16 C: M[m:.
17 M: [.hhh to try an' come t'some sort of an agree:ment of: ways you can go
18   fo:rward.

In contrast to extract 3, in this case the mediator explains mediation as a process, and in terms of what it does, rather than what it does not do. The evidence that this explanation is 'working' is in the caller's regular responses as each component of the explanation is produced. Note that the mediator does not hide from the caller that they will talk to their neighbour, but neither do they invoke notions of 'sides'. They describe the process as impartial, in a way, but do not explicitly articulate it as ideology. Overall, mediators are able to see directly how to engage prospective clients from the evidence playing out in front of them. The research (Stokoe 2013b) showed that *procedural* rather than *ideological* explanations of mediation were more effective in getting callers to become clients of their service, and that effectiveness could be assessed within the call itself.

Not only did the research underpin telephone training for mediators, but it has also underpinned wider interventions in the way that mediation services promote and explain mediation on their websites and leaflets. In 2014, we provided consultancy input into the UK Ministry of Justice to change the wording and design of their promotional mediation materials. What is important about our intervention is that, rather than test the efficacy of website wording in focus groups, where participants are not invested in becoming a client *right now*, for a *particular* reason, *today*, and then decide that the wording 'works', we were able to provide evidence-based input into wording and design. We were able to draw on our research about what works to engage prospective clients, to engage people who would (or would not) become clients of mediation in a live interactional moment.

Interactional Nudge

The interactional data presented above allows us to measure, within the interaction itself, the impact and outcome of particular forms of language, designs of questions, and so on. In this way, it pulls conversation analytic research towards the territory of behavioural change (e.g. Dolan et al. 2012; Thaler and Sunstein 2008), which is of key interest to policy makers around the world. Thaler and Sunstein define a 'nudge' as 'any aspect of the choice architecture that alters people's behavior in a predictable way without forbidding any options or significantly changing their economic incentives'. There are many well-known examples of nudge theory in action, and many of these are language-based. For example, Goldstein, Cialdini and Griskevicius (2008) examined the relative effectiveness of different signs in hotel bathrooms about towel recycling using a randomized design. They found that 'Appeals employing descriptive norms (e.g., "the majority of guests reuse their towels") proved superior to a traditional appeal widely used by hotels that focused solely on environmental protection' (p. 472), in that statistically significantly more hotel guests recycled in the first condition.

What is missing in the 'nudge' literature, and therefore what CA can contribute, is the interactional basis for randomized controlled trials – for those who require statistical confidence in research findings. Compare the next two sets of extracts, again from calls to mediation services. In extracts 5–7, the mediator explains mediation using a particular word from its ideology – it is 'voluntary':

Extract 5: HC-2
1 M: U:h (0.5) an:d (.) we:: (0.4) it's a voluntary process, .hh so that (.) if your
2   neighbours were: (0.4) unwilling: (.) t'be involved in .h (.) mediation then
3   there: (.) is nothing more (.) we could do:.

22 C: I've seen her out doin' the fishwife bit shoutin' at all the other residents in
23   the street. so that's not gonna work. .h
24 M: M:m. It doesn't sound very promising,.h

Extract 6: DG-5
1 M: .hhh so mediation *i*s- is a slightly sort of different process.
2   .hhh uh[m it-] it's a ↑voluntary ↓proce:ss:?=
3 C: [Right.]
4 M: =.hh it's not for everybody? .mhhh .pt uh:m(b) but it's [to-]
5 C: [Yea]h to be honest
6   it does[n't sound] like it's for ↓me,='cause I know it's (uh) gonna be all=
7 M: [(Mhhh)   ]
8 C: =uh- a waste of time,

Extract 7: FMNE-7
1 M: Uh: mediation's voluntary.=so that first appointment is all abou:t:
2   (0.2) .thhh you know. us giving you enough information. .hhh to see
3   whether it's going to work for you.
4   (.)
5 M: .hhh uh::m an:d: as I ↓say it's ↑absolutely voluntary,=so:: (.) you know.
6   (0.2) for b- for each of you. .hhh uh:m if you decide not to proceed that's
7   fine.(m)
8   (0.2)
9 M: .mhhh .ptk uh::m […]

In each case, the word 'voluntary' is closely associated with the caller starting to withdraw more or less actively from the call. In extract 5, the problem with mediation being 'voluntary' is articulated by the mediator himself: 'if your neighbours were: (0.4) unwilling: (.) t'be involved in .h (.)

mediation then there: (.) is nothing more (.) we could do:.'. A few lines later, the upshot of the call is the agreement between caller and mediator that it is unlikely that the caller's neighbour would mediate. Here, the mediator has *offered* the way out of mediation to the caller using exactly the same kind of account that callers themselves use (cf. extract 3c 'I don't think she'd cooperate').

In extract 6, not only does the mediator promote the fact that mediation is voluntary (line 2), she also provides an account that functions as a way out for the caller ('it's not for everybody'). This may be true, but it is not an effective sales pitch! At line 5, the caller does not wait for the mediator to complete her turn before rejecting mediation as a course of action – something that will be a 'waste of time'. Finally, in extract 7, note the lack of alignment from the caller as the mediator emphasizes the voluntary nature of mediation: compare it to extract 4 in which the caller shows her alignment to the mediator's explanation by filling each turn with a 'continuer': 'yes' or 'yeah'. Note also that in extract 4, the mediator does not hide the fact that the process is 'voluntary'; the process is conditional on the participation of the other party ('if they phone up an' say yes'). However, she does not use the word itself.

Finally, consider the following brief extracts. In extract 8, the mediator has explained mediation and is now asking the caller directly if she wants to use the service:

Extract 8a: EC-37
1   M: Does that sound .hhh like it might be helpful to you?
2   (0.7)

We know from line 2 – a gap of 0.7 seconds – that it is likely that the caller is about to produce a rejection-implicative turn. Conversation analysis, by examining talk in such forensic detail, is able to pinpoint key moments in interaction that show trouble ahead. If the caller was enthusiastic about mediation, this would reveal itself at line 2 (e.g. 'that sounds great!'; 'yes it does', etc.). Let us see the caller's response:

Extract 8b: EC-37
1   M: Does that sound .hhh like it might be helpful to you?
2   (0.7)
3   C: I- uh- (0.2) it might be but um:: (0.3) I'm not too sure at this stage about
4   (0.6) you know, how long- y- seein' this: gi:rl, [at all,

The caller's response is indeed a classic 'dispreferred' response, in that it is delayed, it includes an appreciation 'it might be' and an account that starts to invoke the other party ('this girl'). In CARM workshops, we ask mediators to consider what they might do to nevertheless encourage the caller to become their client. 95% of mediators do not come up with what actually works, even though we have found the practice quite regularly across our data corpus. This suggests that people are not good at recalling their experience sufficiently to know what works in these crucial moments, even if they may use it in practice. What works is revealed in extract 8c:

Extract 8c: EC-37
```
1  M: Does that sound .hhh like it might be helpful to you?
2         (0.7)
3  C: I- uh- (0.2) it might be but um:: (0.3) I'm not too sure about
4        (0.6) you know, how long- y- seein' this: gi:rl, [at all,
5  M:                                                    [W'yeah.=↓yeh, but you'd
6     be willin' t'see two of our media[tors jus' t'talk about it all. .hhhh]
7  C:                                  [ Oh of course. Yeah. Yeah         ]
8     definitely.
```

We found that when mediators ask if callers are 'willing', or propose that they are – as in this case – callers' responses are quite marked: it is fast (note the overlap at line 7 where the caller begins to respond, before she has heard all of what is being proposed, that she is willing!) and it is 'more than' – she does not just say 'yes'. The mediator's proposal about the caller is a moral one: the caller, unlike the caller's neighbour (cf. extracts 4 and 5 – 'if your neighbour was unwilling …'), *is* the kind of person who will mediate. Here are some further examples of callers' strong uptake of mediation in response to questions including the word 'willing':

Extract 9: DG-1
```
1  M: I'm sure he would be will:ing t'come in and see our mediat[or:?
2  C:                                                            [Oh yeah:
```

Extract 10: CFM-3
```
1  M: I just- wanted to see if you would be willing to attend a: a session as well.
2  C: I'm more than happy to go down that route.
```

Extract 11: EC-38
```
1  M: Okay then, so would you be willin' f'two of our mediators to call round
2     and talk to you about it all?
3  C: Yeh I'm more than ((willing)).
```

Extract 12: DG-19
```
1  M: =Is that something that you would be willing to [do:.    ]=
2  C:                                                [I would-]=
3  C: =I ↑would be willing to ↓do it.=ye[s:.    ]
4  M:                                   [.ptk (th)at]'s grea:[t.    ]
5  C:                                                        [Just-] (.) do anything
6     just to try and get to see my son,=you know,
```

In each case, note that the caller responds immediately and with more than a 'yes' response ('Oh yeah'; 'I'm more than happy'; 'I'm more than willing'; 'I would…'). Indeed, in extracts 8 and 9, the 'Oh' indicates that the caller's position preceded the question; that they – unlike their neighbour or partner – were always willing to mediate.

Here, then, we have seen how certain linguistic 'nudges' make it more or less likely that callers will engage in a particular behaviour – or at least take the first step of saying 'yes' on the phone and making an appointment. Conversation analysis provides insights into what works and what is not effective in these and other environments, sometimes scaling up findings statistically. Indeed, we found that, when quantifying the effect of 'willing' compared to other formats used by mediators (e.g., 'Are you interested' 'Do you want' , 'Would you be happy to'), 'willing' was significantly more likely to be followed by a strong uptake than other formats (Sikveland and Stokoe 2016).

In addition to training mediators in CARM workshops, we consulted for both the UK Ministry of Justice and the USA Superior Court Alternative Dispute Resolution Service who, on the basis of our research, changed the language used to describe family and community mediation in government promotional materials online, in posters and on leaflets. These interventions demonstrate the impact of conversation analytic research in surprising settings, and how one might translate findings about effective spoken interaction with the written word. How does one best learn the effectiveness of a service like mediation through a published explanation? One could run focus groups with potential users, but these participants do not have the same stake in evaluating an explanation as a caller, live on the phone, deciding in the context of calling for help. One could ask other professionals, who may give an opinion. Or one can test, live, the effectiveness of an explanation by seeing the outcome in a call such as those illustrated above. Spoken interaction, as a 'naturally occurring experiment', provides the best evidence about what works, in a setting that matters.

Discussion and Implications

This edited collection showcases a number of real world interventions in practice and training based on social science research. Focusing particularly on conversation analysis, we have made four key observations: (1) that conversation analysis and ethnomethodology's methods and theory underpin an empirical research database revealing the systematicity of social interaction; (2) that this systematicity provides the basis for making interventions in practice, through communication training, in myriad social, legal and medical settings; (3) that traditional forms of communication training, often developed top-down from theory, produce egregious guidance and simulated encounters that do not reflect actual interaction, and, (4) that the Conversation Analytic Role-play Method provides a robust, research-based alternative to traditional forms of training.

The applied conversation analytic research described in this chapter has not only helped mediators and other practitioners across numerous domains, in the field, but pushed the scholarly field of CA forward. It starts to debunk the notion that CA is atheoretical (it is grounded in ethnomethodology and is connected to fields like behavioural science) or that it is 'a method without substance' (it is a method with the power to identify and realize social change). Its insistence on studying social life via recordings of actual interaction, rather than relying on post-hoc interviews or simulations, has important pay-offs when it comes to identifying what is effective in workplace communication of all kinds. Although CA's original home was sociology, its remit is inter- and multidisciplinary, with analysts working in settings from medicine to human geography, and from education to business studies. The potential of CA, and CARM, to be a route to impact and intervention is beginning to be realized (Emmison 2013; Sikveland et al. 2016; Stokoe et al. 2016).

One question that arises is whether or not the methods and empirical findings of conversation analytic research can be used to deliver practitioner and user interventions while maintaining the integrity of the academic endeavour (see Stokoe, Hepburn and Antaki 2012). Which sites do we choose to study (see Heap 1990)? On whose 'side' do we intervene? Much CA research focuses on the sorts of 'socially responsible' agencies and social services (e.g. primary medical care in Robinson and Heritage 2014; speech therapy in Beeke et al. 2014; Koole and Mak 2014, welfare services in Drew et al. 2014; neurological diagnosis in Jenkins and Reuber 2014; and telephone helplines in Hepburn et al. 2014). For this reason, CA-based interventions have a ready academic integrity. But, as we have argued in this chapter, CA-based interventions have *epistemic* integrity. In the world of untested communication skills training programmes, for which the simulations used have no empirical basis to their claims of authenticity, CARM and related approaches deliver workplace interventions grounded uncompromisingly in empirical findings about the communicative practices that comprise the setting.

In the last four years, CARM's reach and impact has proliferated. CARM workshops were accredited by the UK College of Mediators and the Royal College of Paediatrics and Child Health, meaning that participants are awarded 'Continuing Professional Development' points ('CPD') which practitioners must accrue each year. The route to CPD is one way of developing wider audiences and demand for training interventions, as well as generating interest in CA research and changing the culture of communication training (see Meagher 2013 on the impact of CARM). Furthermore, CARM has recently been commercialized as a not-for-profit social enterprise (www.carmtraining.org), securing private as well as public sector clients, and generating income to employ researchers and cross-subsidize workshops for third-sector organizations. It also won an Enterprise Award (2013), has been the subject of numerous public engagement activities including a TED talk (2014), and won a WIRED Innovation Fellowship (2015).

Such enterprise activities might be steps too far for some. Yet, in a world of limited research funding, it generates income to support research and researchers. It has provided researchers with a tried-and-tested method for intervention that was developed with research council funding, providing leverage for further funding. It shows how what we refer to as 'designedly large-scale qualitative research' can create impact, and underlines the clear differences between CA and more traditional qualitative forms of inquiry. It also brings CA to wide audiences who begin to understand the power of studying interaction scientifically.

CARM's unique contribution brings together ethnomethodological theory, conversation analytic method and applied practice. CARM projects are, crucially, user-driven, in that practitioners (police officers, medics, mediators, salespeople, etc.) approach us to design projects that deal directly with communication problems (e.g. hostage negotiation, general practice front-of-house appointment making, securing clients). In this way, theory, practice and intervention remain closely integrated throughout projects. Yet they also evolve organically rather than purely instrumentally; because CA is thoroughly inductive, we cannot know ahead of looking at practice what findings will emerge, and therefore what 'trainables' we may identify for any subsequent intervention. In conclusion, we hope to have showcased work that manages to address contemporary academic pressures to conduct research with impact, while maintaining academic integrity and scholarly endeavour.

Elizabeth Stokoe is Professor of Social Interaction in the Department of Social Sciences at Loughborough University. She won a Wired Innovation Fellowship for her development of the Conversation Analytic Role-play Method and has spoken about the science of talk at TED and the Royal Institution.

Rein Ove Sikveland is a Research Associate in the Department of Social Sciences at Loughborough University. He is an expert in phonetics and conversation analysis, and is co-developing the Conversation Analytic Role-play Method in commercial and healthcare settings.

References

Andresen, H. 2005. 'Role Play and Language Development in the Preschool Years', *Culture & Psychology* 11(4): 387–414.

Antaki, C. (ed.). 2011. *Applied Conversation Analysis: Intervention and Change in Institutional Talk*. Basingstoke: Palgrave Macmillan.

Beeke, S., F. Johnson, F. Beckley, C. Heilemann, S. Edwards, J. Maxim and W. Best. 2014. 'Enabling Better Conversations between a Man with Aphasia and his Conversation Partner: Incorporating Writing into Turn Taking', *Research on Language and Social Interaction* 47(3): 292–305.

Benwell, B.M. and E. Stokoe. 2006. *Discourse and Identity*. Edinburgh: Edinburgh University Press.

Billig, M. 1999. 'Whose Terms? Whose Ordinariness? Rhetoric and Ideology in Conversation Analysis', *Discourse & Society* 10(4): 543–58.

Boden, D. 1990. 'The World as it Happens: Ethnomethodology and Conversation Analysis', in G. Ritzer (ed.), *Frontiers of Social Theory: The New Synthesis*. New York, NY: Columbia University Press, pp. 185–213.

Booth, S. and D. Swabey. 1999. 'Group Training in Communication Skills for Carers of Adults with Aphasia', *International Journal of Language & Communication Disorders* 34(4): 291–309.

Chomsky, N. 1965. *Aspects of the Theory of Syntax*. Cambridge, MA: MIT Press.

Coser, L. 1975. 'Presidential Address: Two Methods in Search of a Substance', *American Sociological Review* 40(6): 691–700.

Dolan, P., M. Hallsworth, D. Halpern, D. King, R. Metcalfe, I. Vlaev. 2012. 'Influencing Behaviour: The Mindspace Way', *Journal of Economic Psychology* 33(1): 264–77.

Drew, P. and M. Sorjonen. 1997. 'Institutional Dialogue', *Discourse as Social Interaction* 2: 92–118.

Drew, P., M. Toerien, A. Irvine and R. Sainsbury. 2014. 'Personal Adviser Interviews with Benefits Claimants in UK Jobcentres', *Research on Language and Social Interaction* 47(3): 306–16.

Edwards, D. 2006. 'Discourse, Cognition and Social Practices: The Rich Surface of Language and Social Interaction', *Discourse Studies* 8(1): 41–49.

Edwards, D. 2007. 'Managing Subjectivity in Talk', in A. Hepburn and S. Wiggins (eds), *Discursive Research in Practice: New Approaches to Psychology and Interaction*. Cambridge: Cambridge University Press, pp. 31–49.

Edwards, D. and J. Potter. 1992. *Discursive Psychology*. London: Sage.

Edwards, D. and E. Stokoe. 2007. 'Self-help in Calls for Help with Problem Neighbors', *Research on Language and Social Interaction* 40(1): 9–32.

Edwards, D., M. Ashmore and J. Potter. 1995. 'Death and Furniture: The Rhetoric, Politics and Theology of Bottom Line Arguments against Relativism', *History of the Human Sciences; Hist.Hum.Sci.* 8(2): 25–49.

Emmison, M. 2013. 'Epistemic Engine versus Role-play Method: Divergent Trajectories in Contemporary Conversation Analysis', *Australian Journal of Communication* 40(2): 5–7.

Frosh, S. 1999. 'What is Outside Discourse?', *Psychoanaytic Studies* 1(4): 381–90.

Garfinkel, H. 1967. *Studies in Ethnomethodology*. Englewood Cliffs, NJ: Prentice Hall.

Goffman, E. 1959. *The Presentation of Self in Everyday Life*. Garden City, NY: Doubleday.

Goldstein, N.J., R.B. Cialdini and V. Griskevicius. 2008. 'A Room with a Viewpoint: Using Social Norms to Motivate Environmental Conservation in Hotels', *Journal of Consumer Research* 35(3): 472–82.

Griffin, C. 2007. 'Being Dead and Being There: Research Interviews, Sharing Hand Cream and the Preference for Analysing "Naturally Occurring Data"', *Discourse Studies* 9(2): 246–69.

Have, P.T. 1999. *Doing Conversation Analysis: A Practical Guide*. London: Sage Publications.

Heap, J.L. 1990. 'Applied Ethnomethodology: Looking for the Local Rationality of Reading Activities', *Human Studies* 13(1): 38–72.

Hepburn, A., S. Wilkinson and C.W. Butler. 2014. 'Intervening with Conversation Analysis in Telephone Helpline Services: Strategies to Improve Effectiveness', *Research on Language and Social Interaction* 47(3): 239–54.

Heritage, J. 1984. *Garfinkel and Ethnomethodology*. Cambridge: Polity Press.

Heritage, J. 2005. 'Conversation Analysis and Institutional Talk', in K.L. Fitch and R.E. Sanders (eds), *Handbook of Language and Social Interaction*. Mahwah, NJ: Lawrence Erlbaum Associates, pp. 103–47.

Heritage, J. 2009. 'Negotiating the Legitimacy of Medical Problems: A Multi-phase Concern for Patients and Physicians', in D. Brashers and D. Goldsmith (eds), *Communicating to Manage Health and Illness*. New York, NY: Routledge, pp. 47–164.

Heritage, J., J.D. Robinson, M.N. Elliott, M. Beckett and M. Wilkes. 2007. 'Reducing Patients' Unmet Concerns in Primary Care: The Difference One Word can Make', *Journal of General Internal Medicine* 22(10): 1429–33.

Hester, S. and D. Francis. 2001. 'Institutional Talk Institutionalised?', *Text* 20(3): 3–9.

Hutchby, I. 2005. 'Conversation Analysis and the Study of Broadcast Talk', in K.L. Fitch and R.E Sanders (eds), *Handbook of Language and Social Interaction*, pp. 437–460. Mahwah, NJ: Lawrence Erlbaum Associates.

Jefferson, G. 2004. 'Glossary of Transcript Symbols with an Introduction', in G.H. Lerner (ed.), *Conversation Analysis: Studies from the First Generation*. Amsterdam, PA: John Benjamins, pp. 13–31.

Jenkins, L. and M. Reuber. 2014. 'A Conversation Analytic Intervention to Help Neurologists Identify Diagnostically Relevant Linguistic Features in Seizure Patients' Talk', *Research on Language and Social Interaction* 47(3): 266–79.

Kelly, A. 2009. 'Articulating Tacit Knowledge through Analyses of Recordings: Implications for Competency Assessment in the Vocational Education and Training Sector', in C. Wyatt-Smith and J.J. Cumming (eds), *Educational Assessment in the 21st Century: Connecting Theory and Practice*. Dordrecht: Springer Science + Business Media, pp. 245–62.

Kitzinger, C. 2008. 'Developing Feminist Conversation Analysis: A Response to Wowk', *Human Studies* 31(2): 179–208.
Koole, T. and P. Mak. 2014. 'Using Conversation Analysis to Improve an Augmented Communication Tool', *Research on Language and Social Interaction* 47(3): 280–91.
Leising, D., D. Rehbein and D. Sporberg. 2007. 'Validity of the Inventory of Interpersonal Problems (IIP–64) for Predicting Assertiveness in Role-play Situations', *Journal of Personality Assessment* 89(2): 116–25.
Llewellyn, N. 2015. 'Microstructures of Economic Action: Talk, Interaction and the Bottom Line.' *British Journal of Sociology*, 66 (3), 486–511.
Llewellyn, N. and J. Hindmarsh (eds). 2010. *Organisation, Interaction and Practice: Studies of Ethnomethodology and Conversation Analysis*. Cambridge: Cambridge University Press.
Lynch, M. 2001. 'Ethnomethodology and the Logic of Practice', in T. Schatzki, T. Knorr Cetina and E. von Savigny (eds), *The Practice Turn in Contemporary Theory*. London: Routledge, pp. 131–48.
Meagher, L.R. 2013. *Research Impact on Practice: Case Study Analysis: Report on ESRC Grant Number RES-189-25-0202 Mediating and Policing Community Disputes: Developing New Methods for Role-play Communication Skills Training*. Available online at www.esrc.ac.uk
Neisser, U. 1962. 'Cultural and Cognitive Discontinuity', in T.E. Gladwin and W. Sturtevant (eds), *Anthropology and Human Behaviour*. Washington, DC: Anthropological Society of Washington, pp. 54–71.
Parker, I. 2005. *Qualitative Psychology: Introducing Radical Research*. Buckingham: Open University Press.
Powell, M.B., C.H. Hughes-Scholes, C. Cavezza and M.A. Stoove. 2010. 'Examination of the Stability and Consistency of Investigative Interviewer Performance across Similar Mock Interview Contexts', *Legal and Criminological Psychology* 15(2): 243–60.
von Prondzynski, F. 2009. 'A University Blog: Diary of a University President'. Available online at http://universitydiary.wordpress.com/2009/07/09/pure-or-applied.
Robinson, J.D. and J. Heritage. 2014. 'Intervening with Conversation Analysis: The Case of Medicine', *Research on Language and Social Interaction* 47(3): 201–18.
Rogan, R.G., M.R. Hammer and C.R. Van Zandt (eds). 1997. *Dynamic Processes of Crisis Negotiation: Theory, Research and Practice*. Westport, CT: Praeger. ABC-CLIO.
Rosenbaum, M.E. and K.J. Ferguson. 2006. 'Using Patient-generated Cases to Teach Students Skills in Responding to Patients' Emotions', *Medical Teacher* 28(2): 180–82.
Royal College of Paediatrics and Child Health (RCPCH). 2004. *Withholding or Withdrawing Life Sustaining Treatment in Children: A Framework for Practice*. 2nd edn. London: RCPCH.
Sacks, H. 1992. *Lectures on Conversation*. Oxford: Blackwell.
Sacks, H. 1984a. 'Notes on Methodology', in J.M. Atkinson and J. Heritage (eds), *Structures of Social Action*. Cambridge: Cambridge University Press, pp. 21–27.
Sacks, H. 1984b. 'On Doing "Being Ordinary"', in J.M. Atkinson and J. Heritage (eds), *Structures of Social Action*. Cambridge: Cambridge University Press, pp. 413–29.
Schegloff, E.A. 1996. 'Issues of Relevance for Discourse Analysis: Contingency in Action, Interaction and Co-participant Context', *Computational and Conversational Discourse*. Berlin: Springer-Verlag, pp. 3–35.
Schegloff, E.A. 1997. 'Whose Text? Whose Context?', *Discourse and Society* 8(2): 165–87.
Schütz, A. 1962. *Collected Papers I: The Problem of Social Reality*. The Hague: Martinus Nijhoff.
Shaw, C., E. Stokoe, K. Gallagher, N. Aladangady and N. Marlow. 2016. 'Parental Involvement in Neonatal Critical Care Decision-making', *Sociology of Health & Illness*. doi: 10.1111/1467-9566.12455
Sikveland, R.O. and Stokoe, E. 2016. 'Dealing with Resistance in Initial Intake and Inquiry Calls to Mediation: The Power of "Willing".' *Conflict Resolution Quarterly* 33(3), 235–254.

Sikveland, R., E. Stokoe and J. Symonds. 2016. 'Patient Burden during Appointment-making Telephone Calls to GP practices'. *Patient Education and Counseling* 99(8): 1310–1318.

Stokoe, E. 2008. 'Categories and Sequences: Formulating Gender in Talk-in-interaction', in K. Harrington, L. Litosseliti, H. Saunston and J. Sunderland (eds), *Gender and Language Research Methodologies*. Basingstoke: Palgrave, pp. 139–57.

Stokoe, E. 2009. 'Doing Actions with Identity Categories: Complaints and Denials in Neighbor Disputes', *Text & Talk* 29(1): 75–97.

Stokoe, E. 2010. '"I'm Not Gonna Hit a Lady": Conversation Analysis, Membership Categorization and Men's Denials of Violence towards Women', *Discourse and Society* 21(1): 59–82.

Stokoe, E. 2011. 'Simulated Interaction and Communication Skills Training: The "Conversation Analytic Role-play Method"', in C. Antaki (ed.), *Applied Conversation Analysis: Intervention and Change in Institutional Talk*. Basingstoke: Palgrave Macmillan, pp. 119–39.

Stokoe, E. 2013a. 'The (In)Authenticity of Simulated Talk: Comparing Role-played and Actual Interaction and the Implications for Communication Training', *Research on Language & Social Interaction* 46(2): 165–85.

Stokoe, E. 2013b. 'Overcoming Barriers to Mediation in Intake Calls to Services: Research-based Strategies for Mediators', *Negotiation Journal* 29(3): 289–314.

Stokoe, E. 2014. 'The Conversation Analytic Role-play Method (CARM): A Method for Training Communication Skills as an Alternative to Simulated Role-play', *Research on Language and Social Interaction* 47(3): 255–65.

Stokoe, E. and D. Edwards. 2009. 'Accomplishing Social Action with Identity Categories: Mediating Neighbour Complaints', in M. Wetherell (ed.), *Theorizing Identities and Social Action*. London: Sage, pp. 95–115.

Stokoe, E., A. Hepburn and C. Antaki. 2012. 'Beware the "Loughborough School" of Social Psychology? Interaction and the Politics of Intervention', *British Journal of Social Psychology* 51(3): 486–96.

Stokoe, E., R.O. Sikveland and J. Symonds. 2016. 'Calling the GP Surgery: Patient Burden, Patient Satisfaction, and Implications for Training', *British Journal of General Practice*, bjgpnov-2016. DOI: 10.3399/bjgp16X686653

Thaler, R.H. and C.R. Sunstein. 2008. *Nudge*. New Haven, CT: Yale University Press.

Van Hasselt, V.B., S.J. Romano and G.M. Vecchi. 2008. 'Role Playing Applications in Hostage and Crisis Negotiation Skills Training', *Behavior Modification* 32(2): 248–63.

Vecchi, G.M., V.B. Van Hasselt and S.J. Romano. 2005. 'Crisis (Hostage) Negotiation: Current Strategies and Issues in High-risk Conflict Resolution', *Aggression and Violent Behavior* 10(5): 533–51.

Wetherell, M. 1998. 'Positioning and Interpretative Repertoires: Conversation Analysis and Post-structuralism in Dialogue', *Discourse & Society; Niscl.Soc.* 9(3): 387–412.

Whitworth, A., L. Perkins, and R. Lesser. 1997. *Conversation Analysis Profile for People with Aphasia*. London: Whurr.

Wittgenstein, L. 1963. *Philosophical Investigations*, translated by G.E.M. Anscombe. [A reprint of the English translation contained in the polyglot edition of 1958.]. Oxford: Basil Blackwell.

Chapter 4

MAKING THEORY, MAKING INTERVENTIONS
Doing Applied Scholarship at the In-between in Safety Research

Sarah Pink, Jennie Morgan and Andrew Dainty

Introduction

While it is increasingly agreed that applied practice and theoretical scholarship should mutually inform each other, this commonly happens through the 'use' of existing theory/ies to frame the design or analysis of an applied research project, or the subsequent use of applied research materials for the development of academic work. In this chapter we outline and discuss an alternative model, which we argue generates a more complex relationship between applied practice and theoretical scholarship. This model constitutes an *in-between* where the ethnographic-theoretical dialogue can produce alternative ways of understanding the realities of the everyday worlds that applied research focuses on, thus generating new ways of creating innovative applied interventions that advance both theory and practice. Anthropologists might protest at this point that we are suggesting nothing new; that in fact anthropological ethnography has always developed through a dialogue between ethnography and theory – which happens throughout the process of research and representation, and subsequently places 'analysis' across these practices rather than establishing it as a distinct phase. It is certainly true that this ethnographic-theoretical dialogue is at the core of anthropological ethnography, and for Sarah Pink and Jennie Morgan, both of whom are trained as anthropological ethnographers, this was a 'normal' way to work. However, our claim is not simply to have worked in a conventional anthropological fashion to build theory with ethnography. Rather, our argument is that the ethnographic-theoretical dialogue needs to be an acknowledged element of applied research, and that is where applied anthropology (and indeed other applied disciplines discussed in this book) has a key role to play. Working with Andrew Dainty, who has used ethnographic methods in organization and management studies research, gave us an opportunity to take new steps together in this field. Having made this point, we insist that debate and reflection is needed about where this dialogue should be situated in the research and intervention process – which we acknowledge is also contingent on the parameters of specific research projects.

In developing our discussion, we draw on examples from an applied research project in which we were responsible for an ethnographic strand of research: The Management of OSH in Networked Systems of Production or Service Delivery. This project was undertaken with an interdisciplinary team of colleagues at Loughborough University, U.K., and funded by the Institution for Occupational Safety and Health, IOSH (also in the U.K.). The context of our project is the question of how to reduce the number of workplace accidents and injuries by developing a better understanding of how OSH knowledge is engaged by people who work in organizations. These insights are to provide the basis for a range of recommendations aimed at informing OSH professional practice. The particular sectors we look at include health care, where there is an overarching stereotype of workers putting patient safety over their own; construction, which is the most dangerous industry to work in; and logistics (customer deliveries), which involves hazards associated with the mobile nature of the work. Given the importance of these sectors and the risks that working in them entails, it is perhaps surprising that these questions are infrequently approached ethnographically by researchers who wish to combine applied research with theoretical scholarship. One explanation for this is what Watson (2011) has referred to as there being in organization studies, a 'discomforting necessity for ethnography' – a need to get close to the action. However, he highlights that there are difficulties in doing ethnography (and getting it published) within the organization studies field. This, he suggests, is because ethnographic research (or at least the way in which it is written up) falls below the levels expected of the genre. He sees raising the status of ethnography as an important step in addressing this, but it also about paying attention to what he terms the 'technicalities and aesthetics of research writing'. Through our collaboration, we have been able to come to these issues both through the organization studies field, but also through anthropology. Here, the ethnographic-theoretical dialogue offers an advantage particularly in terms of helping to form the thick descriptions that are a cornerstone of good ethnographic writing.

OSH as a Field of Research

OSH research is a field that is little theorized from a social science perspective. This is unsurprising, given that the field has traditionally emphasized applied approaches, which typify those found within social and organizational psychology (Guldenmund 2000). There are some exceptions, such as the study of OSH as part of sociological work on risk (e.g. Hutter 2001, and the work of Gherardi and Nicolini noted below). However, in contrast to other important research topics, such as climate change, that attract many theoretically oriented scholars and researchers, on the surface OSH appears to attract little attention. Indeed, it seems that OSH is more likely to be an everyday frustration to academics trying to get researcher safety protocols through approval boards, than the topic of funding applications that bring together theoretical scholarship and applied practice. This is quite ironic when we consider that in the U.K. the Health and Safety Executive (HSE) reported that in 2012–13, '148 workers were killed at work … and 175,000 reportable injuries (defined as over 7-day absence) occurred, according to the Labour Force Survey' (HSE 2012–13).

It is, perhaps, an acknowledgement of the apparent ineffectiveness of existing dominant approaches to OSH that theoretical debates around the production of safety knowledge have begun to emerge in recent years. Dekker (2003) highlights the philosophical differences in what he terms Model 1 perspectives (characterized by rationalist rote rule following) and Model 2 perspectives (associated with substantive cognitive activity). At the heart of Model 1 thinking is the notion that compliance with procedures leads to safer working practices, and that safety therefore relies upon knowledge of such procedures. In Dekker's view, this produces a series of tensions in safety practice in that procedures can never account for every circumstance, and are often not required to produce safe outcomes. A Model 2 perspective, on the other hand, acknowledges that procedures are themselves shaped by subtle, localized judgements. In other words, actors can account for the situated nature of the hazards that they confront in contingent ways. Dekker reveals how these bifurcated perspectives on OSH lead to a double bind for those confronting emergent hazards; inflexible rule following can lead to procedures that fail, whereas procedural adaptations might themselves fail. In their analysis of how these two perspectives play out in safety research, Hale and Borys (2013) highlight how a gap emerges between the abstracted rules that govern OSH and the lived realities of how it is practised. It is by understanding the gap between procedures and practice that organizations can establish the interventions that help their employees to work safely (Dekker 2003). One way that this can be achieved, of course, is to understand the actualities of safety practice, and the complex ways in which rules and adaptation enmesh together through practical activity. Within OSH research this has been emphasized in recent provocations provided by Hollnagel (2014), who espouses a focus on what goes right (termed Safety-II), rather than on avoiding problems (Safety-I). As Hollnagel states, Safety-II 'start[s] from a different position because it tries to understand how everyday work succeeds'. Although relatively nascent within the OSH field, such debates highlight the need for consideration of the situated, everyday practice of safe and healthy working, and accounting for this in the policy-making process.

Applied anthropology, we argue, has a role to play in both making sense of and crafting possible interventions in this field. Yet, we insist that this needs to be a kind of applied anthropology that does what anthropology often does best – that is to look under the surface of what is already being asked in this field, to twist around the research question, and to problematize what we think we already know. To achieve this, we propose, the ethnographic-theoretical dialogue is essential. It is the 'what if' of theory that proposes alternative understandings of the world, and it is ethnography that both helps us to have these understandings, and to make sense of them through 'real' scenarios developed on the basis of our fieldwork experiences. It is by playing in this zone where theory and ethnography make each other that the creative insights of our work as anthropologists emerge. It is these insights that we argue need to contribute to questions relating to life and death issues in the workplace – rather than a service ethnography that will answer the managerialist questions that often inform research about how to 'improve' what is called OSH compliance; that is, the idea that OSH will improve if workers comply with the regulatory procedures that are designed to ensure that accidents should not happen. As we illustrate through examples below, the ethnographic-theoretical dialogue can lead to the design of unexpected practical interventions, and 'solutions' to 'problems', the parameters of which are not predetermined but are revealed through the research process itself.

In the above, what has been depicted as a Model 1 or Safety-I perspective represents a rather extreme view of OSH regulation, which, if actually practised in such a way, would not be viable, or even worse, could exacerbate safety risks. As we have learned from the OSH practitioners who we have met and discussed our work with, although the regulatory frameworks of OSH can be interpreted as part of neoliberal anticipatory logics – like ethics discussed in Chapter 1– in reality there is a recognition that what Pels in the context of ethics has called 'technologies of the self' (2000), or what design anthropologists would see as a form of everyday improvisation, also forms part of the ways in which people stay safe at work. Our criticism is therefore not so much of the OSH community, where this tension is acknowledged to some extent (Hale and Borys 2013). Rather, we are concerned about the lack of formal recognition of OSH as a technology of the self and as part of the improvisatory practice of humans, and indeed, in our publications on this topic we have called for increased formal recognition of these in OSH contexts.

In the following sections we discuss how a sustained ethnographic-theoretical dialogue might contribute to applied research in this field. Indeed, ultimately this goes beyond merely being a dialogue between ethnography and theory, and becomes a conversation that includes application, and sometimes proposals for intervention. Additionally, practice-based insights rooted in ethnography can, and do, like any academic ethnographic project, challenge theory, and as such participate in disciplinary or interdisciplinary theory building. The model we explain here will not be suitable for all applied research projects, and is most appropriate for longer-term projects and projects where team work can allow different researchers to be differently distanced from research materials during the research process. However, as we suggest in the conclusion, the insights gained from a discussion of this way of working also have implications for projects that need to be modelled in different ways and according to shorter timescales.

In the next section we outline our involvement in the Management of OSH in Networked Systems of Production or Service Delivery project, the field of OSH research that we see our work as responding to, and the contrasting approach that we wished to take to explore how OSH was experienced, learned, performed, known and shared. We then outline how in practice we developed a way of working across ethnography and theory, and how this dialogue became a conversation with the applied element of our work. In this project we used ethnographic materials from short-term fieldwork in occupational safety and health in the health care, logistics and construction sectors to develop theoretical scholarship that contributes to material culture studies, human geography, mobility studies, organization studies and other academic fields, some of which would not initially appear directly relevant to occupational safety and health research. However, as we show, this theoretical work is not simply an alternative output for our research. It is in fact also part of our work as applied anthropologists, in that it has enabled us to develop new routes to conceptualizing how people already stay safe at work (or, as Hollnagel (2014: 176) defines it, the 'other story' of how work succeeds). Through this we have been able to offer safety and health experts alternative concepts through which to think about how to develop and implement OSH policies, and to offer workers new insights on their everyday practices that (typically, within safety management and research) are neither acknowledged nor reflected on as contributing to safe working.

Finally, we argue that this approach enables us to engage theory to consider practical problems in ways that go beyond conventional applications. Instead it involves using applied ethnographic research materials, which focus on very mundane elements and activities in everyday working life, to develop theoretical work that advances academic fields of scholarship. It then brings these advances to bear on the development of new ways to approach practical applied problems relating to central societal issues – including, as in this case, potentially fatal accidents at work. Our agenda was to make applied research thoroughly theoretical and theoretical scholarship thoroughly applied. Indeed, a subtheme of our argument is that when applied research seeks to address 'real' problems that are experienced in the world – like the problem that too many people die in accidents at work – it offers to theoretical scholarship a complex state of affairs that can tell us more about contemporary society than merely how OSH operates as part of it.

Being Anthropological in an Interdisciplinary Context

Some anthropologists have developed commentaries related to OSH. For instance, most notably Hannah Knox and Penny Harvey have discussed OSH in relation to their analysis of the relations and rituals of road building in Peru. We concur with their general approach and argument, and in particular share an interest with them in the anticipatory nature of OSH regulations and the ways in which they deal with uncertainty (Knox and Harvey 2011: 145) (Pink et al. 2015). However, our work is rather differently positioned to traditional anthropological scholarship. It was undertaken in an interdisciplinary context working alongside academics from the fields of engineering, safety, logistics, health and ergonomics. It was also developed in dialogue with research partners in and gatekeepers to the industries with which we were collaborating.

In this section we first outline our involvement in the project, the research questions we were responding to, and our own critical interrogation of these questions. The questions were also of our own making, in that we contributed to writing them in response to the brief for our project. Yet we also knew that the anthropological theory that would guide our research design, and what we were actually likely to find when we did the research, would most likely challenge the concepts that the research was intended to explore. For example, while our research project was in part concerned with questions around if and how OSH knowledge 'flows' in organizations, we needed to examine the notion of knowledge and the idea that it would flow, theoretically. This does not mean that the idea of knowledge flow is not a good metaphor for thinking about ways of learning and knowing about OSH, but rather that for many anthropologists this is a difficult compromise. What this meant for us was that in order to be able to answer a question about knowledge flow, we needed to translate this into concepts that could be researched ethnographically. These concepts also needed to be able to bridge points of difference between our theoretical commitments and the guiding logics through which the practitioners and OSH experts understand the realities of their everyday work contexts. This resulted in our focus being on how OSH was experienced, learned, performed, known, shared and communicated. Here we briefly set out some of the differences in expectations of the concepts that were involved in our project, and how we sought to resolve these in our research process. In a later section we will reflect further on how we then used our findings to re-engage with the research questions.

OSH Knowledge

One of our tasks was to produce a new or deeper understanding of how knowledge about OSH flows in organizations. While on the one hand we were committed to the principle of understanding how OSH was manifested, learned and passed between participants in our research, the concept of OSH knowledge and its transferral between people was more challenging. From an anthropological perspective this notion is challenging in part because the question of knowledge, its transmission and the relationship between concepts of knowledge and knowing have generated much debate in the discipline. If disciplines are what Marilyn Strathern has called 'communities of critics' (2006) then anthropology is particularly powerful in this sense. The anthropological debate around the concept of knowledge transmission is no less so. Here, the debates and differences of emphasis tend to fall between those who favour cognitive theory and those who lean towards phenomenology, or an approach that focuses more on the experiential. Yet, as Trevor Marchand has put it, in describing work drawn together around the concept of knowledge in anthropology, although there was divergence 'in theory and method, there is mutual recognition that knowledge-making is a dynamic process arising directly from the indissoluble relations that exist between minds, bodies, and environment' (Marchand 2010: S2). The discussion also involves the relationship between the concepts of *knowledge* on the one hand and *knowing* on the other. Anthropologists have sought ways to understand how embodied and often unspoken ways of knowing might be learned between people, through human activity and experience of the world, in movement and as incremental processes (Ingold 2000; Harris 2007; Marchand 2010; Pink 2015). These ideas also resonate strongly with work in organization studies that (like this field of anthropology) draws on Lave and Wenger's approach to situated learning and communities of practice (Lave and Wenger 1991; Wenger 1998). As such Davide Nicolini, Silvia Gherardi and Dvora Yanow's (2003) edited volume *Knowing in Organisations*, Gherardi and Nicolini's (2002) work on the culture of safety practice in construction, and more generally work in the field of organizational aesthetics, take a more sociological perspective to organization studies, while following the same critical shift from the concept of knowledge towards that of knowing. In relation to this strand of theoretical scholarship about knowledge therefore, we understood knowledge to be a concept that stood for an objectified entity – a representational category that can be documented and verbalized. Knowing, in contrast, we understood to be an embodied and experiential way of sensing the world. The kinds of knowing we were most interested in researching were performative; they might be verbalized, but we suspected that those that we would find most interesting and informative for our project would be those that were habitual, and perhaps never or almost never spoken about. In particular we were interested in how OSH as representational and OSH as performed would be relational to each other.

Flows

The concept of flow is likewise an important way of thinking in the social sciences and humanities. It has been used variously to speak about flows of capital, power and the making of global realities (e.g. Appadurai 1996), as well as to understand the flow of everyday life as a kind of processual ongoingness, difficult to represent (discussed in Pink 2012), and also to understand smaller-scale environments such as home and the ways in which intangible or invisible elements flow around them, such as air, heat, smells and sounds. For us the idea that knowledge as an objectified entity – in the form of representations of OSH knowledge – might flow was difficult to reconcile with our understanding of knowing outlined above. While cognitive theorists might understand mental representations as being transmitted between people, the position that we take offers a different approach, as Ingold, inspired by the work of ecological psychologist James Gibson, puts it: 'For what is involved, ... is not a transmission of representations, as the enculturation model implies, but an education of attention' (2000: 37).

Moreover, although the concept of flow did not match these anthropological theories of knowledge, we were mindful that for our funders, our industry partners and many research participants (particularly safety experts and managers), notions of flow offer a useful model for understanding how OSH knowledge circulates within their organizations, and informs the design of workplace learning and communication techniques. For example, in the construction industry a classroom style of induction for new workers (using verbal, textual and audio-visual instruction) is widely held to be an effective means of ensuring good workplace OSH, as modelled on notions of knowledge passing from trainer to trainee and 'flowing' out onto and around the building site. To undertake research in this sector we were required by our industry partners to participate in training modelled around notions of flow before commencing our ethnographic fieldwork. Jennie studied for and sat an online health, safety and environment test administered through the U.K.-based Construction Skills Certification Scheme (CSCS, http://www.cscs.uk.com/) to acquire a site visitor card, and took part in on-site induction training. We thus sought to develop an approach that was not critical of the OSH community itself, nor dismissive of local ways of understanding everyday workplace realities, but that rather enabled us to work collaboratively and creatively 'in between' these points of difference to develop new ways of understanding occupational safety: ways that would re-engage both our stakeholders *and our own* theoretical and practical preconceptions about how safety operates in these organizational settings. Indeed, while these categories were theoretically challenging for us, we shared with the wider team of researchers, IOSH, the industry stakeholders and research participants the desire to understand how OSH was understood and performed, and what this would tell us that would help to make workplaces safer. In this sense the categories of knowledge and flows worked as shared stopping points that we could use to talk across the project.

In response to the project brief, we developed an approach informed by phenomenological anthropology and anthropology of knowing, which framed the way we designed our fieldwork and analysis. A key document through which we consolidated this approach was our research proposal: submitted initially to our funders, used as a platform for our ethics submission, and later shared in a summary version with our advisory boards to seek critical feedback. In the proposal we used an appendix to provide details (beyond the project-level description) about the ethnographic strategy, methodologies and experience base we would draw on. This was not simply a pragmatic 'how to' discussion, but informed by our conceptual commitments and biography of applied scholarly work, it set up the theory-research interplay that would subsequently guide our ethnography. For example, we explained how our choice of specific research techniques (including the visual and task-based methods discussed below) were inseparable from our aim of understanding everyday OSH practices to conceptualize the interrelationship between individual action, knowing and the environments in which these are routinely performed. We presented this anthropological approach at several meetings at the outset of the project to our interdisciplinary colleagues, industry ('steering group') and academic ('scientific consultation panel') partners. To communicate our strategy, we focused on three key concepts that had emerged from our reading (outlined above) of a phenomenological anthropological approach to knowing and learning: those of *perception, movement* and *place*. We explained to attendees that these concepts provided an analytic prism through which we would explore tacit – or taken-for-granted and usually not spoken about – ways of knowing how to undertake work in safe and healthy ways. While these concepts emerged from our reading of academic scholarship, they also provided practical 'ways into' designing the fieldwork, and around which we could begin our dialogue 'in between' theory and applied research. These concepts had methodological implications for our project, in that they pointed us towards researching occupational safety in particular ways. For instance, studying OSH not only as abstracted representation encountered in organizational guidelines and procedures but as adaptive embodied practice. To enact this move from theory to applied methodology we thus needed to translate these concepts into (as we described to attendees at these meetings) a set of empirical realities that we intended to explore through our ethnographic fieldwork. Here, *place* encouraged us to consider how the spatial, physical, material and social environment of the workplace interacts with knowing about safety; *movement* encouraged a focus on action and experience to explore how tasks are performed in practice; and *perception* encouraged an interest in bodily, sensorial and perceptual practices of knowing that go beyond what can only be observed or spoken about. These meetings were also an opportunity to build our partners' expectations into the fieldwork design and to co-create an approach that would be acceptable in the field as well successful in achieving our research objectives. We asked, for example, what outcomes they were especially interested in, and what their experience of working across sectors would suggest may emerge from our research or challenge our proposed methods. We learned that while our theoretical commitments challenged dominant OSH perspectives, these were not incompatible with partner expectations. They were interested, for instance, in the potential of our ethnographic attention to 'how everyday work succeeds' (Hollnagel 2014), to identify the specific features of a workplace, and the persons, things and activities that come together to create the environments needed for learning, sharing, communicating and enacting effective OSH. Such insights held potential to be harnessed by practitioners to identify enablers and barriers to safe working within their sectors and organizations.

The Ethnographic-Theoretical Dialogue: Through the Practice and Representation of Fieldwork

Having considered how we critically interrogated our research questions through the process of designing the project and beginning dialogue with our industry and academic stakeholders, in this section we outline how – through the practice and representation of our anthropological fieldwork – we further developed a way of working 'in between' ethnography and theory.

To research worker-OSH we developed an intense short-term ethnographic methodology, which was collaborative, participatory and theoretically informed. We undertook fieldwork within the United Kingdom at two building projects, a logistics warehouse and a health care trust, spending up to six weeks at each. Our intent, here, is not to outline this method in detail (instead, see Pink and Morgan 2013) but rather to reflect on aspects of this practice that fostered the ethnographic-theoretical dialogue central to our work as applied anthropologists. Certainly, short-term ethnography as we have advanced it is characterized not only by shorter time frames than the (typically) year-long immersion of more traditional anthropological approaches, but also by 'a sharply focused dialog [sic] between research and theory' (Pink and Morgan 2013: 352).

One way that we achieved this dialogue was through structured and interventional ethnographic techniques. In addition to more conventional interview and observational methodologies we employed visual (video and photography), re-enactment and walking techniques. These were deeply influenced by our conceptual commitment to examining situated practice and the non-representational elements of everyday life, yet also thoroughly applied in that they were collaboratively developed as appropriate to the problem of OSH knowledge flows and specific to the workplace settings in which we were working. These methodologies represented and enabled us to communicate to participants our research interests, thus facilitating mutual reflection on core issues. Indeed, as Sarah Pink (2006a: 14) has acknowledged elsewhere in her writing about applied organizational ethnography:

> in the absence of existing manuals or guides to how to operate in these institutional or organisational cultures, it means applying one's anthropological eye to the institutions for whom one might work or carry out consultancies in order to inform our own actions and practices of representations within them.

We recognized, for instance, that given the particular circumstances of our research it would not be ethically or pragmatically possible to film or photograph workers undertaking tasks *in situ* in health care or logistics settings when patients/customers were present (although this is possible for other research approaches – see for example Chapter 4, this volume). Instead we used re-enactment techniques to create intense ethnographic encounters through which to explore, with our participants, the unspoken, tacit or otherwise routine and habitual elements of their OSH practice. These methodologies were not new, the trajectories having developed through our own (e.g. Pink and Leder Mackley 2014) work, yet they took on specific inflections in the context of our project, research questions and theoretical interests.

In the health care fieldwork, Jennie asked community nurses and therapists to show on video camera how they applied disinfectant hand gel, and in the logistics fieldwork she asked customer deliveries workers to show, while she photographed, techniques for lifting and moving goods. By asking workers to re-perform these practices set apart from usual workplace activity, and to articulate how they 'knew how' to do so effectively, rich insight on the embodied, sensory and affective knowing involved in staying safe at work was revealed. Our rejection of the concept of OSH flow was also further confirmed, as ethnographic materials demonstrated working safely to be a situated, embodied and incremental process involving individual moments of improvisation and tacit knowing as much as explicable, shared practices. For example, we found that manual handling by logistics workers was guided not only by taught organizational techniques (accessed through training and handbooks), but emerged from a subtle individual process of intuitively perceiving what 'feels' safe and adapting lifting, holding and carrying techniques in response to a complex interplay of material, bodily and even climatic (when moving outdoors) environmental features.

Thus, as this discussion has begun to highlight, a sharply focused ethnographic-theoretical dialogue was achieved by bringing our emerging findings into conversation with key research concepts, including those we were seeking to unsettle, such as OSH flow. Here we see (typical of anthropological ethnography) how fieldwork and analysis were not distinct phases in our project but entangled across research and representation. While the above focuses on how we achieved this through our fieldwork, this dialogue was likewise pushed through writing academic articles contributing to scholarship not usually connected to in safety research. This representational work was not (as we introduced earlier) considered an alternative output for our research (over and above the project reporting detailed below), but was at the core of how we work as applied anthropologists, in that it enabled us to conceptualize OSH in new ways, and on the basis of the analytical work undertaken in these articles identify possible routes for where and how practical interventions might best be made. Indeed, we found it *necessary* to connect our ethnography to theoretical scholarship to begin revising the agenda of applied safety research in a way that more conventional approaches did not enable. Thus, writing articles (similar to the core concepts outlined earlier) functioned as vital 'stopping points' to probe creatively in between theory and ethnography, and was continually undertaken during the project, rather than being confined to a discrete phase. Several articles were written, submitted and/or published while we were conducting our fieldwork, and these were read by our project funders and relevant research participants, who supplied feedback, which further helped connect our thinking and writing with applied outcomes (e.g. Pink and Morgan 2013; Pink et al. 2014a, 2014b, 2015).

One example is our writing on 'the safe hand' (Pink et al. 2014b). This theme emerged directly from our fieldwork with workers in a U.K.-based health care trust, and is a theme through which interests in our research questions held by our interdisciplinary colleagues, funders, industry stakeholders and participants converged. When Jennie accompanied nurses and therapists on community health care visits she was encouraged (despite not having any *actual* contact with patients) to adopt their everyday hand hygiene routine of using disinfectant gel. Recognizing the predominance of this practice, we designed a visual-ethnographic research activity around it, and to communicate our emerging research themes and methodologies to funders and academic stakeholders, designed a participatory 'feedback' exercise (called 'Are your hands clean?') for a reporting workshop hosted by IOSH. At this workshop, Jennie supplied attendees with bottles of hand gel, invited them to apply it, and asked them to consider a range of questions intended to elicit insight on the institutional, material, sensory and affective 'know how' that informed this practice (e.g. 'how do you apply the hand gel?', 'how do you know you are doing so correctly?', 'how does using it make you feel?', 'what do you think it is protecting you from?', 'how do you know that it will protect you?').

Yet, to 'twist around' this practice we also found it necessary to connect our ethnographic work to scholarship that would enable us to better understand how the use of material substances (like gels, gloves and uniforms in health care) is part of how safety is routinely performed, and to consider the meanings attached to such practices and materialities. In writing an article on this topic we looked to material culture studies and phenomenological anthropology, which directed our attention to 'the qualities and affordances of the materialities of organizational safety cultures' (Pink et al. 2014b: 426). We did not put ethnography in the service *of theory* but, guided by an applied agenda questioning how OSH is learned, shared and enacted, brought it into conversation *with theory* to generate new understandings about how safety is achieved. Specifically, this scholarship helped us to reconsider subtle ambiguities of hygiene practices that we had observed during fieldwork: for example, a practitioner creatively adapting the working uniform by removing the fingertip of a glove to engage tactile knowing to take a blood sample safely (Pink et al. 2014b: 437). It inspired us to analyse such ambiguities not through the predominant safety research lens of worker compliance, but taking a phenomenological anthropological approach, as attunements to the unique entanglements of materialities, sensory perceptions, moralities, social relationships and affective moralities from which workplace scenarios emerge. Moreover, by recognizing the uncertain and continually changing nature of everyday life (as this scholarship collectively encourages) we came to see how the ability of workers to adapt and improvise towards safety is crucial to effective OSH. Writing this chapter, and other articles on the topics of mobile media and OSH (Pink et al. 2014a) and safety in other people's homes (Pink et al. 2015), was crucial to our analysis and reporting. However, our conceptual work was inseparable from our applied goal of identifying potential routes for practical interventions. By theorizing the relationship between the hand, tactile knowing, materialities and safety we concluded that the real challenge for OSH managers and experts is to support and ensure that workers adapt towards (not away from) safety, rather than designing interventions around increased regulatory measures. Or 'to consider not how interventions might be made to "improve" OSH through producing more standardized "correct behavior" but instead to consider how interventions might enable health care workers to make safe materially mediated innovations' (Pink et al. 2014b: 439).

From Journal to Report: Working 'in between' Disciplinary Perspectives for Applied Outcomes

Core to our research was incorporating our ethnographic findings and anthropological understandings into a final report submitted for publication by our project funders with an interdisciplinary and practitioner-focused readership (Gibb et al. 2015a). We did not conceive of the report as the endpoint (or ultimate representation) of our ethnographic work, but rather another key stopping point in an ongoing ethnographic-theoretical dialogue used to talk across the project. This conversation continues beyond the project's formal lifespan – determined by funding and staffing arrangements – as we continue to develop our conceptual work through ongoing writing projects (including this book chapter).

In the report we re-engage with the core questions supported by our funders about OSH flow[1] through several interrelated ethnographic concepts, all of which were foreshadowed and developed through our project planning, stakeholder dialogue, fieldwork and academic articles (outlined above). These concepts are: *knowing about safety (rather than knowledge)*, *learning about OSH*, *dealing with uncertainty*, and *improvising towards safety*. Space, here, does not permit us to deal with these concepts individually, but the important point to be made is that this practitioner-orientated and project reporting output again illustrated the impossibility of separating the theoretical from the applied in our research. We invite practitioners to re-evaluate the question of how to make workplaces safer and healthier through these concepts, and encourage them to consider the implications of these understandings for identifying practical interventions.

One example is how our ethnographic insights on *learning about OSH* challenge assumptions about knowledge acquisition and communication inherent to notions of OSH flow. Our ethnographic encounters with health care, construction and logistics workers, and our own reflections on learning how to research safely in these fieldwork contexts, show that people learn not only through what they read or are told, but through their ongoing embodied, sensory and affective interactions with the people, things, spaces and places that constitute the workplace. In the report we translate these ethnographic insights into new applied understandings by bringing these together with theories of learning, which encourage us to conceive of OSH as situated and performed. This includes those that (as introduced above) draw on Lave and Wenger's (1991; also Wenger 1998) notion of situated learning and communities of practice (e.g. Fors et al. 2013), but also Ingold's phenomenological anthropology, which argues that learning involves 'training in everyday tasks whose successful fulfilment requires a practiced ability to notice and to respond fluently to salient aspects of the environment' (Ingold 2000 166–67). Learning is understood to emerge incrementally from an ongoing interplay between practical activity, embodied and sensory perception and the environment, and this approach enables us to move beyond the transmission model of learning (outlined earlier) to report instead on how 'knowing OSH' happens at this intersection as workers attune their responses to specific workplace contexts and scenarios. Our reporting on ethnographic materials is thus informed by these theories, yet we do so by reconfiguring concepts into a set of applied questions focused on learning about OSH (e.g. 'What is it that workers, in different contexts, learn to be attentive to, in order to make decisions (consciously or unconsciously) about safety and health? What are the usually unspoken ways of performing OSH, and what prior learning do they draw on?'). Moreover, by setting out this sustained anthropological argument we encourage OSH practitioners to use this alternative understanding (i.e. that people learn incrementally and from diverse sources including the tacit) to consider its applied implications for (re)designing OSH management and training strategies. In the construction sector, for instance, this might point towards the value of scenario-based training, site-specific rather than generalized information, and inductions undertaken moving through the work area rather than (as is common practice) a classroom style of training set apart from, and usually prior to workers encountering, the site. These suggestions do not respond to managerial agendas or OSH abstractions, but were arrived at in a roundabout (or 'twisting') way through an ethnographic-theoretical dialogue: they are thoroughly theoretical, shaped by our phenomenological anthropological understanding about how learning happens and in what moments, and ethnographic, emerging from our attempts to make sense of everyday workplace realities. They were also shaped through participatory dialogue with our practitioner partners. Indeed, without the creative and playful moving between research, theory and the applied approach outlined in this chapter, we doubt it would have been possible to arrive at project reporting proposals like these.

Crucially, the report also created a space to work 'in between' disciplinary perspectives. Through discussion with our colleagues, it was decided that the ethnographic research would be treated in a stand-alone section rather than being integrated with materials generated by team members working from alternative disciplinary starting points. This had the benefit of constructing a space from which to probe between disciplinary expectations and conventions, to capitalize on the complementary yet distinctive perspectives that our project team offered to the applied problem of how to improve workplace safety. One example in the final report is the team's engagement with the key theme of adaptation and OSH. This theme cut across the project findings: in the ethnography reporting through the concept of *improvising towards safety*, and in the structured interviews and focus group reporting (undertaken and written by our colleagues) the notion of *workarounds*. It also connected to a question that our industrial partner steering group were especially interested in, and that they challenged us to engage with throughout the research: 'Why do people not do what they know they should do?'[2] While our anthropological commitments point towards understanding improvisation as a necessary aspect of working safely in continually changing sensory, material, social and affective configurations, our colleagues working with different methodologies (focus groups, structured interviews), participants (OSH managers), disciplinary perspectives (human factors, organizational psychology), and theoretical commitments (especially to knowledge flow) understand adaptation through the more conventional safety research and management concept of workarounds. One perspective, sometimes espoused within the safety management and research literature, is that workarounds are considered to demonstrate worker 'failure' to comply with institutional OSH, leading to greater risk of severe injury (e.g. Halbesleben 2010). However, working 'in between' these perspectives through collaborative writing in the discussion section of the report generated more nuanced understandings by encouraging the team to consider (as we introduced earlier) how the relationship between OSH as representation and OSH as performed are always relational. Or, as was reflected on in the report:

> The ethnographic work ... suggests that workers will always make changes to the 'formal' procedures and that this is a normal part of human behavior and should not be seen as negative. The interviews and focus group data would suggest a small, but significant change to this claim, namely that these changes should not 'automatically' be seen as negative (Gibb et al. 2015a: 119).

By working between these perspectives it was not the team's ambition to make value judgements about adaptive practices, but rather to reflect on what this relational understanding might productively offer for how OSH is understood and managed. The report argues that the real challenge for safety managers and policy makers is to acknowledge that adaptation 'will happen', and given its inevitability an effective management strategy (rather than focus on increased regulation and tighter compliance measures) is to 'consider behaviour as a resource' that can be successfully applied to the challenge of avoiding accidents in the workplace (Gibb et al. 2015a: 120). Drawing on work by Hollnagel on 'Safety-II', the team concluded that OSH practitioners would be well advised to shift their focus 'from "everything" going right to "enough" going right, and from avoiding failure to ensuring success' (Gibb et al. 2015a: 121). These applied conclusions do not just integrate but *emerge precisely from* the dialogue between the different theoretical standpoints, disciplinary perspectives and fieldwork materials through which our project team approached our core research questions.

Conclusion: For an Applied-theoretical Scholarship

In this chapter we have set out one way in which an applied ethnographic-theoretical scholarship has been developed. As we pointed out at the beginning of this chapter, the model we have developed in this project is not the only possible version. This model is more suited to longer-term projects, where there are enough researchers available to be able to 'see' the project from different distances and directions during an intensive research process. Our ethnography was, as we have described it, 'short term' (Pink and Morgan 2013), but this was not necessarily because there was urgency to report on our ethnography within a short timescale. Rather it was related to the wider project funding and structure, within which we had allocated six weeks of fieldwork to each site, and dedicated the rest of the time to analysis and report writing. Our academic theoretical writing was thus part of our analytical and reporting process. Far from it simply being a case of academics wishing to get some publications out of an otherwise applied project, for us the theoretical work was completely inseparable from the applied process – and vice versa.

Other projects might not offer this luxury; often, in order to meet research partners' deadlines we may need to report on ethnographic findings before undertaking in-depth theoretical work. Such projects do not necessarily 'suffer' from this configuration – we are not making an argument for how it *should* be. Rather, in such work the ways in which theoretical analysis is embedded will be less explicit, but can both inform the way ethnographic findings are presented to research partners and be developed further in later works. Indeed, it is important to realize that applied research and theoretical and methodological development should not necessarily be thought of in an isolated project-by-project sense. Instead, what we learn and theorize as an outcome of one piece of research is part of an incremental process of contextual and contingent generation of theory, methodologies and practical applications. It is never alone, but always relational to other work that we do. The biographies of methods (Pink and Leder Mackley 2012), approaches and theoretical fields of debate happen over time, and feed in and out of projects. The question becomes therefore not how applied-theoretical research *should* be done, but what we can learn from it when it is configured in particular ways in relation to researchers' and scholars' existing bodies of knowledge and ideas, methods and the new work that will emerge with it. This is where and why a reflexive approach to the ways in which we work as applied scholars is important. Since if we do not understand how we ourselves produce and share knowledge, or the implications of this for the sites we wish to understand and intervene in, then we stand little chance of being able to comment on how other people's knowledge 'flows' in their organizations.

Sarah Pink is Professor of Design and Emerging Technologies, and Director of the Emerging Technologies Research Lab, at Monash University, Australia. Her work is interdisciplinary and brings together academic scholarship and applied practice. Her recent publications include the books *Digital Ethnography: Principles and Practice* (2016) and *Digital Materialities: Anthropology and Design* (2016).

Jennie Morgan is a social anthropologist based in the Department of Sociology at the University of York. She is a postdoctoral researcher on the AHRC (U.K.)-funded Heritage Futures project (2015–19). Her recent work is published in journals such as *Museum and Society, Journal of Material Culture, Environment and Planning A*.

Andrew Dainty is Professor of Construction Sociology and Director of Loughborough University Graduate School. His research focuses on human social action within project-based sectors and particularly the social rules and processes that affect people working as members of project teams. He is co-author/editor of nine books and research monographs and over one hundred refereed journal papers.

Notes

1. The project, as established in the funded bid, 'looks at what types of OSH knowledge and evidence circulate and work in organizations involved in networked delivery systems, how organizations interpret information and, in turn, how this influences OSH'.

2. This question has also characterized industry interest in a follow-on project that we have been involved in, which explores OSH in micro, small and medium-sized enterprises (discussed in Gibb et al. 2015b).

References

Appadurai, A. 1996. *Modernity at Large: Cultural Dimensions of Globalization*. Minneapolis, MN: University of Minnesota Press.
Dekker, S. 2003. 'Failure to Adapt or Adaptations That Fail: Contrasting Models on Procedures and Safety', *Applied Ergonomics* 34(3): 233–38.
Fors, V., Å. Bäckström and S. Pink. 2013. 'Multisensory Emplaced Learning: Resituating Situated Learning in a Moving World', *Mind, Culture, and Activity: An International Journal* 20(2): 170–83.
Gibb. A., A. Finneran, A. Cheyne, A. Dainty, J. Glover, J. Morgan, M. Fray, P. Waterson, P. Bust, R. Haslam, R. Hartley and S. Pink. 2015a. 'Occupational Safety and Health in Networked Organisations: Management of OSH in Networked Systems of Production or Service Delivery: Comparisons between Healthcare, Construction and Logistics'. Prepared for the IOSH at Loughborough University.
Gibb, A., J. Pinder, P. Bust, A. Cheyne, A. Dainty, M. Fray, A. Finneran, J. Glover, R. Hartley, R. Haslam, W. Jones, J. Morgan, S. Pink, P. Waterson and E.Y. Gosling. 2015b. *Engagement of Micro, Small and Medium-Sized Enterprises in Occupational Safety and Health*. Prepared for the IOSH at Loughborough University.
Gherardi, S. and Nicolini, D. 2002. 'Learning the Trade: A Culture of Safety in Practice', *Organization* 9(2): 191–223.
Guldenmund, F.W. 2000. 'The Nature of Safety Culture: A Review of Theory and Research', *Safety Science* 34(1): 215–57.
Hale, A. and Borys, D. 2013. 'Working to Rule, or Working Safely? Part 1: A State of the Art Review', *Safety Science* 55: 207–21.
Halbesleben, J.R. 2010. 'The Role of Exhaustion and Workarounds in Predicting Occupational Injuries: A Cross-lagged Panel Study of Health Care Professionals', *Journal of Occupational Health Psychology* 15(1): 1.
Harris, M. (ed.). 2007. *Ways of Knowing: New Approaches in the Anthropology of Experience and Learning*. Oxford: Berghahn.
Hollnagel, E. 2014. *Safety-I and Safety–II: The Past and Future of Safety Management*. Farnham: Ashgate Publishing.
Health and Safety Executive (HSE). (2012–2013). Health and Safety Executive (Annual Statistics Report for Great Britain). Retrieved on 10 September 2016 from http://www.hse.gov.uk/STATISTICS/overall/hssh1213.pdf
Hutter, B. 2001. *Regulation and Risk: Occupational Health and Safety on the Railways*. Oxford: Oxford University Press.
Ingold, T. 2000. *The Perception of the Environment: Essays on Livelihood, Dwelling, and Skill*, reissued edition. London: Routledge.
Knox, H. and P. Harvey. 2011. 'Anticipating Harm: Regulation and Irregularity on a Road Construction Project in the Peruvian Andes', *Theory, Culture and Society* 28(6): 142–63.
Lave, J. and E. Wenger. 1991. *Situated Learning: Legitimate Peripheral Participation*. Cambridge: University Press.

Marchand, T. H. 2010. 'Making Knowledg: Explorations of the Indisoluable Relation between Minds, Bodies and Environment', in *Journal of the Royal Anthropological Institute*. 16: S1–S21.

Nicolini, D., S. Gherardi and D. Yanow (eds). 2003. *Knowing in Organizations: A Practice-Based Approach*. New York, NY: M.E. Sharpe.

Pels, P. 2000. 'The Trickster's Dilemma: Ethics and the Technologies of the Anthropological Self', in M. Strathern (ed.), *Audit Cultures: Anthropological Studies in Accountability*. London: Routledge.

Pink, S. 2006a. 'Introduction: Applications of Anthropology', in S. Pink (ed.), *Applications of Anthropology*. Oxford: Berghahn, pp. 3–26.

Pink, S. 2006b. *The Future of Visual Anthropology: Engaging the Senses*. London: Routledge.

Pink, S. 2012. *Situating Everyday Life: Practices and Places*. London: Sage.

Pink, S. 2015. *Doing Sensory Ethnography*, second edition. London: Sage.

Pink, S. and K. Leder Mackley. 2012. 'Video as a Route to Sensing Invisible Energy', *Sociological Research Online*, February 2012, available online at http://www.socresonline.org.uk/17/1/3.html

Pink, S. and K. Leder Mackley. 2014. 'Reenactment Methodologies for Everyday Life Research: Art Therapy Insights for Video Ethnography', *Visual Studies* 29(2):146–54.

Pink, S. and J. Morgan. 2013. 'Short-term Ethnography: Intense Routes to Knowing', *Symbolic Interaction* 36(3): 351–61.

Pink, S., J. Morgan and A. Dainty. 2014a. 'Safety in Movement: Mobile Workers, Mobile Media', *Mobile Media and Communication* 2(3): 335–51.

Pink, S., J. Morgan and A. Dainty. 2014b. 'The Safe Hand: Gels, Water, Gloves and the Materiality of Tactile Knowing', *Journal of Material Culture* 19(4): 425–42.

Pink, S., J. Morgan and A. Dainty. 2015. 'Other People's Homes as Sites of Uncertainty: Ways of Knowing and Being Safe', *Environment and Planning A* 47(2): 450–64.

Strathern, M. 2006. 'A Community of Critics? Thoughts on New Knowledge', *Journal of the Royal Anthropological Institute* 12: 191–209.

Watson, T.J. 2011. 'Ethnography, Reality, and Truth: The Vital Need for Studies of "How Things Work" in Organizations and Management', *Journal of Management Studies* 48(1): 202–17.

Wenger, E. 1998. *Communities of Practice: Learning, Meaning, and Identity*. Cambridge: Cambridge University Press.

PART III

WORKING IN INTERDISCIPLINARY TEAMS

Chapter 5

From Emplaced Knowing to Interdisciplinary Knowledge
Sensory Ethnography in Energy Research

Kerstin Leder Mackley and Sarah Pink

Introduction

In this chapter we advance discussions of the use of a sensory ethnography approach in interdisciplinary research. One of the frequent issues in interdisciplinary projects is the lack of coherence between the theories and concepts used to understand the worlds that we work in and the ways in which knowledge is produced across different disciplines. At the same time, scholars and researchers from these disciplines nevertheless need to find ways in which to work together and indeed create relationships between their research findings. In this chapter, we interrogate this question through focusing in on how interdisciplinary connections might be achieved at the stage of analytical processes. This is an area of ethnographic practice that researchers often find difficult to document. However, we argue that it is a key site that we need to interrogate in order to understand how interdisciplinary applied work can be undertaken successfully. This is particularly so, because for interdisciplinary practice to be effective, it may need to involve the intersection of disciplines not simply through their findings, but at different moments in the research process.

To do this, we reflect on the example of an interdisciplinary energy research project, which has demanded an increased sense of reflexivity about the kinds of knowledge that video-based sensory ethnography can produce. This has meant not only bringing our own self-awareness about methodological process to the fore, as media and social science scholars, but thinking about this in terms of our relationships and collaborations with scholars from other disciplines and orientations. In contrast to stand-alone ethnographic projects by single researchers, the work we discuss in this chapter has involved sharing and providing entry points into research materials (cf. Pink 2009: 121), both between the authors and with an interdisciplinary team of colleagues in engineering and design. As such, the analytical process and production of (routes to) knowledge entail related questions of modes of representation.

In what follows, we therefore address two issues: one explores how we have engaged analytically with verbal and non-verbal forms of knowing and representation in the context of a video ethnography that attends to the senses; the other considers the role that sensory-ethnographic knowledge can play in relation to applied and interdisciplinary energy research. Such contexts for interdisciplinarity are often characterized as difficult. In their report on one recent interdisciplinary energy project, Transition Pathways, Hargreaves and Burgess conclude that 'A major unresolved question is … how far does willingness to do interdisciplinary work extend before real conceptual limits are reached?' (2009: 37). In this chapter we argue that, to some extent, this question can be addressed through a focus on the analytical process.

In the case of sensory-ethnographic practice, Pink has previously reflected that 'the analysis of experiential, imaginative, sensorial and emotional dimensions of ethnography is itself often an intuitive, messy and sometimes serendipitous task' (Pink 2009: 119). The analytical processes of ethnography are indeed notoriously difficult to document, in contrast for instance to those of conversation analysis or social semiotics. As is commonly stressed in ethnographic methods textbooks, analysis is an ongoing part of the ethnographic process rather than a stage in its own right. As soon as we engage with participants and their life worlds, from recruitment to in-depth research encounters, we begin to analyse, and in doing so we create an ethnographic-theoretical dialogue that often rests at the core of our work. As we follow research participants during our fieldwork, we (con)test existing knowledges and expectations and reframe what we think we know, often in light of the unexpected (cf. Slater and Miller 2007). Sensory ethnography provides important room for such serendipity, which means that analytical thought can be difficult to track and isolate as separate from the ongoingness of the research process.

Simultaneously we often produce research materials – in the form of field notes, photographs, and audio or video recordings – which can themselves be analysed both as evocations of the research encounter (Pink 2009; Pink and Leder Mackley 2012) and as representations of knowledge that, depending on the analytic lenses we apply, may elucidate important idiosyncrasies and complexities or direct us towards wider themes and patterns. Our responsibilities as ethnographers require us to be accountable to each other, to scholars inside and outside our disciplines, to participants and, increasingly, to industry stakeholders and the wider public, to be able to demonstrate *how we know*. Furthermore, we argue that it is precisely through our engagement with how we arrive at ways of knowing that we can also hope to communicate these to others.

In this chapter, we respond to the above context by examining how the issues it raises are actually played out in practice. Rather than proposing specific tools or strategies for sensory-ethnographic analysis, which themselves depend on research modes and questions, we reflect on the role of analysis and representation in the applied context of our research into everyday consumption of energy and digital media use in the home. The focus of the chapter is thus methodological, rather than empirical, as we contemplate the challenges and opportunities that come with video ethnographies and related methods in this study.

There is moreover a certain politics to this context. Our research is not immune from wider issues of the role of anthropology and the social sciences in energy research (see, for example, Henning 2005; Wilhite et al. 2000; Wilhite 2005). As will become clear in the course of this chapter, it is partly our sensitivity towards these wider debates that often causes us to pause and reflect on the nature and status of our knowledge. In particular, it reminds us to strike a balance between producing ethnographic work in its own right and serving the needs of other disciplines. In our experience, some of the most important research developments have occurred at moments when the two intertwine.

We begin by introducing the theoretical sensitivities that underpin our sensory-ethnographic approach before contextualizing these in relation to Low Effort Energy Demand Reduction (LEEDR) – an interdisciplinary project in which we participated at Loughborough University, U.K., between 2010 and 2014.

Attending to the Senses

Sensory ethnography, as we understand and practise it, is a theoretically informed 'critical methodology' (Pink 2009: 8), which puts the sensory, experiential and affective elements of lived reality to the forefront of research design, conduct, analysis and representation. It is not, however, intended as a method that can be implanted from a textbook or from one project to another, but one that evolves in use. In the context of the research project discussed here, we developed elements of Pink's sensory ethnography approach to focus on everyday life through three prisms: place/environment, movement/practice and the senses/perception. Because our research was centred in the homes of our participants, we articulated this through a focus on different elements of the relationships between people, what they do, feel and say and the material and sensory environment of home. In this context, the three prisms shaped the way we did the ethnography *and* served as analytical entry points.

Video-based sensory ethnography requires a mode of investigation that allows us to directly engage and familiarize ourselves with participants' experiences, actions and environments during the ethnographic encounter. It also enables us to continue to imagine these lived realities through analytical reviewing of the materials and seeking to communicate these to others by inviting them to equally imagine participants' experiential realities – albeit in guided ways (see Pink and Leder Mackley 2012 to experience this). As researchers, we make sense of participants' lives and contexts through our own sensing bodies in ways that are intuitively empathetic, while, at the same time, attending to how people's lived experiences are culturally represented and constructed through language. Analysis is thus always multi-layered, allowing us to find different entry points into materials. More broadly, through its attention to the ongoingness of lived reality, of processes, change and interrelations, our ethnography also provides a specific mode of research that scrutinizes seemingly given concepts, categories and ways of seeing. As we show below, this was one of our key contributions within the interdisciplinary exchange.

Applied Sensory Ethnography: Energy Research

The LEEDR project, from which the examples discussed in this chapter are derived, combined longitudinal energy monitoring with in-depth qualitative research to explore in detail how and why families use energy in their homes, and through this to prototype digital mobile device apps that might help people to reduce domestic energy consumption (Buswell et al. 2015; Buswell, Webb and Mitchell 2015). Readers are invited to explore our website, Energy and Digital Living, at http://energyanddigitalliving.com, where we show how the ethnographic and design teams worked together in this project towards the production of the prototype interventions. Twenty U.K. family households volunteered to participate in the project. As part of this they had their homes' electricity, gas and hot water flows measured for up to three years. Due to technical requirements all families were home owners, but they differed in family size, age, ethnicity, income and education. Energy use was monitored at meter level as well as on individual appliances, such as washing machines, toasters and media sets. Homes also contained sensors to detect temperatures, movement, hot water consumption (Buswell 2013; Buswell et al. 2013) and the opening of doors and windows.

LEEDR was funded through a U.K. Research Council grant, which set out to foster interdisciplinary research on digital solutions for a more sustainable future. An initial focus of the team was to make visible and meaningful, in a number of discipline-specific ways, the use of energy in the contexts of participants' everyday lives. The engineering-led disciplines that carried out the energy modelling and analysis used monitoring data to explore where, when and how much energy was consumed, in order to identify potential energy savings, but also to generate compact representations of consumption patterns that could be used as inputs to larger building simulation tools (e.g. Marini et al. 2014). Numerical modelling approaches can be used to understand observed 'behaviours' and to numerically model the potential effectiveness of changes to devices or device use in the home. To our engineering colleagues, energy use was initially made 'visible' and digestible by plotting time series data and calculating specific metrics (e.g. kWh of electricity used per day) on graphs and in spreadsheets. Occupancy data provided a loose understanding of people's movements and activity levels around the home. The analytic lens could be adjusted to studying overall energy-use patterns or individual appliances (or appliance groups) in relation to other factors, such as time of day, day of week, season, weather, construction type, heating system and so on (e.g. Cosar-Jorda et al. 2013).

The design team initially sought an understanding of families' histories, values and activities through semi-structured interviewing and interactive tasks, which invited participants to map everyday movements and activities per family member on a floor plan of their house, thus tracing these according to times of the day and week (see Mitchell et al. 2015). Consequently, the design data firstly existed in the form of mapped floor plans, along with audio recordings and transcripts. The team's attempt to understand families' views, hopes and motivations, through thematic analysis and attitudinal mapping, began to identify the kinds and contexts of interventions that would make sense in people's lives. Subsequent analysis included the development of family 'personas' for use in future-gazing scenarios (Wilson et al. 2014).

Our ethnographic fieldwork was designed to mutually build understandings with the engineering context and to inform the design of bespoke digital interventions. It initially comprised two stages. First, we explored each home with video, asking participants to guide us through their houses and describe and show to us what they would commonly do to make their homes 'feel right'. This form of collaborative home video tour is firmly rooted in the sensory-ethnographic endeavour of investigating participants' everyday activities through the interaction between people and the sensory and material contexts of their homes. As such, we were interested in how participants maintained the 'sensory aesthetics' (Pink 2004; Pink and Leder Mackley 2012) of their homes, through conscious and active negotiation but also, inevitably, through their everyday movements and practices. Learning about floor surfaces, decorative choices, cleaning, heating and lighting preferences, and about the management of sounds and smells, gave us insights into how energy use was implicated in the creation of the sensory home. It also revealed how different everyday practices were entangled in the wider project of making home. Although energy use was on participants' minds during the tour, we purposefully shifted emphasis away from direct questions of energy consumption and towards mundane domestic tasks. As part of the tour, we asked participants to re-enact everyday routines around bedtime and getting up in the morning, as well as leaving and returning home. Here, we were particularly interested in whether participants followed specific routes and patterns in preparing the home for the night or day. Often they did, and their re-enactments tapped into embodied and habitual ways of maintaining the home that participants followed but would not usually talk about.

The home video tours, which preceded the engineers' monitoring installation, produced videos of around forty to a hundred minutes. They were complemented by written field notes about our own experiences of homes and research encounters, especially regarding sensory reflections, conversations and other observations that were not 'caught' on camera. These have helped to situate and contextualize our video materials. Video tours were followed by a second visit to families' homes to discuss with participants the experience of the tour, invite comments from other family members, ensure participants had a chance to edit materials (following our ethics procedure) and discuss any changes since the tour. The latter underlined an observation from the video tours themselves, that homes are always places in transition.

The second ethnographic stage, post-energy monitoring installation and partly informed by themes emerging from the tours, explored everyday domestic activities through which energy is consumed, with a focus on laundry, cooking, bathroom activities and digital media use in eleven households. We used video to record participants in their homes (where individuals felt uncomfortable with video, we combined audio recordings with still photography). At the request of our engineering colleagues, we also photographed activities across the home at the beginning of each visit. This was designed to provide the visual context of what was necessarily going on 'off-camera' and, simultaneously, to validate energy monitoring data. Depending on participants' preferences, we aimed to spend most of up to two days with them, attending to activities as and when they occurred, or we visited families when they engaged in specific activities. Our questions attended to the often tacit and embodied knowledge that participants drew on in going about their everyday activities, for instance how they knew an item needed washing or a saucepan had reached the right temperature. We explored how activity was situated in and interconnected with people's wider sensory environments, and paid careful attention to how particular activities were interwoven with each other, and the contexts in which they became entangled, for instance by focusing on how using heating and media related to laundry, bathroom or kitchen activities.

We have outlined our research processes in some depth as they form an important backdrop to the kinds of materials we produced with participants and how these related to research activities across the team. To us, our video ethnographies sought to provide phenomenological detail and emplaced knowledge that would be difficult to tap into through interviews or observation alone. However, in communicating our experiences and findings to our engineering and design colleagues, we were faced with a number of challenges that impacted on *how* we analysed, and how we represented our knowledge. This partly concerned the nature and status of our videos as 'data', and the questions that the wider team sought to answer through our videos. Drawing out analytic insights and framing the viewing of our videos seemed crucial. In the next section, we examine the status of the knowledge produced through sensory ethnography in relation to knowledge/data expectations that exist in other disciplines.

Sharing Sensory Ethnography

While visual materials have much potential to communicate across disciplines in their capacity to invite viewers to empathetically engage with the experience of both filmmaker and participant (see MacDougall 1998, 2006; Pink 2009), this is sometimes difficult to achieve. For instance, in *Doing Anthropology for Consumer Research*, Sunderland and Denny comment on some of the challenges of making ethnographic videos meaningful to clients, pointing out an assumed 'transparency of meaning', as though ethnography were just a matter of observation (2007: 251). Citing an *Adweek* article, they take issue with the notion that 'With a video camera you can see the difference between what people say they do and what they actually do' (ibid). Their attempt to use video to gain additional non-verbal knowledge and make visible the 'sociocultural texture' of people's lives is rooted in visual anthropology and closely linked to our approach. To understand, then, how our materials and analysis might become meaningful to colleagues from other disciplines, we have focused on the assumptions that these have brought to our research. We are interested here in the question of how the 'strangeness' of other disciplinary approaches has enabled us to mutually achieve further understanding by working *with* our colleagues: it is not just a matter of seeking to persuade colleagues from other disciplines to attend to our sensory approach, but also of us needing to understand their work practices and meanings.

In the early days of the project, engineering colleagues mapped out diagrammatically a possible relationship between our video materials and energy monitoring data, seeking to foster interdisciplinary debate and form the groundwork for a project database. This was an important part of the learning process as it clarified how, from an engineering perspective, our 'social data' would help illuminate the meanings behind the energy monitoring. As we explain below, we do not see our videos as 'data' in the way portrayed in the diagram. Yet the diagram was important because it enabled us to rethink the kinds of 'ways of knowing' that we could actually offer our colleagues concerning the relationship between monitoring data and human experience, and how best to present these.

The use of the video camera did indeed mean that participants could show us what they 'do', in embodied action and in the contexts of their homes, sometimes but not exclusively at times that coincided with their usual activities. Care was taken to time-stamp all audio-visual recordings and photographs, so as to make possible 'real-time' data links between videos and energy measurements. In the case of the everyday activity videos, this offered a way in which to validate and interpret some of the monitoring data. However, what the above-mentioned (purposefully simple) graphic implied was a treatment of the footage as self-explanatory and an understanding of the video materials as linear and simultaneous recordings, as though we were working with CCTV (cf. Martens 2012). While these analytical uses of the materials enabled connections between disciplines, it was important for us to ensure that they could then be developed in relation to our perspectives on what the monitoring data would tell us about the technological, sensory and material environments that our participants were sensing and perceiving.

To us, the video materials are not objective or transparent records of what people do, but audio-visual manifestations of co-constructed ethnographic encounters. As such, they cannot be seen as monitoring tools in the same way as the households' energy use sensors. But rather we see them as entry points into people's lifeworlds and experiential realities, which can be interrogated from a number of angles. They document and evoke the ethnographic encounter and thus serve as aide-memoires for the emplaced sensory and social experience of the researcher, which allow us to revisit and reconnect with the event (Pink 2009). They also represent parts of the ethnographer's gaze which, through video, is always split between the flip-out screen of the digital camera and the wider environment. Further, depending on analytic priorities, the videos could help us construct empirically grounded stories of life in the home. These stories were informed by the researcher's attention to the sensory, social and material environment and by understandings gained from engaging participants in conversation.

Energy monitoring data often tends to be explained through psychological models of behaviours and motivations, leading to arguments for behaviour change campaigns (see our discussion of this context below). A sensory ethnography approach instead considers how energy monitoring data emerges from the sensory, affective, routine and contingent aspects that are part of the ongoingness of everyday life. With regard to our materials, the empathetic element of video viewing is important in how we aim to communicate experiences across and beyond our team. Indeed, as a design colleague put it soon after joining the team:

> As a researcher who probably won't get an opportunity to meet the … households prior to designing for them, such source material affords a level of *empathic understanding* and realistic contextual *texture* that is otherwise missing from thematic analysis and other written reports (Personal correspondence, our emphasis).

For us, this goes beyond providing the kind of context that shows *what is happening when energy is consumed*. Instead, we turn the research question around by seeking to understand how and why our participants need to consume energy in the process of creating the specific sensory aesthetic of home. Therefore, here it is not the measurement that defines the story about energy consumption, but the ongoing sensory and emplaced process of making the home 'feel right' that may implicate different energy uses.

At the same time, whereas to us as sensory ethnographers video recordings stand for our own and the participant's sensory and embodied experiences of place and movement, we need to acknowledge that in other contexts they might be understood as realist data. One option is to seek to educate audiences to our viewing position. Another is to seek other culturally appropriate methods through which to make the elements of the research experience that we wish to communicate accessible. Responding to this context, to share sensory-ethnographic insights from the home video tours with the wider team, Kerstin began writing out narrative portraits of homes and tours. This involved turning the video into words in a way that would continue to evoke the place-event of home (Pink and Leder Mackley 2012) by attending to experiential, social and material detail, all the while drawing out how energy use was implicated in the creation of the sensory home. The narrative portraits were successful in that one design colleague commented:

> The narrative gives a very rich account of the [video tour] experience and the households ... While reading each of them I really felt like I was walking through the house with 'them'. I know some of our families ... better because I was [there] during their [first meeting] ... But I have to say that [for] the ones in which I wasn't present, the [video tour] portrait has given me a very 'vivid' experience of [what] they are like as a family (I got to know them better!) and [what] their household might look like. I also find that this 'vivid experience' certainly contributes – as designers – to understanding how our potential design interventions would fit into their lifestyles (Personal correspondence).

From a critical visual anthropology perspective, the translation of images to words would be framed as an objectification of the visual (non-verbal) to the verbal. However, we would distance our work from the notion that 'for the interpretation of [visual data] "it is the act of describing that enables the act of seeing"' (Price (1994: 5) in Ball and Smith 2001: 308), as this would imply a question of semiotics. Rather, our use of written narratives is a choice of genre for telling research stories that fit the context and engage our audiences in the most appropriate way by evoking and helping to imagine a form of reality while distancing the audience from the (apparent) realism of the videos. The narratives thus invited alternative understandings of the situatedness of people's everyday experiences and practices, enabling design and engineering colleagues to develop new appreciations of the lived realities we described, through detailed insights into otherwise inaccessible idiosyncrasies, interrelations and contradictions that make up domestic life.

Rather than as outputs of thematic analysis, then, we see these as analytically informed texts. By 'analytically informed' we mean they were informed by the ongoingness of the analysis, which was continuous throughout our video tour stage. In a foreword to Clifford and Marcus' *Writing Culture*, Kim Fortun argues that 'Texts need to be imagined as we move through the field, directing our attention to the kinds of material we will need to *perform* an analysis. This means that we must also imagine narration and argument as we go, even while remaining open to the field's beckoning. The prospect of writing can orient without determining our inquiries' (2010: xii, original italics). We would add two points: first, it is not only texts that need to be imagined during fieldwork, but also viewing contexts and audiences. Thus, we have developed additional sensitivities to how we frame participants and contexts, and how to make interconnections between different elements of the ethnographic encounter, to ensure viewers have appropriate entry points into materials. Second, part of the fieldwork process entailed an ethnographic-theoretical dialogue, whereby our ongoing practice as scholars, which involves reading, writing and engaging with theoretical literatures and concepts, was not separate from our similarly ongoing thinking during the fieldwork.

A series of ethnographic-theoretical relationships began to emerge as our video tours progressed, and continued through our practice studies. These included notions of flow, movement, invisible architectures, material agency and everyday change, some of which we discuss below. Yet our research was also structured rather differently to that of the traditional ethnographic participant observation variety that tends to be the subject matter of the *Writing Culture* scholars. Thus we also needed to develop a thematic analysis of what we could call the findings of video tours across all twenty households. This process drew on the processual analysis that had emerged during the research process, in that concepts and ideas had arisen through our experiences of particular tours (where they were heightened or more obvious) and were then tracked through other households. However, this analysis was more formal and involved working through the materials to respond to our core research questions concerning how people 'needed' to use energy to create and maintain a particular sensory aesthetic of home, to make their homes 'feel right'.

Two themes that emerged from the more formal analysis, but which had already become relevant through the ethnographic-theoretical fieldwork dialogue, were movement and flow. We have introduced both concepts to design and engineering colleagues in discussions and internal reports, and through sharing writing-in-progress that employs them as categories through which to research domestic consumption. In doing so, we have sought to advance them as new ways of thinking about what people do in their homes, and subsequently as ways of conceptualizing the kinds of activities that are being designed for. As such, alongside the aforementioned concepts for invisible architecture and everyday change/innovation, they endured through the project to inform the digital design interventions, as documented on the Energy and Digital Living website.

Movement was a leading concept in our research design, emerging from Pink's earlier work on the senses (Pink 2009) and on everyday life practices and places (Pink 2012). In the LEEDR research we suggested that one way to understand energy consumption is as something that happens as we move along the pathways of everyday life, that is, along the habitual (and sometimes less habitual) routes that our participants take through their homes. This, for instance, led us to the routes that people follow when going to bed, getting up in the morning and doing their laundry. We were interested in how, as they follow these routes, people were both sensing their environments as they moved, but also maintaining these environments through the making of a sensory aesthetic of home. This could involve the sensory/material organization of the home through the distribution of laundry through it, or the use of media through the home when getting up in the morning. If consumption happens in movement, as we sense the environments of which we are both part and contribute to the making of, then movement through the home might likewise be considered as a route through which to develop design intervention concepts (Pink and Leder Mackley 2016).

Flow emerged as a concept during our fieldwork (Pink and Leder Mackley 2014). Because we were interested in the question of how the sensory home was made, we developed an interest in what we call the 'invisible architectures of home'. We did not see these as static but rather as sensory and experiential elements of the texture of home that were made through the flows of sound, smell, warmth and other elements. In relation to this, we proposed to the LEEDR team that if we conceptualized people as the directors of such flows in their homes, this could offer a new way of considering what it is that people *do* in their homes that goes beyond conventional divisions of domestic activity into practices of, for example, doing the laundry, cooking or showering.

These concepts and categories that initially emerged from the video tours, narratives and the more formal thematic analysis across households in turn continued to inform our fieldwork and analytical processes during the study of everyday activities in the home. Again, rather than just focusing on what happens in a household through specific instances of energy use, we attended to how energy use is implicated in wider processes of how participants experience, understand and negotiate their sensory environment, and the material and immaterial elements that are part of it.

This part of the fieldwork and analysis has put renewed focus on the often unspoken embodied and emplaced knowledge that participants draw on in performing everyday tasks.

Communicating findings from this second stage of our work to colleagues in engineering and design involved a combination of ethnographic narrative detail and the illumination of conceptual entry points across households, along with sharing visual materials. Simultaneously, being conscious of the categories and practices that would be meaningful to other disciplines, we responded to these by attending to details that would aid their approaches. This included practical information (about washing machine settings, domestic roles and routines), which has informed some of the monitoring data analysis. Moreover, we revisited materials in light of particular design prototypes that were presented to the group, to consider how our analytic concepts and processes might interpret the implications of possible interventions. Below we provide some more detail on the ways in which our sensory-ethnographic concepts and concerns became entangled with the other disciplines' own analytic thinking and approaches.

(Re)framing Analytic Attention

While the LEEDR project allowed researchers from different disciplines to pursue discipline-specific research questions and agendas, interdisciplinary debate was actively fostered and enhanced through the sharing of analytic and visual materials and discipline-specific publications, but also opportunities to co-author across disciplines and exchange data and ideas through a series of team workshops. It was specifically through collaborating on publications (see also Leder Mackley and Pink 2014) and workshops that we were able to negotiate interdisciplinary discrepancies and connections, building forms of mutual understanding and framing problems and solutions across disciplinary boundaries. While the focus on movement and flow initially appeared abstract to our engineering colleagues – partly, because it could not be traced easily in the vast body of energy monitoring data – it eventually aided some of their thinking around, firstly, the meanings and significance of everyday routines and, secondly, the interrelations between energy-related activities and appliances. For instance, thinking began to evolve around the relationships between laundry or bathroom use and heating, making new connections between otherwise separate sections of the dataset. In response to our ways of understanding everyday life and the sensory aesthetic of home, our engineering colleagues began to reconsider traditional engineering concepts, such as 'ventilation' and 'thermal comfort', to also take into account some of the less tangible aspects of how people experience and manage their homes.

Bringing together the quantitative and qualitative elements of our research continues to be a challenge and has, for instance, resulted in an interdisciplinary design tool: PORTS – People, Objects and Resources across Time and Space (Wilson et al. 2014). PORTS developed in part through our emphasis on contingencies, movement and the changing configurations of people, things and resources in the home. It seeks to explore such interrelations at specific points during participants' everyday activities, represented through ethnographic narrative, and to investigate related energy demand measurements and implications. Moreover, our design colleagues adapted their approach to the construction of family 'personas' to take into account the sensory and material contexts of their homes, advancing what would traditionally be largely psychological profiles (see also http://energyanddigitalliving.com/design-in-practice/). As we continue to collaborate on related projects, we are likewise learning from our engineering and design colleagues about their analytic pathways and their understanding of relevant research 'knowledge'. Within this process, we keep returning to individual video excerpts to make tangible some of the more abstract concepts, and to firmly (re)ground our academic analysis in the context of people's everyday lives.

The above team interactions did not follow a straightforward path, and we acknowledge moments of serendipity and retrospective reflection elsewhere (Pink et al. 2016). In the next section, we address how we came to consider the situatedness of sensory ethnography in the wider interdisciplinary project.

Sensory Ethnography as a Route to Interdisciplinarity

As noted above, in the field of energy research, qualitative social research has historically been situated as providing mere context, or a route to understanding human behaviour with a view to ultimately changing it. Within this framework, human behaviour has tended to be seen as a 'barrier' to the success of technological innovations (see, for example, Darnton 2008; Lilley 2009; Guy and Shove 2000), and social scientists have been drawn on as 'people experts' (Henning 2005) to help overcome such barriers. As Wilhite put it:

> The main role of the few anthropologists and sociologists who have entered the energy arena has been reactive, mostly confined to investigating why the

policies or predictions associated with economic and attitudinal approaches fail to accomplish what they set out to do. The subject of energy use is in dire need of theoretical innovation, and is going nowhere as long as economic and attitude models serve as the centrepiece of research, while other social scientific approaches peck away at the periphery (Wilhite 2005: 2).

Accordingly, social scientists are increasingly critical of the notion that they should serve the agendas of technologically driven disciplines, as indeed they have become of the interdisciplinary project itself (Shove and Wouters 2005). A growing literature about what is variously called inter/trans/supra-disciplinarity (see Everett 2009) points towards the institutionally driven top-down agenda of interdisciplinarity, but also to 'bottom up' interdisciplinarity, by which groups of researchers focus on their shared interests across disciplines. The revisionary argument that 'interdisciplinarity may not be so much a desired state of being projected into the future, as a process that generates variation in the evolution of disciplinary research programmes' suggests that it may simply 'be seen as a property of disciplines rather than as their negation' (Shove and Wouters 2005: 6). As we have shown in this chapter, interdisciplinarity can be considered not as a concrete model to be aspired to but as a process and negotiation that evolves. It can go beyond simply bringing together two or more disciplines and can develop critical frames on existing interdisciplinary pacts, to lead to new perspectives.

Therefore, interdisciplinary engagement can create routes to theoretical innovation. Working with other disciplines not only helps us challenge the categories that are imposed externally, but it also makes us reflect on our own. As we have suggested above, it moreover inspires us to develop concepts and categories in new ways as shared spaces where we can 'talk to' colleagues across disciplines. This is precisely what we have tried to achieve in our development of concepts of movement and flow. Neither of these concepts is original to us, both are part of key theoretical debates and turns in phenomenological anthropology and processual geography. Yet both of these concepts have emerged in our work through the ethnographic-theoretical dialogue that was part of the ongoing analytical process during fieldwork, and have been relevant to the interdisciplinary dialogue.

While existing research has shown how many of the assumptions and practices that behaviour-change paradigms engage are problematic (see Shove 2010; Strengers 2011), approaches rooted in psychological models are often fused with design research agendas, and indeed sit neatly with the project of design as instigating change. Here we have demonstrated how a sensory ethnography approach helps us to reframe questions of what people achieve in their everyday domestic tasks, offering a critical perspective on the idea of social research as providing mere behavioural 'context'. This helps us to reflect differently on how we conceive of behaviour and how we might imagine 'change'. By creating a critical approach that is made accessible to design and engineering colleagues through our analytical process, we have thus evaded complying with what has been called the 'subordination-service mode' of interdisciplinary collaboration between the social and technological sciences. As described by Barry et al.:

> In this mode the service discipline(s) is commonly understood to be making up for or filling in for an absence or lack in the other, (master) discipline(s). In some accounts the social sciences are understood precisely in these terms. They appear to make it possible for the natural sciences and engineering to engage with 'social factors' which had hitherto been excluded from analysis or consideration. Social scientists are expected to 'adopt the "correct" natural science definition of an environmental problem "and devise relevant solution strategies"' (Leroy, 1995, quoted in Owens, 2000, p. 1143, n. 3); or they may be called upon to assess and help to correct a lack of public understanding of science (Irwin & Wynne, 1996) (Barry et al. 2008: 29).

The relationships between disciplines that have emerged from our sensory ethnography research were partly influenced by our determination that they would not follow a 'subordination-service' mode. Yet they were not modelled on the aim of achieving a particular place in the range of typologies that tend to be used for retrospectively defining interdisciplinarity. We would instead see interdisciplinarity as an emergent process, a way of working that explores the in-betweens and the gaps of disciplinary practices, and that invites the introduction of alternative concepts to 'bridge' disciplinary differences in ways that surpass existing debates. These bridging concepts, we argue, need to emerge from the analytical process. In order to achieve this, we need to recognize the ongoingness of analysis and the importance of rooting dialogue within it. The emphasis is on those places where relations between disciplines become productive of ways of knowing about consumption that enable us to move forward in our scholarship and practice. It is about focusing not on the different disciplines and how they do or do not comprehend each other, but instead on the in-betweens where they meld or spark.

Conclusion

In this chapter, we have used our own work and experiences to deconstruct and make explicit the often implicit process of analysis to show how this can become shaped in the context of applied and interdisciplinary energy research. This is important because, as Henning has pointed out, 'In order for us to make a serious contribution to mitigating climate change, we must also be prepared, and equipped, to collaborate and communicate with other than our own charmed circle of social scientists' (Henning 2005: 12). A sensory ethnography approach and the analytical possibilities that a focus on sensory experience enables play a specific role in this. We argue, however, that such interdisciplinarity does not happen simply when we bring the findings of different disciplines together into critical relief, but that it also becomes embedded in the ongoingness of analytical process.

The sensory video ethnography approach enabled us to explore the environments we are part of, to follow consumers and the things that they consumed, and to consider the experiential and the particular. It attended to the material, sensory, tacit and verbalized elements of home as well as to how these were experienced. It enabled us to situate consumption as part of place, movement/practice and perception, and to explore how the contingencies of these combined to define how people actually consumed: it thus took more than one entry point into considering where and how consumption might happen. This was an inherently interdisciplinary approach, in terms of its development through an interface between visual anthropology, applied consumer research, philosophy, anthropology, geography and sociology. It is also related to *applied* visual anthropology (Pink 2007), which offers examples of how video and photography practice can serve as what Chalfen and Rich (2007) call 'cultural brokerage', enabling communication between different groups of people. This notion of cultural brokerage can likewise be applied where video enables us to work at in the in-between of 'different' disciplines. As we have seen above, our video tours and the written summaries thereof enabled different routes of communication and to interdisciplinary knowledge.

A focus on how the relationalities and in-betweens of disciplines become woven through the ongoing analytical process of sensory ethnography can enable us to produce applied knowledge that 'matters'. The unpicking and deconstructing of research in ways that acknowledge how analytical process is shaped in relation to such interdisciplinarity, through ongoing ethnographic-theoretical dialogue, enables us to better understand and situate both the nature of the knowledge we are producing and its applied potential. A sensory video ethnography approach offers one way through which to achieve this that is theoretically and methodologically informed in ways that can build bridges between disciplines and their concerns. Such sensory ethnography analysis might be understood as ongoing and situated at the intersection of theoretical, ethnographic, applied and interdisciplinary conversations.

Acknowledgements

This chapter is an adapted version of an article originally published as Leder Mackley and Pink (2013) 'From Emplaced Knowing to Interdisciplinary Knowledge: Sensory Ethnography in Energy Research' for *Senses and Society* 8(3): 335–53. The interdisciplinary LEEDR (Low Effort Energy Demand Reduction) project, based at Loughborough University, was jointly funded by the U.K. Research Councils' Digital Economy and Energy programmes (grant number EP/I000267/1). For further information about the project, collaborating research groups and industrial partners, please visit www.leedr-project.co.uk. The authors would like to thank all the households who generously participated in this research. In the context of this chapter, we also thank our LEEDR colleagues, especially Richard Buswell, for offering their comments in relation to this text.

Kerstin Leder Mackley is a Research Associate at the Loughborough Design School. She has applied a keen interest in people, emerging technologies and everyday life to a range of sustainability projects, including energy demand reduction (LEEDR – Low Effort Energy Demand Reduction, 2010–14) and hot water consumption (Hothouse, 2014–17). Kerstin is a co-creator of the Energy and Digital Living website (www.energyanddigitalliving.com) and has published in peer-reviewed journals, including *Media, Culture & Society*, *TOCHI* and the *Journal of Design Research*.

Sarah Pink is Professor of Design and Emerging Technologies, and Director of the Emerging Technologies Research Lab, at Monash University, Australia. Her work is interdisciplinary and brings together academic scholarship and applied practice. Her recent publications include the books *Digital Ethnography: Principles and Practice* (2016) and *Digital Materialities: Anthropology and Design* (2016).

References

Ball, M. and G. Smith. 2001. 'Technologies of Realism: Ethnographic Uses of Photography and Film', in P. Atkinson, A. Coffey, S. Delamont, J. Lofland, L. Lofland (eds), *Handbook of Ethnography*. London: Sage, pp. 302–19.

Barry, A., G. Born and G. Weszkalnys. 2008. 'Logics of Interdisciplinarity', *Economy and Society* 37(1): 20–49.

Buswell, R.A. 2013. 'Uncertainty in Whole House Monitoring', in *Proceedings of the 13th International Conference of the International Building Performance Simulation Association*, Chambery, France, 25–28 August 2013: 2403–2410.

Buswell, R.A., D. Marini, L. Webb and M. Thomson. 2013. 'Determining Heat Use in Residential Buildings Using High Resolution Gas and Domestic Hot Water Monitoring', in *Proceedings of the 13th International Conference of the International Building Performance Simulation Association*, Chambery, France, 25–28 August 2013: 2412–2419.

Buswell, R.A., L. Webb and V. Mitchell. 2015. 'LEEDR Household Recruitment Procedures, Materials and Methods'. Loughborough University. Available online at https://dspace.lboro.ac.uk/dspace-jspui/handle/2134/16860.

Buswell, R.A., L. Webb, D. Quiggin, P. Cosar-Jorda, D. Marini, K. Osz, R. Moroşanu, S. Pink, K. Leder Mackley, G.T. Wilson, M. Hanratty, V. Mitchell and T. Bhamra. 2015. 'LEEDR: What are the Results? Participant Feedback for H99'. Loughborough University. Available online at https://dspace.lboro.ac.uk/dspace-jspui/handle/2134/18528.

Chalfen, R. and M. Rich. 2007. 'Combining the Applied, the Visual and the Medical: Patients Teaching Physicians with Visual Narratives', in S. Pink (ed.), *Visual Interventions: Applied Visual Anthropology*. Oxford/New York: Berghahn Books, pp. 53–70.

Clifford, J. and G.E. Marcus (eds). 2010 [1986]. *Writing Culture: The Poetics and Politics of Ethnography*. Berkeley, CA: University of California Press.

Cosar-Jorda, P., R.A. Buswell, L. Webb, K. Leder Mackley, R. Moroşanu and S. Pink. 2013. 'Energy in the Home: Everyday Life and the Effect on Time of Use', in *Proceedings for the 13th International Conference of the International Building Performance Simulation Association*, Chambery, France, 25–28 August 2013: 1722–1729.

Darnton, A. 2008. 'Reference Report: An Overview of Behaviour Change Models and their Uses', *GSR Behaviour Change Model Review*. Available online at http://www.civilservice.gov.uk/wp-content/uploads/2011/09/Behaviour_change_reference_report_tcm6-9697.pdf.

Everett, G. 2009. 'Annotated Bibliography: Interdisciplinarity'. Project Report, National Centre for Research Methods. Available online at http://eprints.ncrm.ac.uk/780/.

Fortun, K. 2010. 'Foreword to the Twenty-Fifth Anniversary Edition', in J. Clifford and G.E. Marcus (eds), *Writing Culture: The Poetics and Politics of Ethnography*. Berkeley, CA: University of California Press, pp. vii–xxii.

Guy, S. and E. Shove. 2000. *The Sociology of Energy*. London: Routledge.

Hargreaves, T. and J. Burgess. 2009. 'Pathways to Interdisciplinarity: A Technical Report', CSERGE Working Paper EDM 10–12. Available online at http://www.cserge.ac.uk/sites/default/files/edm_2010_12.pdf.

Henning, A. 2005. 'Climate Change and Energy Use: The Role of Anthropological Research', *Anthropology Today* 21(3): 8–12.

Leder Mackley, K. and S. Pink. 2013. 'From Emplaced Knowing to Interdisciplinary Knowledge: Sensory Ethnography in Energy Research', in *Senses and Society*, 8(3): 335–353.

Leder Mackley, K. and S. Pink. 2014. 'Framing and Educating Attention: A Sensory Apprenticeship in the Context of Domestic Energy Research', in M.L. Arantes and E.

Rieger (eds), *Ethnographien der Sinne: Wahrnehmung und Methode in Empirisch-Kulturwissenschaftlichen Forschungen*. Bielefeld: Transcript, pp. 93–110.

Lilley, D. 2009. 'Design for Sustainable Behaviour: Strategies and Perceptions', *Design Studies* 30: 704–720.

MacDougall, D. 1998. *Transcultural Cinema: Selected Essays*, edited by L. Taylor. Princeton, NJ: Princeton University Press.

MacDougall, D. 2006. *The Corporeal Image: Film, Ethnography, and the Senses*. Princeton, NJ: Princeton University Press.

Marini, D., L.H. Webb, G. Diamantis and R.A. Buswell. 2014. 'Exploring the Impact of Model Calibration on Estimating Energy Savings through Better Space Heating Control', in *Proceedings of Building Simulation and Optimization: Second Conference of IBPSA-England, Conference in Association with CIBSE*. London: International Building Performance Simulation Association, pp. 1–8.

Martens, L.D. 2012. 'The Politics and Practices of Looking: CCTV Video and Domestic Kitchen Practices', in S. Pink (ed.), *Advances in Visual Methodology*. London: Sage, pp. 39–56.

Massey, D. 2005. *For Space*. London: Sage.

Mitchell, V., K. Leder Mackley, S. Pink, C. Escobar-Tello, G.T. Wilson and T. Bhamra. 2015. 'Situating Digital Interventions: Mixed Methods for HCI Research in the Home', *Interacting with Computers* 27(1): 3–12.

Nader, L. 2010. 'Barriers to Thinking New about Energy', in L. Nader (ed.), *The Energy Reader*. Oxford: Blackwell.

Pink, S. 2004. *Home Truths: Gender, Domestic Objects and Everyday Life*. Oxford: Berg.

Pink, S. (ed.) 2007. *Visual Interventions*. Oxford/New York: Berghahn Books.

Pink, S. 2009. *Doing Sensory Ethnography*. London: Sage.

Pink, S. 2010. The Future of Sensory Anthropology/The Anthropology of the Senses', *Social Anthropology* 18(3): 331–33.

Pink, S. 2012. *Situating Everyday Life: Practices and Places*. London: Sage.

Pink, S. and K. Leder Mackley. 2012. 'Video and a Sense of the Invisible: Approaching Domestic Energy Consumption through the Sensory Home', *Sociological Research Online* 17(1): 3. Available online at http://www.socresonline.org.uk/17/1/3.html.

Pink, S. and K. Leder Mackley. 2014. 'Flow in Everyday Life: Situating Practices', in C. Maller and Y. Strengers (eds), *Beyond Behaviour Change: Intervening in social practices for sustainability*, London: Routledge.

Pink, S. and K. Leder Mackley. 2016. 'Moving, Making and Atmosphere: Routines of Home as Sites for Mundane Improvisation', *Mobilities* 11(02): 171–187.

Pink, S., K. Leder Mackley, V. Mitchell, C. Escobar-Tello, M. Hanratty, T. Bhamra and R. Moroşanu. 2013. 'Applying the Lens of Sensory Ethnography to Sustainable HCI', Special Issue: Sustainable HCI through Everyday Practices, *ACM Transactions on Computer-Human Interaction*.

Pink, S., K. Leder Mackley, V. Mitchell, G.T. Wilson and T. Bhamra. (2016). 'Refiguring Digital Interventions for Energy Demand Reduction: Designing for Life in the Digital Material Home', in S. Pink, E. Ardevol and D. Lanzeni (eds), *Digital Materialities: Design and Anthropology*. London: Bloomsbury.

Richardson, I., M. Thomson, D. Infield and C. Clifford. 2010. 'Domestic Electricity Use: A High-Resolution Energy Demand Model', *Energy and Buildings* 42(10): 1878–1887.

Shove, E. 2010. 'Beyond the ABC: Climate Change Policy and Theories of Social Change', *Environment and Planning A* 42: 1273–85.

Shove, E. and P. Wouters. 2005. 'Interactive Agenda Setting in the Social Sciences – Interdisciplinarity', Workshop Discussion Paper. Interdisciplinary Fields and Fashions:

Making New Agendas. Available online at http://www.lancs.ac.uk/fass/projects/iass/files/iass_workshop3_Interdisciplinarity_Discussion_PAPER.pdf.

Slater, D. and D. Miller. 2007. 'Moments and Movements in the Study of Consumer Culture: A Discussion', *Journal of Consumer Culture* 7(1): 5–23.

Strengers, Y. 2011. 'Negotiating Everyday Life: The Role of Energy and Water Consumption Feedback', *Journal of Consumer Culture* 11(19): 319–38.

Sunderland, P.L. and R. Denny. 2007. *Doing Anthropology in Consumer Research*. Walnut Creek, CA: Left Coast Press.

Wilhite, H., E. Shove, L. Lutzenhiser and W. Kempton. 2000. 'The Legacy of Twenty Years of Energy Demand Management: We Know More About Individual Behavior but How Much Do We Really Know About Demand?', in *Conference Proceedings from the 2000 ACEEE Summer Study on Energy Efficiency in Buildings*. Available online at http://www.eceee.org/conference_proceedings/ACEEE_buildings/2000/Panel_8/p8_35.

Wilhite, H. 2005. 'Why Energy Needs Anthropology', *Anthropology Today* 21(3): 1–2.

Wilson, G.T., K. Leder Mackley, V. Mitchell, T. Bhamra and S. Pink. 2014. 'PORTS: An Interdisciplinary and Systemic Approach to Studying Energy Use in the Home', in *UbiComp 2014 Adjunct: Proceedings of the 2014 ACM International Joint Conference on Pervasive and Ubiquitous Computing*, 13–17 September 2014, Seattle/USA, ACM: 971–978.

Chapter 6

WORKING ACROSS DISCIPLINES
Using Visual Methods in Participatory Frameworks

Susan Hogan

Introduction

The Birth Project is a sophisticated research project that seeks to draw together applied practice and theoretical scholarship in an interdisciplinary framework using visual methods. The project is concerned to give those connected with birth the opportunity to make art in a variety of formats. Obstetricians, midwives, doulas, birth partners and new mothers have been given the opportunity to explore their experiences of compassion fatigue, stress, birth suffering and post-natal readjustments using the arts: phototherapy, photo diaries and art elicitation in groups, which then joined together in 'mutual recovery' events in which perspectives have been shared, primarily through elucidation of the works of art produced. Narratives from interviews have also been combined into a theatre piece (viewed by all participants). Films that have been edited to produce narrative sequences that explore the key research questions are also a major output.

This project challenges the usual dichotomy between expert healer and patient and acknowledges that all are subject to different stresses. Furthermore, hospital protocols, coupled with the unpredictability of birthing itself, can override what women want and expect in terms of a birth experience, leaving some women frankly in shock, which then can have a knock-on effect on infant development. The arts have been used to interrogate this complex topic.

Key impacts for the project are as follows:

- To shape and draw attention to new approaches to policy formulation and service delivery.
- To bring about a radical shift in how communities of people with mental-health difficulties, informal carers and health, social care and adult education personnel can connect more creatively to advance mutual recovery.
- To play a significant role in addressing the problem of mental health and well-being issues and so help restore the humanity to healthcare.[1]

To achieve these aims required working across disciplines. However, as this chapter explores, working across disciplines is fraught with complexity. Contrasting epistemologies and consequently different ideas about how to judge knowledge claims lie at the heart of this. These competing knowledge claims in turn affect how we conduct the research. So, methodology is concerned with both the underlying principles and the rules which determine how to proceed with the enquiry. These rules often have disciplinary perspectives, including perspectives on visual methods. Methodology includes the rhetoric of the study (the tone and tenor of projects), and this represents and reflects a complex range of values and sensitivities of the researcher, embedded in methodological assertions and underpinnings that might not be explicit.

Methodological orientations (often resulting in methods being implemented in particular ways in particular disciplines) have consequences for notions of 'validity', the appropriate role and ethical positioning of the researcher. Moreover, the translation of epistemological position into methodology is not always seamless and disciplinary norms invariably feature in that translation. Furthermore, some methodological models of working may fit certain disciplinary endeavours better than others; moving a method developed in community-development contexts to a broadly sociological endeavour, for example, may provoke unforeseen tensions, or indeed a loosening of customary constraints; it will certainly provoke epistemological questioning as to where the locus of power should be located, or to what extent outputs should be co-constructed by researchers and participants and how this can be achieved.

The use of the arts in research adds its own complexity, especially in relation to participatory ideals. Artists enable communities of people to think about themselves in new ways, and are important in bringing people together, resulting in enhanced social networking as well as the production of art works that are sometimes transient. There is a tightrope to walk between not constraining the creativity of the artists, while ensuring that they do not exploit a particular community or context; the community is not merely the subject matter for the artist to be manipulated for their benefit in the development of their portfolio (Hogan et al. 2015; Hogan 2015b). There may be tensions between participatory expression and aesthetic ideals, or between different notions of appropriate display or between different communicative strategies. Different methodological frameworks have different views about what constitutes valid research 'outputs'. Modes of exposition are inherently political. The locus of power and control in research in relation to disciplinary norms and methodological orientations will receive further attention with reference to research outcomes and dissemination.

New developments are actively exploring the synergies between disciplines and how they can enrich qualitative research. Below I examine the use of arts-based social science methods, which are increasingly being employed. These include: participatory arts, art elicitation using techniques from art therapy, re-enactment phototherapy, and also monologues, dance, art installations, and poetic and theatrical performance. Such work provides new ways of engaging audiences, exploring research questions and enabling academic research to have impact in the world. This chapter will explore the nature of interdisciplinarity and what visual methods can contribute in particular. The section on the *ways* in which visual methods contribute to research projects will also give examples from The Birth Project. Since there is some confusion about the nature of interdisciplinary research, the chapter will explore and define key concepts, before moving on to a detailed discussion about the use of film within The Birth Project.

Interdisciplinarity

Disciplines establish a body of knowledge about a subject, have methods to enquire about it, and theories to help order that knowledge. Disciplines are constantly generating new knowledge and new theories. They are relatively self-contained, having their own communities of experts and specialist trainings. Krishnan breaks this down further, pointing out defining characteristics including: 1) that disciplines have particular *objects* in mind as worthy of research; 2) they develop specialist knowledge *which may be esoteric*; 3) disciplines develop theories and concepts which help *to organise this specialist knowledge*; 4) disciplines develop specialist language, or use language in *very specific ways* in relation to a research subject; 5) they develop methods; 6) there is an institutional manifestation of some kind (2009a: 9). As well as being predisposed to approach questions in particular ways, results are produced 'which are acceptable to particular audiences for validation and recognition' (Whitley 1984: 21). Indeed, the results produced may not communicate beyond the specialist community of interest. Visual methods can be particularly useful in traversing such conceptual divides between disciplinary communities. The notion of the discourse is helpful here, as:

> a particular way of talking (and writing and thinking). A discourse involves certain shared assumptions which appear in the formulations that characterise it. The discourse of common sense is quite distinct, for instance, from the discourse of modern physics, and some of the formulations of the one may be expected to conflict with the formulations of the other. Ideology is *inscribed* in discourse in the sense that it is literally written or spoken *in it*; it is not a separate element which exists independently in some free-floating realm of 'ideas' and is subsequently embodied in words, but a way of thinking, speaking, experiencing (Belsey 1980: 5).

However, disciplinary discourses are not equally mutually impermeable, nor are all disciplines intellectually coherent, or stable.[2] Krishnan (2009a: 5) notes that disciplines continuously change and 'are themselves fragmented and heterogeneous' and that they 'interact with other disciplines in many complex ways'. English literature, for example, is noted to 'lack both a unifying theoretical paradigm or method and a definable stable object of research, but it still passes as an academic discipline' (Krishnan 2009: 10). Some disciplines are themselves interdisciplinary, such as art therapy, which grew as an attempt to combine insights from art practice with ideas about psychological expression, driven forward initially by artists who had read about psychology and anthropology, or had undergone psychoanalysis, or were hired by psychiatrists to form part of psychiatric teams (Hogan 2001). Within the discipline of art therapy as a whole, knowledge claims are made that are rather at odds with each other, if not wholly antithetical, and many disciplines live with such incongruities – or to put it another way, with paradigms at odds with one another. It may be that inhabiting conflicting paradigms is more problematic on some occasions for interdisciplinary endeavour than being located in different disciplines (recall again Belsey's point about ideology as inscribed in discourse).

Some commentators suggest that the social sciences could be refreshed by adopting interdisciplinary approaches 'which would help in overcoming artificial disciplinary boundaries, parochialism and narrow-mindedness and would thus improve the overall quality of social science research' (Krishnan 2009b: 2). Interdisciplinary research is often justified because it gives rise to:

a process of answering a question, solving a problem, or addressing a topic that is too broad or complex to be dealt with adequately by a single discipline and draws on disciplinary perspectives and integrates their insights to produce a more comprehensive understanding or cognitive advancement (Repko 2008: 12).

Interdisciplinarity had been described as:

> a mode of research by teams or individuals that integrates information, data, techniques, tools, perspectives, concepts, and/or theories from two or more disciplines or bodies of specialized knowledge to advance fundamental understanding or to solve problems whose solutions are beyond the scope of a single discipline or area of research practice (U.S. National Academy of Sciences, 2005: 39).

It is a notion of 'integration' that distinguishes interdisciplinary research from a mere dialogue between disciplines, though some researchers use the term in this way (Moran 2001: 16). A dialogue from different disciplinary perspectives aimed at elucidating a phenomenon could become an interdisciplinary method, if it were then incorporated as a research method.

It is obvious from the above definition that the forms interdisciplinarity can take must therefore be varied. When working in interdisciplinary teams, because of the specialised nature of disciplines, we cannot assume that individuals from different disciplines are using language in the same way, as Belsey points out in her discussion of discourses above. So, to take the example of 'participatory research', which will be discussed further, it is likely that researchers within interdisciplinary teams will have different ideas as to how *participation* should be translated into practice. As each discipline will be predisposed to tackle problems in a certain way, even when research teams agree a primary *modus operandi* such as participatory research, there may be quite different expectations within such teams as to how this will be translated into methods for applied research.

The Main Modes of Working Across Disciplines

Krishnan identifies five main modes of interdisciplinary exchange. It is perhaps helpful to give a précis of these to help teams think about how they stand in relation to them and their potential pitfalls and to avoid muddled thinking about what interdisciplinarity means.

1. Multidisciplinarity

Multidisciplinary approaches are those in which different disciplinary components are executed independently and then joined outwardly through editorial links; in multidisciplinary research 'each separately authored component could stand in isolation from the others' (Rossini and Porter 1984: 27). Krishnan puts it thus:

> In multidisciplinary research a team of researchers works towards a common aim or on a common problem, but each represented discipline works independently or in sequence. The contributions of the disciplines are purely complementary to the final product, which may just consist of a compilation of disciplinary research on a common theme or object. Alternatively, this collaboration may result in an integrated research product that synthesizes the disciplinary perspectives into a coherent picture. If it does, it means that the synthesis is carried out as a final step by the principal investigator(s), possibly without any exchange between the disciplines concerned (Krishnan 2009b: 5).

Risks: Krishnan notes that this model of working puts a lot of pressure on the principal researcher to draw together the different components. There is also the risk of misinterpretation and misrepresentation of research data, so some liaison with teams is essential to solicit feedback on the final work done. Positive aspects include that different aspects of a problem can be interrogated from different perspectives, but nuanced findings could be overridden in the final analysis. This model may be seen to be at odds with participatory ideals, since the final analysis may be completed by one researcher who makes executive decisions about what is relevant. It is also hard for the principal researcher to always have a full grasp of all the disciplines involved. If images are being used, a high degree of visual literacy is required to prevent the juxtapositioning of images in certain ways that might create unforeseen and unintended narratives. Those used to working visually are acutely aware that the way in which images are placed in relation to each other can have an impact on the way we assimilate them. Curating is a specialist activity sensitised to meaning making, including a sense of the spectator in the space. In a participatory model (such as participatory action research, PAR) this meaning making should be influenced by the participants. On a pragmatic level, in applied research, if a PAR model is being envisaged in a multidisciplinary frame, then it would need to be a contained and finished piece of work synthesised by the participatory group and then handed over in order to retain its integrity. Krishnan notes that projects in which a summary of disciplinary perspectives is the aim are easier than those which attempt to produce an 'integrated research product that can take into account the various disciplinary perspectives on a given problem', which is extremely challenging.

This description is focused on a hierarchical incorporation of different approaches without overarching synthesis; but when there is an emphasis on disciplines collaborating to develop a common perspective Krishnan calls this interdisciplinarity or supradisciplinarity, below (Krishnan 2009b: 7–8).

2. Transdiscipinarity

Transdisciplinarity is a term that seems to be used differently by different researchers, so is a term to treat with caution.

Rossini and Porter suggest it refers to research that encompasses a number of separate disciplines working together to create an overarching paradigm (Rossini and Porter 1984: 27). Lattuca's (2001: 113–18) understanding of transdisciplinarity, in common with that of Holland, is that it has the aim of applying a concept or method across disciplinary domains so 'as to unify those domains – as in socio-biology' (Holland 2014: 3). Seek to understand how other authors define this term, and define it yourself if you are using it.

Krishnan suggests that transdisciplinary research is always conducted with non-academic partners who are involved in the research process, such as NGOs. These collaborators are actually stakeholders in the results of the research. Krishnan describes it like this:

> Unlike crossdisciplinary and multidisciplinary research, transdisciplinary research is not derived from already existing disciplines or the research agendas of disciplines, but is driven by real-world problems and usually entails the opportunistic selection and use of research methods according to whatever 'fits' the problem (Krishnan 2009b: 6).

Risks: Krishnan suggest that such research can be undervalued and lack prestige. Furthermore, academic collaborators may not determine the final aims of the research and could find themselves in a lesser role as a service provider. This emphasis on real-world issues might work very well with a participatory research model, in which a community, or communities of interest, may lead the research process. There would seem to be rich opportunities for the use of visual methods and visual modes of dissemination.

3. Crossdisciplinarity

Crossdisciplinarity (borrowing knowledge and methods) is the application of methods developed in one discipline to the study of phenomena in a different discipline. How can game theory (from mathematics), for example, help a political scientist understand political institutions?

Risks: Krishnan notes that researchers run the risk of being accused of dilettantism, in applying methods they may not completely understand (2009b: 2). Secondly, he notes that this is an approach which must be handled sensitively, otherwise it can seem imperialistic, as areas of knowledge from one discipline are 'appropriated' by another. Furthermore, the way in which 'imported' methods are applied may result in criticism from the originator discipline. For artists working in social science research, the 'imperialistic' nature of the endeavour can be felt at the outset in project design when they are brought in as 'consultants' or 'community partners' in research bids, rather than as co-investigators (the primary development and management team in bids funded by research councils usually consisting of one principal investigator and one or more co-investigators); not being part of the core management of the project can make artists feel like 'fodder for high-class race horses', as one artist-researcher recently put it to me. Integrating artists into project steering groups can help.

In applied research there can be a clash of values between arts practitioners and social scientists, which it is useful to be aware of. Reductive interpretation of art works by social scientists is a danger. For example, a project researcher might feel that it is acceptable to make up titles for images to help make them more accessible to the general public; this is done with good intentions in an attempt to help make the work more comprehensible and to enhance the impact of the research. The artist or arts facilitator, in contrast, might feel that this process is impoverishing, because images can contain multiple meanings and part of their usefulness is that they are inherently polysemic and *are complex*, so locking down the meaning with reductive titles is at odds with the artist's values and notions about why visual research is useful. Another artist might feel that the research data is thus being corrupted and that the validity of the images as data is being compromised by this well-meaning attempt to make them more accessible through making up titles. Artists following a participatory mandate might argue that it is more appropriate to use the *actual words* of the people who made the artwork as the basis for labels, if they tolerate labels at all. Alternatively, any decisions about labels should surely be made by the participants themselves? In a participatory research model, the display of the works, and decisions about it, should be in the hands of the makers of the artworks and any text generated by them part of their decision making.

4. Interdisciplinarity or Supradisciplinarity

Krishnan also identifies a sustained effort of sharing theories, methods and concepts as interdisciplinarity (corresponding with the definition given above by the U.S. National Academy of Sciences) or as supradiscplinarity. He suggests that examples of supradisciplinarity could include structuralism, deconstruction, poststructuralism, feminism and complexity theory (Krishnan 2009b: 7).

Risks: The irony of all this activity is that most disciplines have formed ideological camps; communication between these 'competing supradisciplinary paradigms' can be problematic. However, if issues of power are also addressed, then there are opportunities here for an open exploration of different conceptual camps (within and between disciplines) and the implications for knowledge construction.

5. Megadisciplinarity

This is the sustained effort to rearrange the disciplines into a smaller number of super disciplines (superdisciplinarity or megadisciplinarity).

For example, it has been proposed to create a discipline of 'earth system science', which could combine many elements of natural sciences and social sciences disciplines in order to understand the earth as an integrated physical and social system. Another example might be a global social theory, which could unify all of the social and behavioural sciences (Krishnan 2009b: 9).

Risks: Unlike in interdisciplinarity, the sharing of concepts, theories and methods, which still respects disciplinary boundaries and leaves the disciplines themselves intact, this approach seeks a merger, which is obviously fraught as the weak may be engulfed by the stronger. On the other hand, it may be a pragmatic way of addressing certain problems.

Working across Disciplines Using Visual Methods: Discussion

Such collaboration is not without its challenges. Although the majority of art therapists and arts facilitators resist indulging in reductive interpretations, it may be the case that there is an inherent tension between the polysemic nature of images and the pressure on research teams to formulate social-policy pronouncements, and simple 'sound bite' report findings when working within certain models. Academic environments do not always know how to incorporate images into their findings, and have a tendency to attempt to 'translate' arts-based research into traditional 'outputs'. Furthermore, where visual outputs are concerned, how these are presented is obviously of crucial importance to the construction of meaning and how the works actually function: as a provocation, educational tool or emollient. It may be the case that project team debates about exhibition strategy contain within them *irreconcilable* aspirations.

Lattuca uses a different set of terms, but identifies fundamental *ways* of approaching interdisciplinary work:

1. *That in which the methods or concepts of one discipline make a contribution to answering questions posed in another discipline* (which corresponds to the definition above of crossdisciplinary research).
2. *Work in which a research question acts as a 'bridge' between one or more disciplines that are interested in the question* (some multidisciplinary work).
3. *Work to unify domains via concepts and methods across disciplinary domains* (some people's definition of transdisciplinary research; interdisciplinary research).
4. *Modes of research that address a research question which has no 'compelling disciplinary basis' and thereby constructs a critique of traditional disciplinary approaches to a particular issue or problem* (Lattuca 2001: 113–18).

This, I would argue, is a useful classification that research teams might consider, and which has different potential impacts for the role of artists and artist-researchers within projects. It is worth spending some time conceptualising and discussing where the art 'fits'. Is the art being used to enhance the communication of difficult ideas, or ask questions differently (as in 1)? Or could the art act as a bridge between disciplines (as in 2)? Could it have a unificatory function (as in 3)? Or could the art be used as a challenge to disciplinary assumptions and approaches (as in 4)? What forms might these different approaches take?

Barry, Born and Strathern (2007) have pointed out in their article on interdisciplinary working that the dominant British funding model for art-science collaboration tends to employ art 'to serve the sciences by communicating them or enhancing public engagement with them' (what Barry et al. call the 'service mode'; p. 3). In other words, they are often employed to enhance the communication of complex ideas beyond the academic and research communities, and also to educate, inform and solicit feedback from the wider community.

Barry, Born and Strathern (2007) also identify an 'agonistic antagonistic mode' of interdisciplinary collaboration, which they suggest 'springs from a self-conscious dialogue with, criticism of, or opposition to the limits of established disciplines, or the status of academic research ... in general ... [to] contest or transcend the given epistemological and/or ontological assumptions of specific historical disciplines'. Antagonism, we suggest, is encountered in the critique of such assumptions, manifest in attempts to propose a new ontology (2007: 3). Recent papers by Hogan and Pink (2010), Pink et al. (2011), Hogan (2011), Hogan and Warren (2012, 2013) and Hogan (2015b) touch on this aspect of interdisciplinary working, asserting the unique value of incorporating art elicitation techniques into ethnographic and sociological research projects to explore states of being and knowing, and also to offer a useful challenge to epistemological disciplinary assumptions. Without full discussion, teams may be working at cross-purposes, with artists feeling that they wish to engage in an agonistic-antagonistic mode of engagement, when other members of the team may view them as service providers with a limited remit.

Visual Methods: Ten Good Reasons to Use Visual Images in Research

As noted above, visual methods[3] can be particularly useful in traversing conceptual divides between disciplinary communities, offering distinctive modes of communication and epistemological exploration.

1. Pictures Can Be Used to Represent and Explore the Ineffable

That which is hard to put into words, including mood tones and feeling states, can often be expressed eloquently by images. Symbols, analogies and metaphors can be sophisticated, and metaphors used in conjunction with one another create complex reverberations within a pictorial frame. The materials themselves can be elegantly expressive. Feelings that are indefinable can find expression in a moment of ontological revelation in the act of making. The image and process of production is potentially illuminating. Moreover, it is not just the art object itself, but subsequent interactions with it which may become of significance. The images created in photo-documentation have been argued to encapsulate 'the textures and tactilities, smells, atmospheres and sounds or ruined spaces, together with the signs and objects they accommodate, [which] can be emphatically conjured up by the visual material' (Edensor 2005: 16). To give another example, one of the midwives participating in The Birth Project was able to explore her aspiration to 'make special' the event using glitter and other

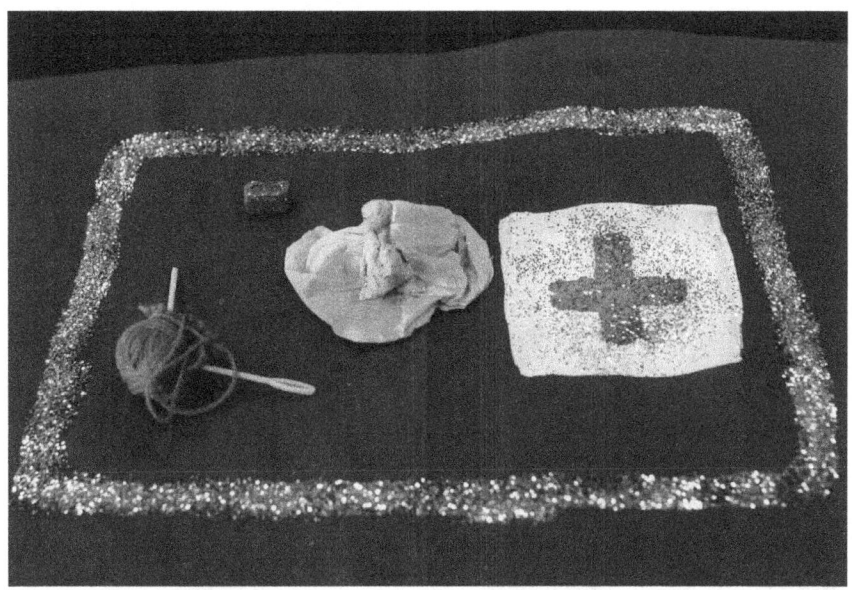

Illustration 6.1: Midwife's art work from The Birth Project.

materials to conjure up her sense of holding and providing a loving magical space – her idealism made evident.

2. Images Can Convey an All-at-oneness (Eisner 1995)

Images can produce a holistic depiction of ideas or feelings. They can also encapsulate eloquently. As images are not linear sequences as are utterances, different levels of meaning can be conveyed simultaneously and contradictory sentiments expressed instantaneously. Equally, images can be used to convey complicated concepts and complex data. The developing field of informatics uses diagrams and images to summarise chunks of information, which would be hard to digest if simply heard, but which are immediately evident when seen. Complicated concepts can be condensed in simple visual formulations, or extended ones such as animations or cartoons. Weber points out that large concepts such 'poverty' or 'war' are often given 'visual exemplars' to enable accessibility (2008: 44). In The Birth Project a midwife was able to reflect that putting down all her conflicting thoughts and feelings on one page in a visual form was revelatory for her as she was able to see contradictions and tensions in a new way.

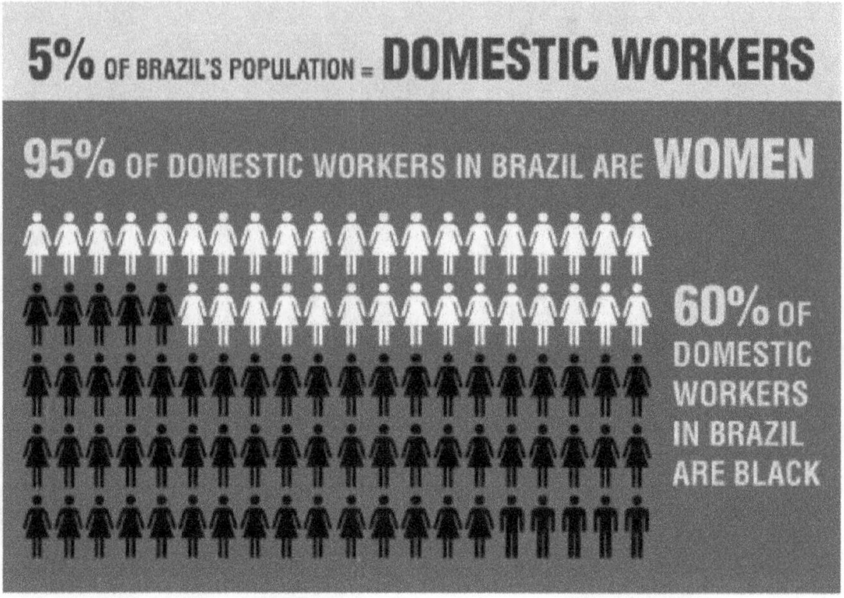

5% OF BRAZIL'S POPULATION = **DOMESTIC WORKERS**

95% OF DOMESTIC WORKERS IN BRAZIL ARE **WOMEN**

60% OF DOMESTIC WORKERS IN BRAZIL ARE BLACK

Illustration 6.2: Infographics. 5% of Domestic Workers by Matters of the Earth. Courtesy of Natalie Foster/Matters of the Earth/Pathways of Women's Empowerment.

3. Images Can Make us Attentive to Things in New Ways

When visual anthropologists or sociologists photograph mundane practices, we are able to see these in a new light. The image can draw attention to previously unnoticed details, but can also enable us to look at objects afresh (Pink 2001, 2015). The images can help us to refresh our sensibilities and to highlight culturally distinctive, but often taken for granted, cultural practices. Similarly, drawing or painting an object can make us look at it intensely. In her photo-elicitation practice, Ruth Beilin has used images to *reveal* landscape conservation issues. In my discussion of this work (Hogan 2012: 58), I note that the images are absolutely revelatory to the viewer who is not used to seeing the land in such a way, and the images and text combine to open out a new consciousness to the reader. Thus an aesthetically pleasing gash in the ground becomes 'land problems at the creek' and a pleasing rolling hill becomes a 'landslip' seen by the photographer as a 'flesh wound' or a 'running sore', the narrative emphasising the challenges of managing the landscape and also evoking 'the intense physical relationship between landscape management and identity' (Beilin 2005: 61). In The Birth Project the birthing room and the birth experience itself were depicted by midwives, allowing them to think about their aspirations for how childbirth should be and their role in the room. They were able to think both abstractly and figuratively about their place.

4. Images Can Be Memorable

From billboards to news footage, it is often iconic images that stay with us. In The Birth Project particular images stayed in participants' minds and triggered particular memories and emotions relating to their experience of childbirth.

5. Images Can Develop Empathetic Understanding and Generalizability

While issues of mass migration or civil war in some far corner of the globe might feel abstract and remote, images can be used to make these issues feel much more immediate. Often this is done by the depiction of individual people to highlight the issues of many, so the story of one family's migration journey stands for many such journeys, for example. Charities such as Oxfam or Amnesty International often use this approach. The daily threat of rape in Darfur may be hard to conceptualise, but the image of the individual who has to put herself at extra risk, leaving the comparative safety of her village, to fetch water for her children makes the day-to-day menace shockingly real; through the image of the individual, the humanitarian issue is given weight and meaning. There may be 'one born every minute', but it is clear from The Birth Project that not having the uniqueness of the event honoured was a source of distress for new mothers. The poignant images of distress (especially from the art therapeutic elicitation group) reach out to create empathetic reactions in the viewers.

6. Images Can be Used to Look at Changes Over Time

Photo-elicitation techniques have been used to look at how neighbourhoods change over time, but also as an ethnographic tool to look at specific cultural phenomena. Clayden et al. (2015) for example, used time-lapse photography to examine the ways that people use space and build informal memorials in natural burial sites. As a sequence, complex changes, which would be laborious to describe, are easily illuminated. Looking at a series of images can also produce unforeseen and revealing narratives. In The Birth Project women produced narrative sequences about their experience of childbirth, exploring their sometimes 'naïve' expectations, the experience of giving birth, their adjustment difficulties to the reality of having a newborn infant and their aspirations for the future.

7. Images May be More Comprehensible Than Most Other Forms of Academic Discourse

People who might not read a broadsheet newspaper or academic article can still engage with images; also as a 'stimulant' to research interviewing, asking a respondent to talk about a photo can provide useful results, replacing abstract or interrogatory questioning (Prosser 2006: 3). In The Birth Project the visceral nature of some of the images was palpably affecting.

8. Images Provoke Action for Social Justice

Images are often used to provoke social change. Images of police brutality in the U.S. and in Greece were used prominently in campaigns for reform and retribution, and are useful to researchers in lending weight to justifications for research activity. Nick Ut's 1972 photo of a little girl naked, screaming with pain and terror after a U.S. napalm attack in Vietnam, is often cited as a powerful example of an image that was used as an anti-war statement. Feminist calls for social justice can be well-met in terms of empowering women, through their ability to bring feelings and experiences of oppression into the public domain (particularly, in The Birth Project, in terms of revealing, exploring and confronting hospital practices with iatrogenic outcomes).

9. Image Making Can Foster the Exploration of Embodied Knowledge

Weber suggests that there 'is an unintentional but automatic and visceral identification with some images; we cannot escape contemplating, or even on some level, experiencing the situations depicted, even if they were previously unfamiliar to us' (2008: 46). Indeed, images can be affecting almost as though through a process of 'emotional contagion' (Hogan and Coulter 2014: 95).

Nor should the kinaesthetic aspects of art or image making be overlooked: Bourdieu, for example, speaks of embodied knowledge as 'habitas'. Others refer to 'muscular knowledge' (for example, I can't remember the numbers I must press to enter a security zone without using the movement of my hand to create the pattern – it isn't the numbers I

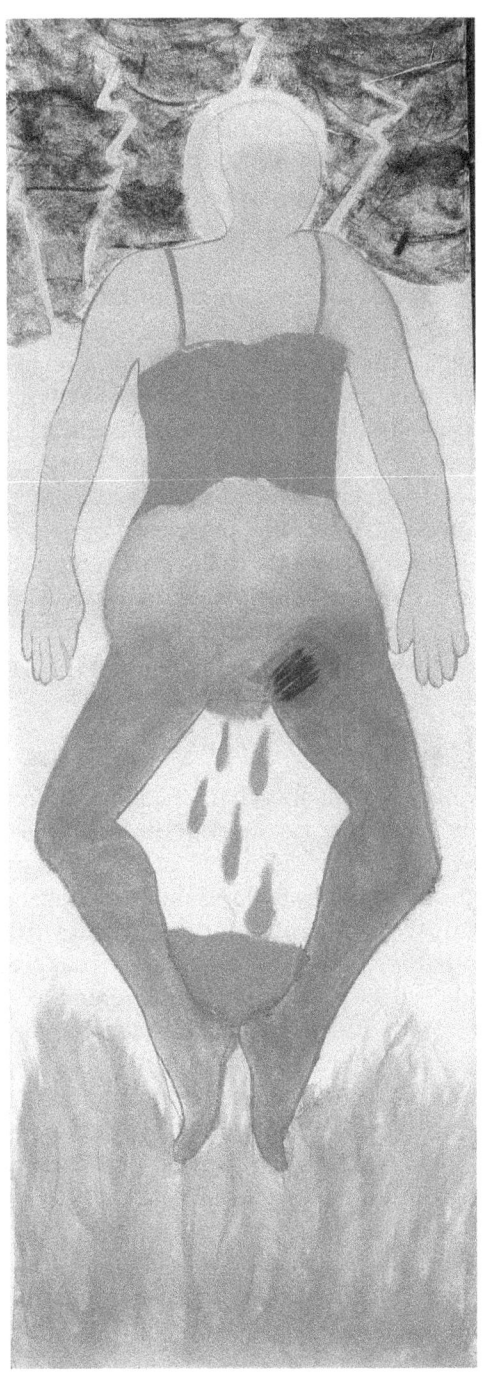

Illustration 6.3: Artwork from the art elicitation group. The Birth Project.

recall, it is the shape and pattern my hand needs to make to press the right numbers. It is embodied knowledge.). See Martens, Halkier and Pink (2014) for a discussion of embodied research practices.

The kinaesthetic qualities of both producing and viewing artwork are of potential importance. One characteristic of an installation exhibition format, for example, is that it uses the total space and invites the viewer to move within it. This physical moving into the discursive space is slightly different qualitatively to simply looking at something on a wall or plinth; it is a more bodily engagement with the artwork and offers a more immersive experience. It is potentially more challenging in its theatrical invitation to the viewer to engage with the subject matter in an embodied way. How the narrative flow unveils itself depends on the participant's movement through the space; one perspective may necessarily cut off another, and new configurations are generated by being at different vantage points in the space. The format evokes uncertainty, anxiety perhaps, and the entire work cannot be viewed from any particular vantage point. In certain conceptual frameworks, such as one that seeks to emphasise heterogeneity, this might be a very appropriate format to prevent the foreclosure of meaning. The embodied nature of childbirth was depicted in The Birth Project and may be enacted in phototherapy techniques.

10. Image Making Can Be Vitalizing

Artworks can be made in a manner that can jolt our mundane sensibilities, using materials in ways that can refresh our outlooks and capture our enthusiasm. Whether art is being made to reflect on a project to enhance reflexivity, or with communities making and reflecting, image making can create a 'potential space', which affords opportunities to be in the moment; this is a moment that is disengaged from one's usual preoccupations and concerns, it is indeterminate. There is rich potential to struggle with the not-knowing-ness of the situation, to move beyond one's comfort zone in terms of ideas about performance, productivity or preconceived ideas about the quality of the artwork. There is the opportunity to be immersed (in the flow) using intuition, serendipity, spontaneously enjoying the tactile embodied nature of the experience – what many call 'creativity' (though often without defining what they mean). In this indeterminate space individuals or groups of people can become highly attuned to what is emerging – it is an emergent space. If working collectively, there are also potentially productive opportunities to explore interpersonal dynamics (for instance, within teams) or to reflect upon the nature of personal authorship. These are spaces of being and becoming, of ontological uncertainty, spaces in which ways of knowing are explored. In the Mothers Make Art Group, one of The Birth Project's art elicitation groups, the ontological nature of art making was at the fore:

> The workshop series was distinctive in tenor and tone and focus. Although structured, it was successful in facilitating the women, some whom had never made art before, towards a sophisticated level of engagement with arts-based practice. Art is a complex event that can engage the ontology of the self and brings about the possibility of something new. ... Watts' art practice with its interest in encounter lends itself to a visceral illumination of the transition to motherhood. This was evident in the way in which the women reimagined significant scenes triggered by Watts' prompts ... whilst handling significant objects. Another example was of experimentation with materials undertaken in pairs, in this case exploring different qualities of paper. This led one pair to make a bed with the paper and then to muse upon the significance of the bed for new mothers and its multiple roles, as well as their experiences of exhaustion. The resulting film work has a fresh dimension, depicting the women making and talking and actually *reconceptualising their experiences* in the moment. This focus on encounter follows the work of Deleuze and Guattari who suggest that that the art encounter can challenge habitual ways of being and acting in the world, ways which are potentially undermined and questioned. They suggest that, our systems of thought can be disrupted and that we may be jolted into thought (Hogan 2015a: 29–30, italics original).

Using Film in the Birth Project: A Case Example of Potentially Challenging Interdisciplinary Issues

Here I focus on part of this process which involved filming by Sheffield Vision as a research method and as a documentation of the research process. The aim of the filming is fourfold:

1. Firstly, as a method to capture the research, which will be used to develop new thinking on contemporary birth experience and practice (it is research data).
2. Secondly, the footage is edited to produce short films which address the research questions. Thus the films are a research output.
3. Thirdly, the short films themselves will also function as teaching and training resources and will be made available for this.
4. Lastly, a documentary film of the entire process is to be made and shown to a public audience.

The notion of using film as research data, familiar to anthropologists, was a foreign idea to some of the research team. The 'authenticity' of the material was questioned, because surely people would put on a 'front' for the camera; of course the same could be said of much qualitative interviewing and there is a lot of literature exploring this subject (Cameron 2001 is particularly eloquent). However, there is something particularly inhibiting about the presence of a film crew; the scrutiny of the lens is qualitatively different to the mere presence of a recording device (until one forgets the film crew is there). There is potential for further inequality between the more extrovert and introvert members of a group (inequalities that a feminist participatory ethos is keen to minimise). Protection of potentially vulnerable participants was an issue, particularly in relation to the thematic art elicitation group with potentially traumatised new mothers, which was facilitated by an art therapist. Although all participants had signed a permission form stating that they understood they were *not* participating in art therapy, it is perhaps inevitable, given the intimate subject matter under discussion, that the group would take on a close and intense character. The facilitator also insisted on emphasising the therapeutic character of the group and was very wary of the film crew, to such an extent that this may have had an influence on the participants themselves. A slightly more upfront briefing might have defused such issues, but the film crew as an intrusion into the safe space seemed to be a dynamic in this case. This had an impact on how much research data we were able to capture and on the integration of that set of participants into the research project as a whole. This was less of an issue with the other art therapist-facilitated group, in which the facilitator had a more relaxed attitude to the presence of the film crew (herself having been a participant in one of my earlier research projects using the same methodology). This was not therefore a disciplinary issue *per se*, though there is a tendency in art elicitation work facilitated by art therapists, for the work to become intense, which is partly its value (as well as the particular appeal and worth in using imagery and tactile materials, as previously outlined and explored). There are inevitably going to be 'boundary' issues that need to be carefully negotiated with participants as to how much access the film crew, or project researcher, can have because of the bounded nature of the art therapy elicitation model.

The notion of collecting raw footage for further analysis was not too alienating *per se*. Delineating further use of the material *was* felt to be potentially problematic. Would the material be used in the documentary or was it merely data for the stated research outputs? How we should word the permission forms in such a way that this was sufficiently clear to participants was something that exercised us, and further clarification was sent around to all participants mid-project to try to ensure that all was as clear as possible.

The footage being edited to produce short films that addressed the research questions was technically challenging, as film relies on coherent narrative flows and the construction of a 'storyline' or the development of 'characters' to create human interest and hold audience attention. Too many disparate people and the filmmaker's craft is disturbed and the film may start to feel fragmented. As the researcher, it was easy for me to mark out sections of footage that answered our research questions, but capturing these and embedding them into a film sequence was technically trying for the filmmaker. I was particularly pleased to be working with an excellent filmmaker who has experience of producing broadcast-quality material, so I was aware that my demands might conflict with her ideas about effective filmic communication strategies and her worthy perfectionism. There are also questions of 'validity' in relation to the films as research outputs. In formal research structures such as the HEFCE REF (Higher Education Funding Council for England Research Excellence Framework), it is uncertain how these films will be regarded in relation to formal research papers for research assessment purposes.

A high ethical bar was adopted. Participants signed permission sheets giving their consent for the footage to be used, but we appreciate that the films were 'constructed' in a way in which original remarks or gestures might be reconfigured. We therefore felt it was essential that participants see the films and re-approve the use of material, and that re-editing then take place where requested by participants. This was also in line with a more participatory and feminist ethos, in which the researcher does not simply wish to run off with the precious data, but rather wishes to negotiate and co-construct outputs. This has implications for resources and is time-consuming, but is essential when working with potentially vulnerable participants in a participatory framework.

Making the short films available as resources may require a certain amount of 'reframing' the material (and the films can be embedded in descriptive material which can help their reception among different audiences via their situation in a website or with verbal framing in presentations). It is useful to make the films available in addressing the impact agenda for the research. They may be used in the training of midwives, and other health professions, as well as trainee therapists, who may end up working with women who have been defined as experiencing postnatal depression.

The documentary film will be a more accessible summary of the issues and concerns of the project and will reach a yet wider audience. The balance between producing an arresting document and imparting research findings has yet to be explored in fine detail, but will raise its own challenges. Certainly, any hope of it being shown on mainstream television depends on certain conventions being adhered to.

Summary and Conclusion

In summary, multidisciplinary, transdisciplinary, crossdisciplinary, interdisciplinary, supradisciplinary and megadisciplinary models may have different implications for the use of visual methods, and although some friction can be productive, here are some aspects to consider:

- Is the team as a whole actually clear about which model of research is being used?
- Tease out how the mode of interdisciplinarity is understood from different standpoints and what its defining features are felt to be.
- Disciplines are recommended to share their thoughts about the project in terms of what *expertise* is felt to be brought to bear.
- Group discussion of the model of research and how it will affect the different components, or stages, of the research is recommended.
- Key terms such as 'participatory' need to be discussed from a disciplinary point of view. It is useful for projects to make a list of key words related to their endeavour and spend a session talking about how these terms are understood from different perspectives. In a recent project these included 'trauma', 'iatrogenic', 'motherhood', 'PND', 'participatory research', 'visual methods' and 'feminism'.
- If art objects are generated, how are they regarded? Are the artworks data? Will they be translated? Are they outputs? Can they be both? Will they be returned to their makers or kept for research purposes? Will they be photographed? Have storage issues been considered?
- The sharing of disciplinary expertise might include running experiential 'taster' sessions of disciplinary approaches.
- It is necessary to consider how key concepts will translate into methods, and not to assume there is a common understanding. If participants will have 'input' into research design or dissemination, what is understood by that?
- Explore how supradisciplinarity is operating within teams with a frank exploration of these different positions. If you are all feminists, then does that help give your team a collective starting point? What is that? Tease it out.
- Don't assume you are approaching ethics in the same way. For example, if you are working with documentary filmmakers, they

won't necessarily think twice about inviting a participant out for coffee to capture extra footage. The project might not have the necessary ethics permission for this to occur, or you might want to put in extra safeguards (where, when, how, backup for if there is distress, referral on to other services ascertained for vulnerable participants, and so forth).
- How is the concept of confidentiality understood from different disciplinary standpoints?
- What 'boundaries' are considered appropriate with groups of participants? Can researchers walk in and out while an art elicitation activity is taking place, for example? Could a camera crew pop in to snatch interview clips?

To conclude, Holland (2014) notes that there is considerable ambiguity about what is meant by 'integration' in much interdisciplinary research, but endorses Bell et al.'s proposal that researchers 'make a conscious effort … to describe to others both the methodological and epistemological foundations of their research and how these are used to interpret their findings in an ongoing effort to 'make their disciplinary contribution mutually intelligible' (Bell et al. 2005: 12). As noted, there are myriad potential tensions in different modes of interdisciplinary working. As elaborated, artwork and film can be used in many ways in applied research.

This chapter should help research teams to think about the principal *ways* in which imagery is functioning within projects. It has also explored in some detail a number of tensions and complexities that arose in The Birth Project. There are particular challenges inherent in using visual methods, which have been elucidated and which need to be considered by research teams. Nevertheless, working with others who have different suppositions and ideas is intrinsically interesting, and gives one pause to inspect one's own preconceptions (Hogan 2012).

Acknowledgements

As Sarah Pink knows, I am often happy to pick up a gauntlet thrown down, so I am thankful for having been prompted to think about this topic further. Thanks also to Sarah and Tom O'Dell for their editorial remarks, which strengthened this chapter. Many thanks to Phil Douglas and Kate Phillips for their comments to improve the legibility of the work. The Birth Project is funded by the Arts and Humanities Research Council's Communities, Cultures, Health and Wellbeing Research Grants, Cross-council Programme (grant ref. AH/K003364/1).

Susan Hogan is Professor of Cultural Studies and Art Therapy and Professorial Fellow, Institute of Mental Health, Nottingham. Publications include: *Feminist Approaches to Art Therapy* (1997); *Healing Arts: The History of Art Therapy* (2001); *Gender Issues in Art Therapy* (2003); *Conception Diary: Thinking About Pregnancy & Motherhood* (2006); *Revisiting Feminist Approaches to Art Therapy* (2012); *The Introductory Guide to Art Therapy* (with Coulter, 2013); *Art Therapy Theories* (2015); *Maternal Ambivalence* (co-edited volume, in press) and *Gender Issues in International Arts Therapies Research* (forthcoming).

Notes

1. http://www.derby.ac.uk/media/derbyacuk/contentassets/documents/ehs/collegeofeducation/centreofsocietyreligionandbelief/Creative-Practice-as-Mutual-Recovery.pdf
2. 'Kuhn coined the term 'paradigm' to express the idea that disciplines are organised around certain ways of thinking or larger theoretical frameworks, which can best explain empirical phenomena in that discipline or field. Results that do not fit into the prevailing paradigm are somehow excluded, for example by limiting the domains of theories, or treated as anomalies the ongoing attempted resolution of which shape its development. Thus paradigms shape the questions scientists ask and also the possible answers they can get through their research. Once the problems with the paradigm become obvious as too many exceptions remain unexplained, a new paradigm that is able to explain more phenomena and / or that is in some sense more efficient might replace the previous one' (Krishnan 2009a: 15). This process of fundamental change within disciplinary paradigms has been called 'paradigm shifts'. One of the arguments for interdisciplinary work is that it can help disciplines see beyond their paradigmatic 'blind spots'.
3. Weber (2008: 44–47) produces a list of reasons to use visual research (which I'm using as an inspiration and starting point, but refashioning along the way, as I felt her categorisations lacked sufficient distinction); however, these categories are not all mutually exclusive.

References

Barry, A., G. Born and M. Strathern. 2007. 'Interdisciplinarity and Society: A Critical Comparative Study. Full Research Report'. ESRC End of Award Report, RES-151-25-0042-A. Swindon: Economic and Social Research Council.

Beilin, R. 2005. 'Photo-elicitation and the Agricultural Landscape: "Seeing" and "Telling" about Farming, Community and Place', *Visual Studies* 20(1): 56–68.

Belsey, C. 1980. *Critical Practice*. London: Routledge.
Bell, S., M. Marzano and D.N. Carrs. 2005. 'Calming Troubled Waters: Making Interdisciplinarity Work'. ESRC Final Report, RES-224-25-0110. Swindon: Economic and Social Research Council.
Cameron, D. 2001. *Working with Spoken Discourse*. London: Sage.
Clayden, A., T. Green, J. Hockey and M. Powell. 2015. *Natural Burial*. London and New York: Routledge.
Eisner, E. 1995. 'What Artistically Crafted Research Can Help Us to Understand About Schools', *Educational Theory* 45(1): 1–13.
Edensor, T. 2005. *Industrial Ruins: Space, Aesthetics and Materiality*. Oxford: Berg.
Hogan, S. 2001. *Healing Arts*. London and New York: JKP.
Hogan, S. 2011. 'Images of Broomhall, Sheffield. Urban Violence and Using the Arts as a Research Aid', *Visual Anthropology* 24(5): 266–80.
Hogan, S. 2012. 'Ways in which Photographic and Other Images Are Used in Research: An Introductory Overview', *Inscape: International Journal of Art Therapy* 17(2): 54–62.
Hogan, S. 2015a. 'Mothers Make Art: Using Participatory Art to Explore the Transition to Motherhood', *Journal of Applied Arts & Health* 6(1): 23–32.
Hogan, S. 2015b. 'Interrogating Women's Experience of Ageing – Reinforcing or Challenging Clichés?', *The International Journal of the Arts in Society: Annual Review* 9: 1–18.
Hogan, S., C. Baker, S. Cornish, P. McCloskey and L. Watts. 2015. 'Birth Shock: Exploring Pregnancy, Birth and the Transition to Motherhood Using Participatory Arts', in N. Burton (ed.), *Natal Signs: Representations of Pregnancy, Childbirth and Parenthood*. Bradford, Ontario: Demeter Press, pp. 272–296.
Hogan, S. and A. Coulter. 2014. *The Introductory Guide to Art Therapy*. London and New York: Routledge.
Hogan, S. and S. Pink. 2010. 'Routes to Interiorities: Art Therapy, Anthropology and Knowing in Anthropology', *Visual Anthropology* 23(2): 1–16.
Hogan, S. and L. Warren. 2012. 'Dealing with Complexity in Research Findings: How Do Older Women Negotiate and Challenge Images of Ageing?', *Journal of Women & Ageing* 24(4): 329–50.
Holland, D. 2014. *Integrating Knowledge Through Interdisciplinary Research*. London and New York: Routledge.
Krishnan, A. 2009a. 'What Are Academic Disciplines?' ESRC National Centre for Research Methods. ESRC NCRM Working Papers Series. University of Southampton.
Krishnan, A. 2009b. 'Five Strategies for Practising Interdisciplinarity'. ESRC National Centre for Research Methods. ESRC NCRM Working Papers Series. University of Southampton.
Kuhn, T. 1996. *The Structure of Scientific Revolutions*, third edition. Chicago: University of Chicago Press.
Lattuca, L.R. 2001. *Creating Interdisciplinarity. Interdisciplinary Research & Teaching Among College and University Faculty*. Nashville, TN: Vanderbilt University Press.
Martens, L., B. Halkier and S. Pink. 2014. 'Researching Habits: Advances in Linguistic and Embodied Research Practice', *International Journal of Social Research Methodology* 17(1): 1–9.
Moran, J. 2001. *Interdisciplinarity: The New Critical Idiom*. London: Routledge.
Pink, S. 2015. *Doing Sensory Ethnography*. Second Edition. London: Sage.
Pink, S. 2001. *Doing Visual Ethnography: Images, Media and Representation in Research*. London: Sage.
Pink, S., S. Hogan, and J. Bird, 2011. 'Intersections & Inroads: Art Therapy's Contribution to Visual Methods', *Inscape: International Journal of Art Therapy*, 16 (1) June, pp. 14–19.

Prosser, J. 2006. 'Researching with Visual Images: Some Guidance Notes and a Glossary for Beginners. Real Life Methods'. University of Manchester and University of Leeds, ESRC National Centre for Research Methods. NCMR Working Paper Series 6/06. Available online at http://eprints.ncrm.ac.uk/ 481/1/0606_researching_visual_images.pdf.

Repko, A.F. 2008. *Interdisciplinary Research: Process and Theory*. Los Angeles, CA: Sage.

Rossini, F.A. and A.L. Porter. 1984. 'Interdisciplinary Research: Performance and Policy Issues', in R. Jurkovich and J.H.P. Paelinck (eds), *Problems in Interdisciplinary Studies: Issues in Interdisciplinary Studies*, 2. Aldershot and Vermont: Gower Publishing, pp. 26–46.

U.S. National Academy of Sciences, National Academy of Engineering, and Institute of Medicine. 2005. *Facilitating Interdisciplinary Research*. Washington, DC: National Academic Press.

Weber, S. 2008. 'Using Visual Images in Research', in J.G. Knowles and A.L. Cole (eds), *Handbook of the Arts in Qualitative Research: Perspectives, Methodologies, Examples and Issues*. London: Sage, pp. 41–54

Whitley, R. 1984. 'The Rise and Decline of University Disciplines in the Sciences', in R. Jurkovich and J.H.P. Paelinck (eds), *Problems in Interdisciplinary Studies: Issues in Interdisciplinary Studies*, 2. Aldershot and Vermont: Gower Publishing, pp. 10–26.

PART IV

LETTING GO AND MOVING FORWARD

Chapter 7

HOW TO GAIN TRACTION?
From Theoretical Scholarship to Applied Outcomes in Energy Demand and Housing Research

Yolande Strengers, Cecily Maller and Larissa Nicholls

Social scientists are increasingly asked to develop 'deeply embedded partnerships' with Science, Technology, Engineering and Mathematics (STEM) disciplines and organizations in order to address the challenges facing our societies (Spoehr et al. 2010: 4). These partnerships are often established to tackle applied or policy problems and are usually funded by commercial or government entities. Some researchers have lamented the large interdisciplinary bucket into which the Humanities, Arts and Social Science (HASS) disciplines are often thrown to satisfy these arrangements, where the aim is to develop 'an integrated holistic approach to a complex problem or set of problems' (Evans and Marvin 2006: 1012). This creates a problematic entanglement and 'mixing' of incommensurable ontological and epistemological assumptions associated with different disciplines, theories and approaches (Blaikie 1991; Evans and Marvin 2006; Shove 2010).

A further challenge of these partnerships is the uneven playing field on which HASS researchers often find themselves. Spoehr et al. (2010: 13) describe the undervaluation of HASS research as 'the elephant in the room', noting that 'few acknowledge that HASS disciplines do not enjoy the high status afforded to STEM disciplines in the innovation debate'. Social researchers have lamented that they are too often treated as 'subcontracted social data providers' (Sofoulis 2011a: 80), or as providing the 'people' perspective on what are otherwise framed as technical problems and agendas (Guy and Shove 2000).

These challenges are heightened in the neoliberal research environment, in which academics must justify the 'real-world' implications and benefits of their research, and are often required to respond to pre-existing research (and theoretical) agendas with embedded assumptions about social life. Policy makers and partners increasingly demand findings 'which they can handle' – that is, outcomes which are 'defined as "concrete, achievable and manageable"' (Shove 2010: 1281), leaving little room for interpretative, complex or nuanced understandings of the social world. This not only affects the type of funded research, the theoretical orientations that inform it, and the ways in which it is conducted, it also reproduces specific social realities at the exclusion of others (Law 2009).

At the same time, most social scientists *want* their research to 'make a difference', be it to reduce homelessness, curb domestic violence, shave energy consumption, improve housing conditions or design better neighbourhoods. Applied or partnered research is not only desirable but often necessary to achieve this outcome. How then, can social scientists ensure our work has impact in the organizations, governments and companies where it has the potential to make a difference, without compromising or deserting our ontological and epistemological positions? How do we gain traction in an environment that remains dominated by positivist traditions and agendas? How do we not only provide the 'people perspective', but fundamentally *reshape* research and policy agendas, potentially reproducing new realities and intervening in the world?

We explore these questions in this chapter by reflecting on our own applied social research in the energy and housing fields, conducted under the banner of the Beyond Behaviour Change (BBC) research programme over the past seven years (Strengers et al. 2014a). The BBC programme was born partly out of frustration with the positivist behavioural theories which dominate the fields in which we work. In establishing BBC, we were interested in expanding the parameters and understandings of social change in household (and other) settings, where programmes, developments and policies seek to achieve reductions in energy and resource use, or improve neighbourhood residents' health and well-being. Theoretically, we wanted to incorporate a perspective that would provide a dynamic and performative understanding of the role of 'materials' in everyday life, such as the appliances, houses, neighbourhoods, trees, pets, devices and infrastructures that are central to the practices we seek to understand and potentially change. For this we turned to post-humanist theories of social practice (Reckwitz 2002; Shove et al. 2012; Warde 2005), which understand social change as an outcome of participation in shared social practices.

Bringing these theories to bear on projects with partners who are heavily subscribed to the theoretical orientations of behaviour change – along with the positivist methodologies of STEM disciplines these are often associated with – has generated a suite of challenges. In discussing these below, we do not intend to judge or be disrespectful to our partners, to whom we are very grateful for their support, insights and funding. Nor do we seek to position one theoretical orientation (namely theories of social practice) as inherently better than another (theories of behaviour). As Pink and Leder Mackley (2014: 167) note, all academic constructs – be they behaviours, practices or some other analytical category – are 'elusive as an empirical reality'. Thus, this chapter is not a debate between behaviour and practice, but rather about how to *gain traction* with any theoretical orientation that challenges accepted, dominant and inherently more highly valued ways of knowing.

We are aware that we are not the first to contemplate these issues. Numerous scholars have written reflexively about the challenges working across positivist and post-positivist disciplines (Connelly and Anderson 2007; Sharp et al. 2011), conducting interdisciplinary projects (Evans and Marvin 2006), 'triangulating' research findings (Blaikie 1991), 'connecting' the HASS and STEM sectors (Sofoulis 2011a) and attempting to 'intervene' in STEM-dominated environments (Browne et al. 2013; Browne et al. 2014). We contribute to this discussion by reflecting on our own experiences and strategies in working with partners where these challenges are an inherent reality of 'getting the job done'.

We approach this task first by introducing our partners and their agendas, and by outlining more explicitly the ontological and epistemological assumptions that underlie these. We provide contrast with our own research agendas, assumptions and theoretical leanings. We frame this discussion through the common ground we hold with our partners – namely a commitment to understanding and changing social action. The chapter then turns to four strategies we have developed in our research projects to navigate, disrupt and question our partners' assumptions. Here we draw on specific examples to present strategies intended to make our research more 'appealing' or cognisant to our partners. We conclude by reflecting on the different ways that we can conceptualize our role in this process – describing it as a potential form of compromise, strategy and/or intervention, before asking what our reflexive analysis can tell us more broadly about how to transform theoretical scholarship into applied outcomes.

Partnering Up

Within the BBC research programme we work alongside a range of partners, notably housing developers, energy utilities and policy makers in the environmental and housing fields. People working for these companies, departments and organizations typically have STEM or 'STEM-like' qualifications – particularly in engineering, construction, planning, public health, policy, marketing or economics. By 'STEM-like' we mean that they identify with the same or similar positivist assumptions about the social world as traditional STEM disciplines. The 'people' dimension is most often understood using marketing or cognitive psychology approaches, which are imbued with positivist residues,[1] discussed in more detail below.

Similar claims have been made by other housing and energy researchers, who describe the disciplines dominating the environment and housing sectors as operating under a 'techno-economic' paradigm (Guy and Shove 2000) or a 'physical-technical-economic model' of consumption (Lutzenhiser 1993). Terms commonly applied to explain the 'human dimension', such as 'household demand management', 'users', 'consumers' and 'customers', reflect these techno-economic orientations, and seek to extend them to understandings of people and social phenomenon (Sharp et al. 2011; Sofoulis 2011b).

Typically our research is positioned as social 'input' into larger and predetermined technological or construction projects, such as the development of a master-planned housing estate, or the roll-out of smart energy meters. Thus, we often find that our role and purpose has been predetermined before the partnership is formed and before research proposals and agreements have been drawn. In many cases we tacitly or explicitly accept this position in order to 'win' the work and form a partnership, reflecting the practical realities of applied researchers who are not always in financially secure positions, and who want to contribute to better environmental and housing outcomes. However, the risks of accepting a predefined social 'box' are many. Guy and Shove (2000: 8–9) have previously argued that when sociologists 'come to the rescue', to provide a 'human perspective' to energy or problems, they 'tacitly accept their sponsors' two-part view of the world in which proven energy-saving technologies confront a reluctant social world'.

This does not mean that we are always epistemologically and ontologically poles apart from our partners. In any partnership we form, both parties are interested in achieving an agreed outcome, whether to reduce peak electricity demand, curb greenhouse gas emissions from residential buildings, or improve health and well-being. However, the ways in which we conceptualize these problems and think they should be approached, studied and potentially intervened in can differ quite markedly. This is not to say that our partners are not interested in, and/or enthusiastic about, our approach and perspective, but rather that it can deeply challenge strongly held assumptions that do not always make 'room' for, tolerate or accept alternative social realities.

A first point of difference is theoretical orientation. Typically our partners – and most policy makers and programme managers working in similar sectors – understand the social world through cognitive theories of behaviour, broadly defined. Shove (2010) brought considerable attention to this prevailing theoretical perspective in her seminal paper on the 'ABC' of climate change policy, where she argued that most policies and programmes are premised on theories of social action and change that prioritize people's attitudes, behaviours and choices (their ABCs). This dominant theoretical orientation has been widely critiqued in the environment sector for failing to result in behavioural policies or strategies that achieve long-lasting or convincing change (Burgess et al. 2003; Moloney and Strengers 2014). Our issue here is not with these theories, which do have impressive track records and achievements in some areas, but rather in the uniform perspective they provide of social reality. In prioritizing a *different* theoretical perspective that focuses on the practices people participate in and perform, we seek to reproduce a *different* reality with alternative avenues for change (Spurling et al. 2013). We also seek to collapse the common distinctions between 'technical' and 'behavioural' research, instead viewing these as inseparable – or rather as composites or elements of social practice.

In environment and housing research, the practice perspective is gaining ground as a mode of understanding social and environmental problems, such as energy consumption and well-being, as outcomes of social practices. Practices can be conceptualized as an *entity* – such as running, cooking or laundering, each of which are made up of several elements, namely *meanings* about the value or ideas of a practice, *competences* about how to undertake it, and *materials* such as things, tools and infrastructures which necessitate their existence (Shove et al. 2012). Practices persist and change through their recurrent performances by the *carriers* of practices, who are the people who perform them (Reckwitz 2002). Further terms help describe and conceptualize how practices link together into loose-knit *bundles* or more tightly sequenced *complexes* (Shove et al. 2012), branching out to form an overarching ontology that sees the entire social world as a *plenum* of social practice (Schatzki 2014). There is nothing, some theorists argue, bearing up or down on practice – rather practices constitute the whole social world, thereby collapsing divisions between structure and agency to generate a 'flat' ontology (Schatzki 2014). While this, too, is an analytical construct, it is different from the dominant ABC view of social action, and therefore provides an alternative perspective on our understanding of social phenomena.

Theories of social practice also provide different perspectives for thinking through how to intervene in social life. There is now an emerging body of work dedicated to articulating intervention possibilities through theories of social practice, proposing alternative but also sometimes similar modes of intervention to those that emerge through the dominant ABC perspective (Evans et al. 2012; Maller and Strengers 2014; Spurling et al. 2013; Strengers and Maller 2014).

A second point of difference from our partners is epistemological and methodological: how we go about studying social life to produce knowledge, and indeed what we think constitutes knowledge. Our partners' assumptions about the generation of knowledge reflect their positivist orientations. Positivists view the world as an objective social reality which is predictable and relatively stable, and which can be known through a set of accepted instruments targeted primarily at people (Sharp et al. 2011). Table 7.1 outlines assumptions commonly held by our partners, and makes explicit the positivist origins of these. In pointing out the problems with these assumptions in the far right column, we highlight our own post-positivist position, through which we view the world as complex, dynamic and open to interpretation. Rather than seeking to determine one knowable reality which a definable set of instruments can understand, predict and ultimately regulate or govern, our own position views the social world as being constituted by *multiple* realities, which research helps to generate and perform (Law 2009).

The qualitative methods employed in our projects, such as in-depth conversational or semi-structured interviews, in-home tours (Maller et al. 2011; Maller and Strengers 2013; Strengers et al. 2014b), diaries (Strengers 2009) and photo 'scrapbooks' (Maller and Strengers 2015) reflect our preoccupation with uncovering the complexity of the social world and how change takes place within it. As is common in qualitative research, we recognize our own agency in this process (Bazeley 2013), and assume that all knowledge of social life is subjective, even that which is steeped in the scientific tradition (Latour 1987).

In past work we have suggested that these different theories and methods of understanding and knowing social phenomena and change can be conceptualized as different *practices* of what it means to 'do' social change (Strengers et al. 2014a). We have argued that our partners share common meanings, competences and materials about acceptable modes of understanding social reality and making change happen within it,

Table 7.1: Studying social life: epistemological and methodological assumptions.

Dominant assumption	Origin	Problems with these assumptions
If you can't count it, it doesn't count	Positivist perspective where knowledge is captured and made through numbers, formulas, equations and causal or correlational relationships	Assumes that complex phenomena can be simplified into numerical form; creates 'statistical smoothing'; statistical constructs and assumptions can be confused with social facts (Ang 2011; Law 2009; Sofoulis 2011b)
Everything can and should be compared and benchmarked	Positivist perspective where groups and phenomena are tested and compared with another, e.g. control groups	Assumes social 'variables' are identifiable, controllable and comparable
Problems can be reduced to external and internal barriers and drivers	Emerges from scientific traditions which understand natural phenomena as existing and changing through measurable and knowable 'inputs' and 'outputs'	Simplifies and precludes relationships between social phenomena; separates social world into agency (individual drivers/barriers) and structure (external barriers/drivers); can generate an unlimited list of 'factors' with no method or theory to understand their history, interdependence, 'dynamic qualities' or 'their precise role in promoting and preventing different behaviours' (Shove 2010: 1275)
Demographics adequately capture diversity and complexity	Emerges from scientific traditions that understand natural phenomena through their known characteristics and attributes and use these to predict future behaviour and relationships	Demographics cannot explain all social difference or patterns; ignores other ways in which diversity and change can be understood (Sofoulis 2011b)

Table 7.1: *continued*

People should be the focus of research and interventions	Prioritizes ABC theories – assumes individual attitudes, behaviours and choices explain human action and change	Precludes understandings of social change that do not prioritize individual agency; ignores diversity of social theory (Shove 2010)
Segmentation accurately deals with diversity and complexity	Emerges from scientific traditions that assume the existence of natural 'groupings', which can be determined through individual attributes	Can create a 'weak and misleading semblance of cultural studies notions of a society containing a diversity of cultures and subcultures' (Sofoulis 2011b: 803)
Everything can be 'scaled up'	An engineering concept where small-scale models are trialled before building large-scale models (Sofoulis 2011a); assumes knowledge is cumulative (Sharp et al. 2011)	Communities cannot always be extrapolated upwards (Sofoulis 2011a); ignores spatial, material and cultural differences and diversity; assumes a 'sameness' and replicability about social phenomena
One reality can be known	Emerges from positivist belief in 'an independent and objectively accessible world'; assumes reality can be known through 'general laws describing regularities in nature and/or society' (Connelly and Anderson 2007: 213)	Precludes other possible realities; ignores ways in which social research can generate, prioritize and reproduce some realities over others (Law 2009); presupposes a 'fantasy of seamless knowledge integration' (Sofoulis in press)

which differ from our own. We have conceptualized our own role as agitators or facilitators in these dominant social change practices, in which we seek to disrupt normal practice by introducing different theoretical and methodological orientations – thereby facilitating alternative social change practices. In the following section we provide four examples of such 'agitations' employed in our research with applied partners. We consider these approaches as ways to navigate through, and in some cases duck, the inherent assumptions of our research partners in order to gain traction in applied research.

Gaining Traction: Four Strategies

Counting Something Different

The impetus to quantify everything has emerged from positivist disciplines that prioritize statistics, representation, causes and correlations. It reflects a scientific epistemology that is applied to the social sciences (Ang 2011). Within this epistemology, countable or measurable knowledge is viewed as more rigorous and valid (hard) than non-countable or immeasurable (soft) knowledge. This 'hard' evidence is in turn 'enabling' for policy and decision makers; it provides an illusion of certainty that enables it to be acted upon in 'concrete' ways (Ang 2011). Most often it is people and their individual attributes that are counted – particularly demographic features, attitudes, behaviours and relationships – through instruments such as large-scale surveys. This again reflects the dominance of cognitive psychology and marketing disciplines in making sense of the human world (Shove 2010).

Increasingly people are also being quantified by the data collected about them, tracking things like their consumer choices, geographic movements, or consumption of resources. Devices such as smart meters not only seek to know people through numbers and big data (Mayer-Schönberger and Cukier 2013), but also seek to change social conditions and reality *through* data, reflecting a less acknowledged positivist view that numbers are not only necessary to *know* the social, but also required to change and govern it (Strengers 2013). The common engineering and business dictum, 'you can't manage what you can't measure', reflects this preoccupation with quantification as a source of understanding *and changing* the social world. Hacking (1982: 280–1) describes this obsession with counting as a 'fetishistic collection of statistical data' or a form of 'statistical enthusiasm' which generates an 'avalanche of printed numbers'. Reflecting a variation on Foucault's (1995) concept of the all-seeing panopticon or the 'biopower' of knowledge production, these numbers are not just neutral indicators, but seek to tame, control and subvert a population (Hacking 1982). They are numbers with an agenda.

There are many risks associated with this focus on quantification, not least of which is the devaluing of people's experiences and self-understandings about their own social realities (Sofoulis 2011b). Anything that cannot be quantified or is difficult to count, such as someone's life history, is easily excluded from measurable realities. More problematically, a social reality generated by numbers and reliant on quantified associations requires extensive assumptions about human experience (Law 2009). Someone must make decisions about who or what to count regarding any given phenomenon. If knowledge or experiences that can't be counted, measured or quantified in some way aren't included as part of any given social reality, a distorted view of the world emerges from which governments and agencies build and deliver policies and programmes (Law 2009).

One research strategy we have developed to counteract this potentially problematic situation is to count or measure something different. In a large (~80 households) qualitative study funded by several energy utilities with employees from primarily engineering backgrounds, we were engaged to provide insight into household energy demand. Following our theoretical approach, we proposed to explore the social practices that constitute energy demand – specifically those practices that are problematic for demand management. In particular, household cooling is the prime contributor to residential peak demand in Australia, and became a key focus of our research. We were interested in how cooling practices were performed in these households, and how they were changing. In the early stages of the research we presented the complexity and diversity of cooling practices to our partners through thematic analysis. However, the validity and relevance of this data was questioned. How representative was it? What could it really tell us beyond the 'stories' being showcased? How could it be 'acted upon' or used to develop demand management programmes? Where was its value? Our presentation of this rich data wasn't 'cutting through' to our research partners or being taken seriously. We tried a different approach.

Following Browne et al.'s (2013, 2014) strategy of quantifying the social practices of bathing and laundering, we attempted to quantify our qualitative data by generating five segments of cooling practices. These segments divided households into *natural comfort and health* (Segment 1, no air conditioning 15%), *aspiring to air-conditioned cooling* (Segment 2, 3%), *passive cooling supplemented with air conditioning* (Segment 3, 55%), *liberal air-conditioned cooling* (Segment 4, 25%), and *automated climate control* (Segment 5, 4%). We could then more easily see where the problem for peak demand lay: the majority of households (55%) were passively cooling their houses by opening windows and doors and using different combinations of shading and other strategies, such as leaving the home to visit cool places. This meant that they only used air conditioning when they 'really needed it' – namely on the very hot days of the year, when peak demand is at its worst. Additionally, we could see that a further 15% of households aspired to passive cooling supplemented with air conditioning, indicating that the peak demand problem may get worse again in the near future when these households acquired an air conditioner. This allowed us to demonstrate some of the diversity in how households cooled their homes, as well as suggest specific strategies for different segments, such as incentivizing passive cooling strategies on very hot days. The presentation of qualitative data in numerical form appealed to our partners and was more readily acceptable and 'actionable' than rich and deep stories.

This strategy does, however, come with problems. In playing the numbers game we potentially misled our partners (and others) into believing that our data was, or could be, representative of a larger population. The percentages for each segment were not representative of any population, nor did they capture all diversity or complexity. Of course all research must simplify or reduce data in some way; indeed, that is the purpose of coding and analysis in qualitative methodologies, but there is a risk that we construe a larger reality here and generalize phenomena in a problematic way. We also risk losing the 'intense, engaging, challenging, non-linear, contextualized, and highly variable' nature of qualitative data (Bazeley 2013: 3). Some may argue that this is an unacceptable compromise in qualitative research that reinforces the positivist practices of research partners by quantifying the *qualities* of social phenomena and attempting to conceal the agency of the researcher. Others may conclude that this is an acceptable (and necessary) way to gain traction in a world in which quantification reigns supreme. We do not seek to declare a position one way or the other, but rather offer this example to provoke reflection about the complexities and compromises that social researchers make when seeking to make their research 'count'.

Comparing Something Else

In establishing the parameters for a longitudinal project seeking to track the health and well-being outcomes for residents living in a master-planned estate, we again met with the positivist assumptions of our research partners. In this project, partners were keen to quantify residents' experience of living in the new estate as well as to compare their health and well-being with residents of another 'similar' estate or estates to generate 'actionable data'. Their interest in comparison was intended with a clear goal in mind: to assess (and ideally publicly declare) whether their estate was 'better designed' and produced healthier residents than another. Comparison was assumed to add validity to the research by having a 'benchmark' from which to more confidentially establish and declare a social truth, or in this case a definitive outcome.

This desire reflects a preoccupation with control groups and comparison points in some social science where all variables are assumed to be known and are rendered controllable or treatable. However, as other social scientists have noted, the social world does not easily conform to the assumed objective knowability of the scientific realm (Ang 2011). The notion of a 'control' group is problematic for the qualitative researcher who views the world as complex, dynamic and highly changeable. Indeed, for most social scientists, the very notion that a social group can be 'controlled' in an experimental sense is ethically questionable, not to mention virtually impossible in most cases. This does not mean that comparison is undesirable or unachievable. In qualitative research, comparison is carried out and valued for different purposes – to compare across and within datasets and analytical concepts, within or across cases, across different contexts of action, or over time (Bazeley 2013).

In this project we were faced with the conundrum of appeasing our partners' desires for comparison without setting up an impossibly or problematically comparable scenario. Problems we identified in comparing residents of communities in two estates included: (i) having to make an assumption that the communities would be similar in enough ways to reduce unwanted variation, yet different in terms of the features we wanted to study; (ii) that all variables and features being studied would be able to be controlled or monitored in both communities; (iii) that double the resources would potentially be required to study two communities longitudinally instead of one; and (iv) that the findings would most likely stigmatize the community that was found to be doing less well.

Our strategy was to compare something else. Instead of comparing the residents of one estate with another, we proposed and emphasized alternative comparative points. We used a mixed methods design comprising three annual rounds of longitudinal qualitative interviews and a quantitative survey, to study residents and their practices over time – that is, we compared them against themselves over several years as the neighbourhood and estate's infrastructures developed. We also used indicators of health and well-being, such as national smoking rates and physical activity data, as comparative reference points. As this data is nationally representative it gave as a benchmark or comparison that did not involve comparing groups or communities.

Comparisons made the dataset seem more robust and 'solid' than it otherwise might have been, and served to build the partners' confidence in the social research without compromising the integrity of the data and analysis, or our own epistemological position. However, like our strategy of counting qualitative data, we are aware that this approach is one of appeasement, rather than fundamentally challenging the knowledge assumptions held by our partners. It is a way of 'getting around' the 'need' for comparison without disrupting the practices of our partners in any substantial way, while still producing rigorous, qualitative research.

Showcasing Complexity and Interdependency through Practice

In doing applied social research, social scientists invariably confront the assumptions that their partners hold about human action and social change. This also pushes researchers' own assumptions into view and, in some cases, forces us to acknowledge and question them. Knowing what assumptions to challenge and whether it is necessary or worthwhile – that is, whether the effort is 'worth it' – is sometimes difficult to determine.

In the same project as discussed above, one assumption was highly prevalent and problematic – namely that any given social phenomenon can be viewed as an input-output system, in which various external and internal drivers go in, and behaviours or outcomes come out. For example, whether or not residents of a master-planned estate engage in regular running for physical activity can be viewed as an outcome of their personal motivations (internal drivers) and the available physical infrastructure (external drivers). Like historical divides between humans and non-humans, or structure and agency, Sofoulis (2011a) describes the division between external and internal drivers as a form of 'purification' that seeks to reduce the complexity of everyday life to a list of discrete factors which can be acted upon or ignored. She and other social researchers (Ang 2011; Shove 2010) have critiqued this view for erasing much of the complexity of everyday life, and the nuanced relationships *between* 'factors'.

Seeking to avoid these potential pitfalls, our research sought to rethink the relationship between factors through theories of social practice. For example, within these theories, running for exercise can be viewed as being comprised of socially shared (rather than individually motivated) *meanings* about the value and benefits of running and why, where and with whom to run; *materials* such as roads, lights, paths, drinking fountains and running gear; and *competences* such as warming up/down, treating injuries and planning routes. This theoretical position not only gives us a way of accounting for different factors, but provides a meaningful way of grouping them together and understanding how they both reproduce or potentially transform a particular outcome (e.g. physical activity). It also allows us to emphasize the different relationships between practices, and identify bundles and complexes of practice that naturally group together. In particular, the temporal ordering of practices, bundles and complexes generates daily routines. For example, an early morning routine bundle of practices might comprise waking, running, showering, dressing, eating breakfast and journeying to work. In this example, there is a relatively fixed temporal order to these practices, which creates a path dependency such that journeying to work can only occur after the performance of other practices.

In this project, these input-output assumptions about social life were worth challenging and reconceptualizing with our partners because this alternative theorization also shifted the locus of change and intervention – from internal and external drivers or barriers, to the elements of the practice of running, or the relationship between running and commuting as part of early morning routines. Rather than producing lists of external and internal drivers that can be acted upon, we returned to the qualitative tradition of representing our data as rich accounts and narratives of social experience through the lens of practice. In telling this story, we strove to challenge the assumptions our partners held about the ways in which human action is constituted, as well as provide them with an alternative mode of understanding and potentially intervening in certain phenomena to improve social conditions such as health and well-being.

Although this reconceptualization has challenged our partners, they have been able to see that residents' lives are not bounded by the masterplanned estate and that they have responsibilities and perform practices beyond their housing community that the partners and designers have little, or no, control over. Likewise, they have acknowledged the limitations of attempting to intervene in some practices without also intervening in or altering others. For example, attempts to encourage outdoor exercise have been hampered by residents' lack of time spent at the estate caused by long commutes to and from work each day (for many these are more than an hour by car one way). These challenges have facilitated deeper reflection on the complexity of residents' lives and the limited ability of developers and designers to intervene substantially in their health and well-being.

Developing Provocative Personas

A final strategy involves mirroring our partners' assumptions back at them in order to incite reflection and potentially disrupt their own practices. This approach emerged from our research on new smart energy technologies, such as in-home displays, smart meters and other devices intended to help householders control and manage their energy demand. These technologies are premised on questionable assumptions about the relationship between technology, data and social change. In a review of marketing research in this area, we found that a common set of demographic and psychosocial attributes were being collected to determine the desires and characteristics of the 'new' or 'smart' energy consumer (Strengers 2013). Survey questions that asked householders what data they wanted and whether they understood energy terms such as 'kilowatt hour' and 'energy feedback' were embedded with assumptions that this 'energy literacy' was needed in order for householders to manage and change their energy behaviours by making best use of 'actionable data' (Strengers 2013). These assumptions reflect an engineering and economic mindset, or the 'techno-economic' perspective (Guy and Shove 2000), which dominates in the energy industry. It was assumed that the way to reduce and shift household energy demand was to provide households with the same tools and data that economists and engineers use to manage energy systems (Strengers 2013).

In contrast, our own research with households, which prioritized the whole-of-household practices they were participating in and the energy outcomes of these, presents a different reality and perspective on the new 'smart' energy consumer. We found that while men are likely to be more interested in energy data and technologies, women are often at the helm of energy consumption in the home, by virtue of being responsible for the majority of domestic activities and caregiving (Strengers 2013; Strengers et al. 2014b). To showcase these different realities, we created a fictional character – Resource Man – premised on the assumptions embedded in industry and marketing research seeking to understand and target the smart energy consumer. Reflecting the gendered orientations of the STEM disciplines, Resource Man was represented as an imagined, but also potentially emerging, reality. Resource Man reflects the latest energy consumer research – he is interested in and able to manage the energy consumption of his home through accurate data and smart technology. He is unencumbered by the eclectic members of the household, and able to 'take control' of his energy consumption on behalf of the home in a seamless and straightforward manner (Strengers 2014).

In presenting this stereotyped and deliberately provocative persona to our research partners and other interested parties, we reflected their own assumptions back at them and challenged their perspective through humour and storytelling based on social research. We also gained much support for our research and for the limitations of Resource Man – with (male) energy industry professionals often noting that, while they were the epitome of Resource Man, they were often unable to 'control' the practices and energy consumption of their families, despite having high-level technical knowledge of (and access to) smart energy technologies and data. Resource Man encouraged them to reflect on their own social reality in a new way and gave them pause to question their own epistemology, particularly the tools they were drawing on to attempt to understand and intervene in households to achieve energy shifts and reductions. This opened up dialogue for alternative conceptualizations and ways of approaching the energy challenges that the industry is facing, and for seeing other possible realities which don't rely solely and wholly on technology and data.

Compromise, Strategy or Intervention

Rather than declaring the outright success or failure of these approaches, we wish to conclude by offering three different ways of conceptualizing what we are doing when we deliberately seek to appease, 'work around' or challenge our partners' epistemological and ontological assumptions. The first is to see our strategies as compromises, which essentially involves 'giving in' or conceding to the assumptions and expectations of our research partners, thereby muddying the theoretical and methodological terrain. Quantifying qualitative data and comparing our data to something else most readily fall into this category, as they make the least attempt to fundamentally challenge our partners' assumptions.

Alternatively, we could view our approaches as forms of practical strategizing – as ways of finding 'middle ground', which ensures our research is heard and, most importantly, *used* in applied settings. This perspective is most sympathetic to the agendas of applied researchers, whose priority is to make change in the world. In this sense, we 'do what it takes', albeit within clear limits, to try and ensure that our research is taken seriously and has an impact in the world. This requires that we work with and around the dominant realities that exist.

Finally, we could conceptualize our role as a form of intervention into the dominant social change practices of our partners. By working at the boundaries, proposing different approaches, or deliberately and provocatively disrupting the assumptions embedded in our partners' approaches, we are simultaneously disrupting what counts as knowledge and what knowledge should be counted. More profoundly, we are involved in performing different realities of the social world, and therefore creating new social possibilities, through our research. Our conclusion is that, like the multiple social realities that exist everywhere, we can also conceptualize our role as being all three of these realities, which are at times individually performed, and at other times simultaneously.

Regardless of how we and others conceptualize our role in these projects, this chapter has served another valuable purpose: to make explicit the ontological and epistemological differences between researchers and their partners in applied research – a challenging but essential task in any interdisciplinary partnership (Evans and Marvin 2006). We are increasingly hearing the call for 'holistic', 'integrated', 'triangulated' and 'interdisciplinary' approaches, but we rarely stop to reflect on whether this is possible, desirable or inherently better than single-discipline research. We do not wish to suggest that there *is not* value in interdisciplinary research, but we do add to the chorus of scholars cautioning against the impossibilities of merger and incorporation of, at times, incommensurable theoretical and methodological positions (Shove 2010). In making transparent the assumptions implicit in our own partnerships, and in reflecting on the strategies we as researchers have developed to navigate these, we hope to give others pause to reflect on the compromises, strategies and/or interventions social scientists make as they attempt to gain traction with their research in a world where positivist perspectives still take centre stage.

Further we see value in taking up Evans and Marvin's (2006) call to make room for a new class of experts, intermediaries or 'knowledge brokers ... whose expertise lies in translating between different frameworks and paradigms' (Evans and Marvin 2006: 1027). These knowledge brokers need not be external actors or agents; rather we see scope for social researchers to consider themselves as undertaking this role. As highly qualified knowledge experts well-versed in different traditions and origins of knowledge, and trained to recognize and question assumptions, theories and paradigms inherent in their own and others' work, social scientists are well placed to take on this translation task in interdisciplinary partnerships, and make their role *transparent* to all partners. In this way we can move closer to providing greater awareness of and value for the interpretive social sciences, and potentially challenge and disrupt dominant practices of understanding and seeking to change social phenomena. We can also potentially perform and make accessible the existence of multiple social realities.

Yolande Strengers is a Senior Research Fellow at RMIT University's Centre for Urban Research, where she co-leads the Beyond Behaviour Change research programme. Yolande has published *Smart Energy Technologies in Everyday Life* (Palgrave Macmillan, 2013) and an edited collection (with Cecily Maller), *Social Practices, Intervention and Sustainability* (Routledge, 2014).

Cecily Maller is Vice-Chancellor's Senior Research Fellow at RMIT University's Centre for Urban Research. She is co-leader of the Beyond Behaviour Change research programme and a chief investigator for the Clean Air and Urban Landscapes Hub funded by the Australian government. Cecily has published theoretically informed applied work on health and sustainability.

Larissa Nicholls is a Research Fellow at RMIT University's Centre for Urban Research. She has published applied research projects about household practices that use energy and links between urban design, health and community in residential neighbourhoods. Larissa is a recipient of the Peter Harrison Memorial Prize.

Note

1. The American Psychological Association defines psychology as a STEM discipline.

References

Ang, I. 2011. 'Navigating Complexity: From Cultural Critique to Cultural Intelligence', *Continuum* 25(6): 779–94.
Bazeley, P. 2013. *Qualitative Data Analysis*. London: Sage.
Blaikie, N.W.H. 1991. 'A Critique of the Use of Triangulation in Social Research', *Quality & Quantity* 25(2): 115–36.
Browne, A., W. Medd and B. Anderson. 2013. 'Developing Novel Approaches to Tracking Domestic Water Demand Under Uncertainty: A Reflection on the "Up Scaling" of Social Science Approaches in the United Kingdom', *Water Resources Management* 27(4): 1013–35.
Browne, A., W. Medd, B. Anderson and M. Pullinger. 2014. 'Method as Intervention: Intervening in Practice through Quantitative and Mixed Methodologies', in Y Strengers and C.J. Maller (eds), *Social Practices, Intervention and Sustainability: Beyond Behaviour Change*. Abingdon: Routledge, pp. 179–95.
Burgess, J., T. Bedford, K. Hobson, G. Davies and C. Harrison. 2003. '(Un)sustainable Consumption', in F. Berkhout, M. Leach and I. Scoones (eds), *Negotiating Environmental Change: New Perspectives from Social Science*. Cheltenham: Edward Elgar, pp. 261–92.
Connelly, S. and C. Anderson. 2007. 'Studying Water: Reflections on the Problems and Possibilities of Interdisciplinary Working', *Interdisciplinary Science Reviews* 32(3): 213–20.
Evans, R. and S. Marvin. 2006. 'Researching the Sustainable City: Three Modes of Interdisciplinarity', *Environment and Planning A* 38(6): 1009–28.

Evans, D., A. McMeekin and D. Southerton. 2012. 'Sustainable Consumption, Behaviour Change Policies and Theories of Practice', *Collegium: Studies across Disciplines in the Humanities and Social Sciences* 12: 113–29.

Foucault, M. 1995. *Discipline and Punish: The Birth of the Prison*. New York, NY: Vintage Books.

Guy, S. and E. Shove. 2000. *A Sociology of Energy, Buildings and the Environment*. London: Routledge.

Hacking, I. 1982. 'Biopower and the Avalanche of Printed Numbers', *Humanities in Society* 5: 279–95.

Latour, B. 1987. *Science in Action: How to Follow Scientists and Engineers through Society*. Cambridge, MA: Harvard University Press.

Law, J. 2009. 'Seeing Like a Survey', *Cultural Sociology* 3(2): 239–56.

Lutzenhiser, L. 1993. 'Social and Behavioral Aspects of Energy Use', *Annual Review of Energy and the Environment* 18: 247–89.

Maller, C.J., R. Horne and T. Dalton. 2011. 'Green Renovations: Intersections of Daily Routines, Housing Aspirations and Narratives of Environmental Sustainability', *Housing, Theory and Society* 29(3): 255–75.

Maller, C.J. and Y. Strengers. 2013. 'The Global Migration of Everyday Life: Investigating the Practice Memories of Australian Migrants', *Geoforum* 44: 243–52.

Maller, C.J. and Y. Strengers. 2014. 'Conclusion: Transforming Practice Interventions', in Y. Strengers and C.J. Maller (eds), *Social Practices, Intervention and Sustainability: Beyond Behaviour Change*. Abingdon: Routledge, pp. 196–200.

Maller, C.J. and Y. Strengers. 2015. 'Scrapbooking as an Interview Method to Understand Past and Present Practices', paper presented to Qualitiative Methods Conference, Melbourne, Australia, 27–29 April.

Mayer-Schönberger, V. and K. Cukier. 2013. *Big Data: A Revolution That Will Transform How We Live, Work, and Think*. New York, NY: Houghton Mifflin Harcourt Publishing Company.

Moloney, S. and Strengers, Y. 2014. '"Going Green"? The Limitations of Behaviour Change Programmes as a Policy Response to Escalating Resource Consumption', *Environmental Policy and Governance* 24(2): 94–107.

Pink, S. and K. Leder Mackley. 2014. 'Flow and Intervention in Everyday Life: Situating Practices', in Y. Strengers and C.J. Maller (eds), *Social Practices, Intervention and Sustainability: Beyond Behaviour Change*. Abingdon: Routledge, pp. 163–78.

Reckwitz, A. 2002. 'Toward a Theory of Social Practices: A Development in Culturalist Theorizing', *European Journal of Social Theory* 5(2): 243–63.

Schatzki, T. 2014. 'Practices, Governance and Sustainability', in Y. Strengers and C.J. Maller (eds), *Social Practices, Intervention and Sustainability: Beyond Behaviour Change*. Abingdon: Routledge, pp. 15–30.

Sharp, L., A. McDonald, P. Sim, C. Knamiller, C. Sefton and S. Wong. 2011. 'Positivism, Postpositivism and Domestic Water Demand: Interrelating Science across the Paradigmatic Divide', *Transactions of the Institute of British Geographers* 36(4): 501–15.

Shove, E. 2010. 'Beyond the ABC: Climate Change Policy and Theories of Social Change', *Environment and Planning A* 42: 1273–85.

Shove, E., M. Pantzar and M. Watson. 2012. *The Dynamics of Social Practice: Everyday Life and How it Changes*. London: Sage.

Sofoulis, Z. 2011a. *Cross-connections: Linking Urban Water Managers with Humanities, Arts and Social Science Researchers*. Canberra, Australia: National Water Commission.

Sofoulis, Z. 2011b. 'Skirting Complexity: The Retarding Quest for the Average Water User', *Continuum: Journal of Media & Cultural Studies* 25(6): 795–810.

Sofoulis, Z. In press. 'A Knowledge Ecology of Household Water Consumption', *ACME: E-Journal of Critical Geographies*.

Spoehr, J., K. Barnett, S. Molloy, S. Van Dev and A.-L. Hordacre. 2010. 'Connecting Ideas: Collaborative Innovation in a Complex World'. Australian Institute of Social Research, University of Adelaide. Report prepared for Department of Further Education, Employment, Science and Technology, Adelaide.

Spurling, N., A. McMeekin, E. Shove, D. Southerton and D. Welch. 2013. *Interventions in Practice: Re-framing Policy Approaches to Consumer Behaviour*. Manchester: Manchester University Press.

Strengers, Y. 2009. 'Bridging the Divide between Resource Management and Everyday Life: Smart Metering, Comfort and Cleanliness', PhD thesis. Melbourne, Australia: RMIT University.

Strengers, Y. 2013. *Smart Energy Technologies in Everyday Life: Smart Utopia?* London: Palgrave Macmillan.

Strengers, Y. 2014. 'Smart Energy in Everyday Life: Are You Designing for Resource Man?', *Interactions* 21(4): 24–31.

Strengers, Y. and C.J. Maller. 2014. 'Introduction: Social Practices, Intervention and Sustainability: Beyond Behaviour Change', in Y. Strengers and C.J. Maller (eds), *Social Practices, Intervention and Sustainability: Beyond Behaviour Change*. Abingdon: Routledge, pp. 1–12.

Strengers, Y., S. Moloney, C.J. Maller and R. Horne. 2014a. 'Beyond Behaviour Change: Practical Applications of Social Practice Theory in Behaviour Change Programmes', in Y. Strengers and C.J. Maller (eds), *Social Practices, Intervention and Sustainability: Beyond Behaviour Change*. Abingdon: Routledge, pp. 63–77.

Strengers, Y., L. Nicholls and C. Maller. 2014b. 'Curious Energy Consumers: Humans and Nonhumans in Assemblages of Household Practice', *Journal of Consumer Culture*. Available online at http://joc.sagepub.com/content/early/2014/05/25/1469540514536194.abstract.

Warde, A. 2005. 'Consumption and Theories of Practice', *Journal of Consumer Culture* 5(2): 131–53.

Chapter 8

THE SOCIAL LIFE OF HOMAGO

Heather A. Horst

Over the past twenty years, attention has turned to the importance of interdisciplinary, collaborative research across the humanities and social sciences, including the need to address questions of relevance outside of academia. This has created new questions around the commodification of knowledge and the ways in which value is being defined and redefined across increasingly intertwined institutional contexts, whether value is articulated through 'impact' and 'partnership' agendas in the university sector (Allen 2014; Bastow, Dunleavy and Tinkler 2014; Oliver 2014), or through a generalized focus upon 'applied' research in a resource-constrained funding environment. Yet, as the introduction to this volume suggests, we have few published examples of the ways in which these kinds of collaborations with partners outside of academia play out in practice or of some of the consequences of such collaborations for understanding the value of academic knowledge.

This chapter focuses upon an example of how research findings can be taken up in practice-based settings. It explores the case study of HOMAGO, a learning concept and theory that emerged out of the findings of a three-year investigation into innovative knowledge cultures, tracing the concept's transformation from a collective research finding to a learning 'theory' and 'principle' for guiding out-of-school curriculum, professional development and learning spaces in the field of education. By analysing HOMAGO's translation over time and across different contexts, this chapter explores the role of translators and knowledge brokers in the process of giving life to concepts beyond their intended use. It concludes with a discussion of how concepts are exchanged and revalued for different ends or purposes.

HOMAGO: An Origin Story

HOMAGO[1] is a concept that emerged out of the findings of the Digital Youth project, a three-year ethnographic investigation of informal learning with over eight hundred youth in the United States, funded by the John D. and Catherine T. MacArthur Foundation as part of the Digital Media and Learning initiative.[2] Building upon sociocultural learning theory (Lave and Wenger 1991; Varenne and McDermott 1998) and research on youth, new media and participatory culture (e.g. Holloway and Valentine 2003; Jenkins 2006; Livingstone 2002), the project involved an open-ended exploration of young people's use of digital media and technology, interpretation and meaning of these practices from the perspective of young people themselves and their potential for shaping how we might think of twenty-first century learning practices across formal and informal contexts.

In the analysis phase of the project, the research team identified different 'genres of participation', the most important of which was the difference between 'interest-driven' and 'friendship-driven' genres of participation. 'Genres of participation' describes differing levels of investments in activities that, at least in part, involve new media. Rather than focusing upon structural categories such as age, educational status, race and ethnicity, school grades, social capital or frequency of media use (e.g. heavy, light, etc.) that reduce users of media to psychological 'types', the research team approached young people's use of digital media more holistically and dynamically. 'Genres of participation' as a framework attempts to account for the ways in which media and engagement and sociocultural categories have become constellations of practices that are in constant negotiation and flux as young people (and others) experiment with new modes of communication and other cultural forms (Ito et al. 2009, 2010).

Drawing upon interviews with youth across the United States, we found that most youth – approximately ninety per cent – spent their time engaging in friendship-driven activities, such as socializing with their friends on their mobile phones, through social networking sites, gaming and across other spaces. While there are important dimensions of socialization associated with friendship-driven genres of participation, interest-driven participation became particularly intriguing from a learning perspective. As we characterized the difference in Ito et al. (2009):

interest-driven genres of participation put specialized activities, interests, or niche and marginalized identities first. ... Youth find a different network of peers and develop deep friendships through these interest-driven engagements, but in these cases the interests come first, and they structure the peer network and friendships. It is not about the given social relations that structure youth's school lives but about both focusing and expanding on an individual's social circle based on interests [that often] ... require more far-flung networks of affiliation and expertise (Ito et al. 2009: 10).

Based on our interviews with youth engaged in interest-driven practices, we identified three forms of participation that young people moved across as they became engaged in more interest-driven activities with digital media and technology: 'hanging out', 'messing around' and 'geeking out' (HOMAGO). 'Hanging out' accounts for the kinds of peer sociability that have occurred since the emergence of youth culture after the Second World War in the United States and other contexts. For most youth in the study, digital media and technology offer a place to create and maintain friendships and to explore and experiment with different forms of identity. With the increasing restrictions to youths' use of public and private (e.g. shopping malls) spaces, social networking sites and other social media now represent key sites of social life for many teens, although there are of course different challenges around surveillance and privacy as the practices play out and persist in networked public cultures. 'Messing around' involves a more intensive engagement with digital media and technology, often driven by a question or interest, tinkering, exploring and extending their understanding by searching for information online, and playing with gaming and digital media production in a situation with few consequences for error or failure. 'Geeking out', by contrast, includes learning how to navigate specialized domains of knowledge and practice and participating in communities that traffic in these forms of expertise. The ability to engage with distributed communities and publics has expanded substantively through digital media and technology. What was important about HOMAGO is that the concept accounts for the identity work tied to media practices in young people's lives without tying young people to a static identity or typology. In addition, and as part of a theory of learning, we identified a relationship between 'messing around' and 'geeking out', with 'messing around' becoming a pathway towards interest-driven learning.

HOMAGO: Into Practice

Towards the conclusion of the Digital Youth project, a series of opportunities emerged to disseminate and translate the findings of the research on young people's informal learning with digital media into a series of applied and/or teacher training contexts. Even prior to the release of the book we began uploading 'Stories from the Field' to our project website (http://digitalyouth.ischool.berkeley.edu), which captured early findings and observations across our field sites. In addition, we participated in a public forum 'From MySpace to HipHop',[3] at Stanford University in conversation with a variety of stakeholders, including Global Kids,[4] a youth development non-profit organization, and Common Sense Media,[5] a U.S.-based non-profit organization that provides practical and policy advice to parents, schools and the public. We also published a version of our final report as an accessible 'White Paper' in the Digital Media and Learning Series with MIT Press that included a two-page executive summary. The executive summary was made available separately from the report and was used in conversations with the media by the principal investigators, members of the research team and representatives of the MacArthur Foundation. The findings were well represented in the media in outlets such as National Public Radio, BBC News and *The New York Times*, as well as local media. The project's findings were captured through headlines such as 'Chill Out, Parents: Time Online Teaches Kids Important Skills, Study Shows' (Noguchi 2008),[6] 'Online Time Is "Good for Teens"' (Shiels 2008), or 'Teenagers' Internet Socializing Not a Bad Thing' (Lewin 2008). All of these activities were focused upon dissemination of the project findings in light of public conversations about the implications of digital media for young people's practices and the broader 'media effects' discourse that tends to dominate media discussions of new media use generally.

Other translation projects were also underway in the final year of the project. For example, Jessica Parker was brought into the Digital Youth project to work with researchers to translate, or interpret for different audiences, the book for teachers that would be published with Corwin Press, a publisher specializing in publications for educators. The result, *Teaching Tech-savvy Kids: Bringing Digital Media into the Classroom, Grades 5–12*, is a how-to guide for middle to high-school teachers trying to understand youth learning, literacy and knowledge within a digital context and the pedagogical possibilities these practices may offer (Parker 2010). It explores how young people use and relate to technology through YouTube, social networking platforms and gaming worlds by providing first-hand accounts of youths' experiences with these tools in order to frame how the everyday use of digital technologies can be incorporated into the everyday practice of teaching youth.[7] Importantly, the book was written in conversation with the researchers and in collaboration with a number of authors of the original HOMAGO text, including danah boyd, Becky Herr-Stephenson and Patricia G. Lange, who worked closely with Parker to translate some of the concepts around networked publics, creative production and online writing communities (Parker 2010). By addressing myths circulating in relation to how young people perceive themselves and use technology, the book stressed socially connected learning as a key framework in progressing teaching practices to be more in tune with the increasing use of media in the lives of students.

A second translation project emerged through the founding of YOUmedia, what is now described as 'an innovative, twenty-first-century teen digital learning space' in downtown Chicago. Initiated in 2009, the YOUmedia initiative involved a collaboration between the Chicago Public Library and the Digital Youth Network, with financial and other forms of support from the John D. and Catherine T. MacArthur Foundation and the Pearson Foundation (see https://www.youtube.com/watch?v=yRG2Bf-me6k). One of the most important features of the initiative was the availability of a 5,000 square foot space on the street level of the Harold Washington Library in downtown Chicago, prime real estate connected to the rest of the city by a range of public transport, which made it accessible to youth throughout the city. Through an agreement between the MacArthur Foundation's Digital Media and Learning Initiative's leadership and the Chicago Public Library, Drew Davidson and other designers from the Entertainment Technology Center at Carnegie Mellon University created physical spaces for the different activities, differentiated by the kinds of furniture, books and technologies located in the space based upon the genres of participation underpinning HOMAGO (Spotlight on Digital Media and Learning 2013). A recent report by Penny Sebring and colleagues (Sebring et al. 2013) characterizes the design and evolution of the YOUmedia programme space:

> The hybrid design of YOUmedia derives in part from the founders' decision to put into practice the seminal ethnographic research conducted by Mimi Ito and her colleagues. Her research found that the most common behaviors teens exhibit around digital media are hanging out, messing around, and geeking out. It was the plan of the founders of YOUmedia to provide physical spaces for all three activities, though they are not sharply delineated. The hanging out area has comfortable furniture where teens can socialize, check Facebook, play games, and browse through the library's young adult book collection. The messing around area is identified by red flooring and also has a gaming console, comfortable seating, reference materials, and kiosks with PC and Mac desktop computers. A studio provides tools to

produce music and other audio recordings. The geeking out area is designed as a more serious work space. It is located far from the chatter of the hanging out space and features moveable conference tables, dry erase boards, and a SMART board. Here teens can use laptops, cameras, and other digital equipment to make digital media products (Sebring et al. 2013: 16).

As a youth-driven space, the library was structured to enable young people to move within and across YOUmedia and, by extension, engage in the structured or unstructured activities afforded in the space. Unlike formal afterschool activities, young people could sit and do their homework, talk to their friends and even eat in the hanging out space. However, staff at YOUmedia and the library did hope that young people in the space would engage in the workshops and geeking out spaces, given the potential for skills development and of engaging in production activities.

In this context, genres of participation effectively became the principles for the design team that were, in turn, combined with the Digital Youth Network's curriculum to enable the theory or principles to come alive. The Digital Youth Network,[8] a programme founded by Nichole Pinkard in 2006 to 'help youth understand how to use digital media for all aspects of their lives' through developing analytical, technical and creative skills, had developed a curriculum framework for engaging with urban youth in the 'geeking out' spaces. Many of the programmes focused upon graphic design, photography, video, music, 2D/3D design, STEM and making, and they worked to connect books, media, mentors, youth and institutions throughout Chicago. The Digital Youth Network's digital literacy, skill development and mentorship curriculum drew upon their extensive experience of working with youth in afterschool programmes in Chicago. In particular, the Digital Youth Network had a well-developed mentorship programme that leveraged youth mentors across the physical spaces of YOUmedia (and other research locations, see Barron et al. 2014) and the online platform, iRemix.[9] iRemix was developed to support young people's engagements outside of school (see *Rethinking Mentorship, Learning Pathways in a Networked Age: A few moments with Nichole Pinkard* 2013; and Barron et al. 2014). The articulation between HOMAGO's principles, the designed space and young people's engagement hinged upon Digital Youth Network-trained mentors' ability to spark interest in the workshops offered in geeking out spaces, which they hoped would facilitate greater engagement with the learning opportunities afforded by the geeking out space over time. As Larson et al. (2013) note:

> the DYN model had been nurtured and developed in spaces with a dedicated youth population and allowed for more structured educational offerings.

Adapting the DYN model to YOUmedia, a drop-in space with a fluctuating youth population, presented several challenges. The primary tension arose from attempting to combine structured program offerings designed to last several weeks – where each week builds on skills learned in previous weeks – with the culture of the library, where teens were not required to attend and could drop in and out of programming at will. This productive tension led to numerous iterations of DYN's instructional goals in order to better align its programming model with the 'hanging out, messing around, and geeking out' principles that underpinned the design of YOUmedia. To this end, YOUmedia mentors and staff have continuously adapted their programs and ways of engaging with youth (Larson et al. 2013: 10).[10]

In particular, the mentorship programme in the Digital Youth Network model adapted to the YOUmedia space by strengthening the professional development of staff working in the space. They also created opportunities for focused activities and projects and brought in artists, musicians and other specialists to the YOUmedia space. Since this time, Chicago Public Libraries have also worked to expand the YOUmedia programme into twelve other libraries throughout the city of Chicago. Yet, without the designed space to define activity spaces, the primary engagement with the principles and practice of HOMAGO comes through the framework of the Digital Youth Network-YOUmedia hybrid curriculum (Sebring et al. 2013). The insights of HOMAGO in practice, its modifications through its on-the-ground interpretation and implementation at YOUmedia, and the responses of youth to the programme design, also shaped the theoretical insights and learning principles of the interdisciplinary Connected Learning Research Network, who used the insights gleaned through the YOUmedia experience to develop their theory of connected learning (see Ito et al. 2013). This represents a move between theory and practice, but also the productive relationships that occur when practice shapes theory.

HOMAGO: Into the DML Community

As the previous section begins to suggest, the research that underpinned HOMAGO entered into a broader suite of activity, some of which was under the banner of the Digital Media and Learning initiative. Other connections occurred through the growing engagement with the practitioner community, which included teachers, museum educators, afterschool programme leaders and practitioners and many others who became involved in the Learning Networks established in New York and Chicago that were later integrated into the Hive Learning Networks (https://hivelearningnetworks.org).[11] Led by the Mozilla Foundation, the

Hive Learning Networks function as a hub for interested parties (educators, designers and community builders) to develop networked learning centres in cities and metropolitan areas. Through its wiki, The Hive Cookbook, a formula is provided detailing how to create and host Hive Events that bring youths and organizations together to test out longer-term possibilities. The formation of Hive Learning Communities seeks to solidify the tools and practices that will support ongoing success in projects, culminating with locally oriented but internationally connected networks of organizations under official Hive Learning Networks that are economically sustainable.

One such organization is the Yollocalli Arts Reach, a youth initiative of the National Museum of Mexican Art. Yollocalli collaborated with Hive Learning Networks to develop a published account of the Yollocalli Arts Reach Experimental Sound Open Studio programme in Chicago and their use of the HOMAGO principles for designing the programme. Their book, *HOMAGO: A Guidebook*, discusses how the principles of technology-focused teen 'drop-in' programmes can be applied to an art-based setting with youth and teaching artists (Hernandez and Marroquin 2013). Hernandez and Marroquin detail how the creation of a HOMAGO space should be approached in relation to its participants, mentors and the organizational and administrative requirements needed to support a functioning programme. Yollocalli typically accept youth who apply to the programme directly or who are recommended by an art teacher or through other community arts programmes, i.e. youth who come with a passion for art. Stress is placed on the sociality and informality of the programme, the key to which is an understanding that art creation can take place through self-paced and self-determined artistic goals. Mentors are expected to be open to challenging their own perceptions of youth, as well as being prepared to guide and support when necessary, as opposed to leading or dominating. The organization itself and its administrative functions focus upon accepting youth on their own terms without the imposition of generalized expectations, while also creating a space that can facilitate specific programme goals across a range of activities and stimulate socialness and informality among its users. Key to the success of this form of collaborative learning space is an explicit commitment to creating a space that is (in their words) organic, intergenerational, collaborative, experimental, process-orientated, safe, social, participatory, empowering, individualized, fun, caring and stress free. Yollocalli Arts Center contrasts this with non-HOMAGO spaces which are 'static, adult oriented, solitary, concrete or fixed, formal schooling, home, adultist, teacher proof, limiting and boring' (Hernandez and Marroquin 2013: 7). Alongside this, ongoing processes of documentation – a form of monitoring and evaluation – are deemed important as they detail the stages of creation across a variety of representational forms beyond completion of an artefact at the end of the programme.

In the case of the Yollocalli Arts Center, HOMAGO was presented as an 'experiential' and 'exploratory learning theory' put into practice in informal afterschool programmes, namely YOUmedia in downtown Chicago. The authors cite the general principles of HOMAGO, but they note that their aim was to adapt the model for 'a space of cultural production and how we could translate it into a method that would be usable by our teaching artists' (Hernandez and Marroquin 2013:3,, http://issuu.com/yollocalli/docs/homagoguidebook) in an open studio programme. One of the biggest points of difference for Yollocalli Arts Center is the shift from thinking about adult teaching artists as the experts who impart knowledge or expertise, to thinking of them as collaborators and mentors, where 'everyone is a teacher and a student' (Hernandez and Marroquin 2013: 20). In addition, members of the centre also had to confront their established ideas of 'what production looks like', opening up their definition to incorporate the creative production activities that young people engage in when they are using their phones and other everyday technologies (Hernandez and Marroquin 2013: 6). The Yollocalli Arts Center guidebook states that the primary sources for their understanding of HOMAGO emerged through an engagement with the Chicago Hive Learning Network, who financially supported their activities through a small grant from the Chicago Trust. In particular the (then) Hive Chicago Learning Network's director Christian Greer worked closely with the centre to interpret and translate HOMAGO's principles into the open studio space. They also worked with members of the Digital Youth Network, who were also involved in the Chicago Hive Learning Network, to develop strategies for mentorship. In effect, the principles of HOMAGO provide a useful catalyst and language for the formation of learning principles in an open artists' studio, and the principles themselves are adapted to the different ends and aspirations of a centre focused upon supporting Chicago's creative community. The guidebook was ultimately produced and shared online to be made available to others engaged in implementing HOMAGO in the Hive Learning Networks and beyond.

In addition to the Hive Learning Networks there has been an expansion of YOUmedia into what is termed the YOUmedia Learning Lab Network, which is:

> a national, open network dedicated to expanding the reach and impact of the Learning Lab model. Learning Labs are transformative spaces—and catalysts—for new kinds of thinking about what learning institutions such

as libraries, museums, and community centers can become in the 21st century. Learning Labs are open, flexible, and highly creative spaces where young people can 'hang out, mess around, and geek out' with the support of mentors and community partners (http://youmedia.org; see also 'Learning Labs in Libraries and Museums: Transformative Spaces for Teens' 2014).

As with YOUmedia, the YOUmedia Network Learning Labs have been developed as a collaboration between the Digital Youth Network and Connected Learning (Ito et al. 2013; Larson et al. 2013).[12]

Regimes of Value in the Social Life of HOMAGO

In the previous sections I have focused upon how the concept of HOMAGO was translated from research and the initial report into specific practice-based initiatives such as YOUmedia and the Hive Learning Network. I have also highlighted their role in brokering the concept of HOMAGO for an open studio and a range of other initiatives. In this section I would like to return to the connection between the forms of value that have been produced, and reproduced as the concept has moved within and across different contexts. Cultural studies scholar Mieke Bal (2002) has argued for greater attention to the origin stories of concepts as they move across disciplinary and interdisciplinary spaces in the humanities and social sciences, in an effort to better appreciate how and why particular concepts were developed, and the 'work' that they have carried out for other disciplines. However, here I am less concerned with the difference and distance from the original principle and theory. Given these unexpected translation opportunities, any imagination we (or at least I) had about its utility outside of academic circles certainly included remixing, to borrow a metaphor from digital culture, as it became salient for the practitioner community. Rather, I am interested here in the ways in which an object (or in this case, a concept) moves through different institutional settings and thus enters into different regimes of value, to follow Appadurai (1998), Myers (2001) and others (Keane 2001, 2008).

The regimes of value associated with academia often revolve around developing new concepts to describe and define young people's engagement with new media, such as the five genres of participation discussed in this chapter. The value or impact in academic regimes is often 'measured' by citation counts of the work, which illustrate its uptake and the relative value of publishers and journal ranking. By these kinds of accounts the book and the notions of interest-driven genres of participation, hanging out and geeking out have gained traction across a range of fields, such as education and related areas of learning sciences as well as fields such as communication and new media studies. They have garnered a strong Google citation count (around 1133 for the book and 618 for the white paper, 10 September 2016) and are recognized as a contribution to the field of digital media and learning through (among other things) the book's publication in the open access series with MIT Press. It has also been assigned in undergraduate courses as a key text. Within the U.S. tenure cycle model where many of the co-authors work, the book could not be used for the tenure process as a key monograph in disciplines such as sociology or anthropology. In addition to being produced prior to the 'tenure clock' (acquisition of a tenure-track job), the lack of recognition of a co-authored policy piece was tied to the difficulty in identifying individual authors' contributions in relation to others' contributions. Indeed, it is often cited as an edited rather than co-authored book. These concerns were less prominent for scholars working in interdisciplinary areas such as education, information studies, media studies and communication studies, or for authors of the book working in contexts outside of the United States.

Yet there were other non-academic meanings and uses tied to the work. From the very beginning of the dissemination phase, different researchers and leaders on the project engaged in *direct translation* of the project's outcomes and findings for a range of different audiences. Although this included other academic researchers, the primary focus was around media and education practitioners. Each of these collective and individual acts involved the acknowledgement of another regime of value. However, the broader value of HOMAGO was based less on individual researchers' (twenty-eight in total) ability to disseminate and translate findings, but rather more intricately tied to the support of programme officers and communication staff at the John D. and Catherine T. MacArthur Foundation. The foundation brokered relationships and created additional opportunities to translate and transform the project's findings for new and non-academic stakeholders. This first occurred through the engagement with Global Kids and Common Sense Media in a public forum and was taken to new heights through the formation of YOUmedia in downtown Chicago. In both cases the value accorded to HOMAGO among youth development, education, media and policy practitioners hinged upon the close collaboration with two of the principal investigators and other researchers. For example, translations involved discussions with members of the design team from Carnegie Mellon University as well as phone calls and meetings with members of the Chicago Public Library, the Pearson Foundation and the leadership of the MacArthur Foundation.

The conversations, support and active engagement in brokering relationships by leading institutional stakeholders had an important effect

– they transformed HOMAGO from an academic concept to an evidence-based theory of practice (or, depending upon the interpretation, theory of change). As an evidence-based theory for policy and practice, practitioners and other stakeholders helped to realize a second regime of value through which HOMAGO could circulate. It circulated through YOUmedia, the Hive Learning Network initiative as well as sites like Yollocalli Arts Center whose exploration of HOMAGO was financially supported by the small grants programme associated with the Chicago Learning Network. Yet, this was not a simple case of appropriation; rather, the framing of HOMAGO as a theory or principle enabled each organization to ascribe meaning to its relevance in their own context. Because HOMAGO was firstly a set of design principles and a theory that hinged upon the importance of context and the social, there was an openness to understanding how it would work in practice as well as an expectation that it would and even should change in relation to different contexts. The translations that occurred through discussions with members of the research team, the foundation and a series of other organizations such as the learning network, all involved interpretation. As Umberto Eco (2008) in *Experiences of Translation* has noted, translation always involves interpretation across different cultures and contexts.

In Fred Myers'account of the relationship between sacred designs in Aboriginal art and its use by the state for the social and economic development of Aboriginals in Australia, he observes that 'different levels of circulation and different forms of inalienability are articulated through the connection of distinct institutional contexts' (Myers 2001: 11). As an evidenced-based theory and principle, the value of HOMAGO rested on its academic rigour, often defined as 'the research' or 'evidence base' supporting its use. This is a point emphasized in the origin videos and narratives that accompany HOMAGO (YOUmedia Chicago). As it moved into a collectively owned vision for practitioners involved in and/or engaged with the DML initiative, it became a new entity whose value was reworked and redefined or, in the words of Nick Thomas, recontextualized (Thomas 1991). Yet, it is also clear that there is movement between the regimes of value tied to academia and the practitioner community. In fact, with the use of a concept like HOMAGO there is also a reinterpretation of its value for academic or academic-relevant ends as evidence of a theory. Indeed, in a recent report focused upon the scaling of YOUmedia, the authors describe the Hive Learning Networks, YOUmedia Learning Labs and other related initiatives as 'key DML test beds for the connected learning approach to design and educational reform' (Larson et al. 2013: 9). Appadurai noted a similar process in relation to commodities when he wrote, 'As commodities travel greater distances (institutional, spatial, temporal), knowledge about them tends to becomes partial, contradictory and differentiated. But such differentiation may itself ... lead to the intensification of demand' (Appadurai 1998: 56). HOMAGO entered into a unique ecosystem where research and practice were in constant conversation. Within this ecosystem HOMAGO took on new material forms, moving from a research report, to a White Paper (Ito et al. 2009), book (Ito et al. 2010), PowerPoint presentations and videos made available online by the original authors of the research to a designed environment (YOUmedia), a teacher guidebook (Parker 2010), programme guidelines and guidebook (Hernandez and Marroquin 2013), as well as further presentations and documents created by authors not involved in the original research. In this case the demand is for research to further assess and examine the efficacy of the theory of learning or, more precisely, the kinds of amendments, modifications and remixes that accompany a theory. In effect, the slippage into and across alternative regimes of value associated with 'theory' and 'practice' works so that the one reinforces the other.

Conclusion

Addressing the life of a concept through regimes of value can, one might argue, be conceived as incommensurate given that academic knowledge and concepts are not often experienced as commodities, particularly in the humanities and social sciences where we have historically been critical of the commodification of knowledge.[13] And compared to the sciences, humanities and social science scholars produce fewer objects that might lead to commercialization. Historically academia has valued research 'for research's sake' and has undervalued applied research practice, especially at Ivy League (U.S.), Research 1 (U.S.), Russell Group (U.K.) or Group of Eight (Australia) institutions. Yet, in a time where public funding of education is changing and the importance of being a globally branded university is increasing (Bell 2009; Davidson and Goldberg 2009; Herr-Stephenson et al. 2011 Sidhu 2009), the ways in which academics are spurred to think about the implications of their work in the world and the ways in which institutions (educational or otherwise) value academic knowledge increasingly frame it as a 'commodity', even if not necessarily recognizable to the practices that spurred debate by Appadurai (1998), Myers (2001), Keane (2001) and Thomas (1991) over the past two decades.

Academia represents a regime of value that, while dynamic, sets a series of expectations for scholars in the humanities and social sciences about the significance of their work and the increasing need to be relevant and meet the needs of other sectors. In the case of HOMAGO, there was not necessarily a top-down drive to be relevant beyond academia. Instead, the focus of the work at its most fundamental level requires an engagement with educators (teachers), youth development practitioners, the media and the public. In other contexts, this may involve understanding the needs and questions of industry and public sector entities. This shift towards the revaluation of academic knowledge and the role of academics and other partners as brokers is particularly pertinent during a time of rapid change in higher education globally.

Heather Horst is Professor of Media and Communication at RMIT University. Her published books include *The Cell Phone* (Berg, 2006), *Kids Living and Learning with New Media* (MIT, 2009), *Hanging Out, Messing Around, and Geeking Out* (MIT, 2010), *Digital Anthropology* (Berg, 2012) and *Digital Ethnography: Principles and Practices* (Sage, 2016).

Notes

1. While I have attempted to present this origin story as accurately as possible, I acknowledge here that origin stories are partial and positioned. In my case, this is shaped by my work on the project as a postdoctoral scholar and later as Associate Project Scientist between 2008–11 at the DML Hub at the University of California, Irvine established to 'build the field of digital media and learning'. I moved to RMIT in Australia in late 2011, in a period often described as 'phase 2' of the initiative. There are certainly other origin stories, which could be told from different vantage points and perspectives.
2. The project was the 'Kids' Informal Learning with Digital Media: An Ethnographic Investigation of Innovative Knowledge Cultures' (2005–08). The principal investigators included the (late) Peter Lyman, Mizuko Ito and Michael Carter, as well as twenty-eight researchers across the University of Southern California and the University of California, Berkeley.
3. 'From MySpace to HipHop: A MacArthur Forum' 23 April 2008. Published by holymeatballs, https://www.youtube.com/playlist?list=PLCC2EF6A461393C86.
4. Global Kids, http://www.globalkids.org, works to develop opportunities and networks for youth leadership.
5. Common Sense Media: https://www.commonsensemedia.org.
6. See also http://digitalyouth.ischool.berkeley.edu/press.html for other engagements with the press.
7. The book won the 2011 Library Media Connection Editor's Choice Award.
8. The Digital Youth Network http://digitalyouthnetwork.org was founded by Nichole Pinkard in 2006. It was originally established at the Urban Education Institute at the University of Chicago and is now located at DePaul University. It also resulted in the formation of Remix Learning. After five years working with YOUmedia and other

initiatives across Chicago, the Digital Youth Network is now providing an advisory paper for a new 'Cities of Learning Initiative', to be spearheaded by former MacArthur Foundation Digital Media and Learning initiative programme officer, Connie Yowell.
9. Remix Learning, the company that supports iRemix, developed an online social networking platform for schools, afterschool programmes and community centres designed to enhance learning: http://remixlearning.com.
10. Sebring et al. (2013) highlight some of the challenges of the merging of different organizational cultures. The Digital Youth Network and YOUmedia formal collaboration ended in December 2013 (see http://youmediachicago.org) as the Digital Youth Network has become increasingly involved in the new Cities of Learning Initiative (http://citiesoflearning.org).
11. Having already established Hive Learning Networks in three U.S. and one Canadian city, Hive Learning communities are being developed in seven other cities, including international sites such as Bangalore and Mombasa, with more planned in the future.
12. Connected Learning activities include the Connected Learning Alliance (http://clalliance.org), the Connected Learning Research Network (http://clrn.dmlhub.net) and Connected Learning TV (http://connectedlearning.tv).
13. This is not to negate the extensive work in 'applied' anthropology and other fields, but as a general statement about academics as practitioners who research and teach.

References

Allen, A. 2014. 'Who Benefits from the Impact Agenda?', *Times Higher Education*, 6 November. Available online at https://www.timeshighereducation.co.uk/comment/opinion/who-benefits-from-the-impact-agenda/2016732.article.
Appadurai, A. (ed.). 1998. *The Social Life of Things: Commodities in Cultural Perspective*. Cambridge: Cambridge University Press.
Austin, K., S.B. Ehrlich, C. Puckett and J. Singleton. 2011. *YOUmedia Chicago: Reimagining Learning, Literacies, and Libraries: A Snapshot of Year 1*. Chicago, IL: University of Chicago Consortium on Chicago School Research. Available online at http://ccsr.uchicago.edu/sites/default/files/publications/6899YOUmedia_final_2011.pdf.
Bal, M. 2002. *Travelling Concepts in the Humanities: A Rough Guide*. Toronto: University of Toronto Press.
Barron, B., K. Gomez, N. Pinkard and C.K. Martin. 2014. *The Digital Youth Network: Cultivating Digital Media Citizenship in Urban Communities*. Cambridge, MA: MIT Press.
Bastow, S., P. Dunleavy and J. Tinkler. 2014. *The Impact of the Social Sciences: How Academics and Their Research Make a Difference*. London: Sage.
Bell, D. 2009. 'Learning from Second Life', *British Journal of Educational Technology* 40(3): 515–25.
Chaplin, H. 2013. 'Q&A: Learning by Design: A Conversation with Drew Davidson'. Spotlight on Digital Media and Learning, 18 June. Available online at http://spotlight.macfound.org/featured-stories/entry/qa-learning-by-design-a-conversation-with-drew-davidson/.
Chicago Public Library. YOUmedia. Available online at http://www.chipublib.org/programs-and-partnerships/youmedia/.
Davidson, C. and D.T. Goldberg. 2009. *The Future of Learning Institutions in a Digital Age*. Cambridge, MA: MIT Press.

Eco, U. 2008. *Experiences in Translation*. Toronto: University of Toronto Press.
'From MySpace to HipHop: A MacArthur Forum'. 2008. Three-part series, published by holymeatballs, 23 April. Available online at https://www.youtube.com/playlist?list=PLCC2EF6A461393C86.
Gallagher, L. 2008. *Assessing Youth Impact of the Computer Clubhouse Network*. Menlo Park, CA: Center for Technology in Learning, SRI International. Available online at http://www.computerclubhouse.org/sites/default/files/CapstoneReportFinal.pdf.
Hernandez, B. and N. Marroquin. 2013. *HOMAGO: A Guidebook*. Yothcalli Open Studios: HIVE Learning Network and The National Museum of Mexican Art.
Herr-Stephenson, B., D. Rhoten, D. Perkel and C. Sims. 2011. *Digital Media and Technology in Afterschool Programs, Libraries, and Museums*. Cambridge, MA: MIT Press.
High, M.M. 2013. 'Polluted Money, Polluted Wealth: Emerging Regimes of Value in the Mongolian Gold Rush', *American Ethnologist* 40(4): 676–88.
Holloway, S.L. and G. Valentine. 2003. *Cyberkids: Children in the Information Age*. London: RoutledgeFalmer.
Ito, M., H. Horst, M. Bittanti, d. boyd, R. Herr-Stephenson, P.G. Lange, C.J. Pascoe and L. Robinson. 2009. *Kids Living and Learning with New Media: Findings from the Digital Youth Project*. Cambridge, MA: MIT Press.
Ito, M., S. Baumer, M. Bittanti, d. boyd, R. Cody, R. Herr-Stephenson, H.A. Horst, P.G. Lange, D. Mahendran, K.Z. Martinez, C.J. Pascoe, D. Perkel, L. Robinson, C. Sims and L. Tripp. 2010. *Hanging Out, Messing Around, and Geeking Out: Kids Living and Learning with New Media*. Cambridge, MA: MIT Press.
Ito, M., K. Gutierrez, S. Livingstone, W. Penuel, J. Rhodes, K. Salen, J. Schor, J. Sefton-Green and S.C. Watkins. 2013. *Connected Learning: An Agenda for Research and Design*. Irvine, CA: Digital Media and Learning Research Hub.
Jenkins, H. 2006. *Confronting the Challenges of Participatory Culture: Media Education for the 21st Century*, with K. Clinton, R. Purushotma, A.J. Robison and M. Weigel. Cambridge, MA: MIT Press.
Kafai, Y., K. Peppler and R. Chapman (eds). 2009. *The Computer Clubhouse: Constructionism and Creativity in Youth Communities*. New York, NY: Teachers College Press.
Keane, W. 2001. 'Money is No Object: Materiality, Desire, and Modernity in an Indonesian Society', in F. Myers (ed.), *The Empire of Things: Regimes of Value and Material Culture*. Santa Fe, NM: School of American Research Press, pp. 65–90.
Keane, W. 2008. 'Market, Materiality, and Moral Metalanguage', *Anthropological Theory* 8(1): 27–42.
Larson, K., M. Ito, E. Brown, M. Hawkins, N. Pinkard and P. Sebring. 2013. *Safe Space and Shared Interests: YOUmedia Chicago as a Laboratory for Connected Learning*. Irvine, CA: Digital Media and Learning Research Hub.
Lave, J. and E. Wenger. 1991. *Situated Learning: Legitimate Peripheral Participation*. Cambridge and New York: Cambridge University Press.
Lewin, T. 2008. 'Teenagers' Internet Socializing Not a Bad Thing', *The New York Times*, 19 November.
'Learning Labs in Libraries and Museums: Transformative Spaces for Teens'. 2014. Washington, DC: Association of Science-Technology Centers Urban Libraries Council. Available online at http://youmedia.org/wp-content/uploads/2014/11/LearningLabsPublication.pdf, accessed 1 October 2015.
Livingstone, S. 2002. *Young People and New Media*. London and Thousand Oaks, CA: Sage.
Myers, F. 2001. Introduction, in F. Myers (ed.), *The Empire of Things: Regimes of Value and Material Culture*. Santa Fe, NM: SAR Press, pp. 3–64.

Noguchi, S. 2008. 'Chill Out, Parents: Time Online Teaches Kids Important Skills, Study Shows', *The San Jose Mercury News*, 20 November.

Oliver, K. 2014. 'What's the Impact of the Research Impact Agenda?', 27 July. Available online at http://www.ucl.ac.uk/steapp/steapp-news-publication/2013-14/impact-agenda-oliver.

Parker, J. (ed.). 2010. *Teaching Tech-savvy Kids: Bringing Digital Media into the Classroom, Grades 5–12*. Thousand Oaks, CA: Corwin Press.

Rethinking Mentorship, Learning Pathways in a Networked Age: A Few Moments with Nichole Pinkard. 2013. Irvine, CA: Digital Media and Learning Research Hub, University of California. Available online at http://dmlhub.net/newsroom/expert-interviews/rethinking-mentorship-learning-pathways-in-a-networked-age/.

Sebring, P.B., E.R. Brown, K.M. Julian, S.B. Ehrlich, S.E. Sporte, E. Bradley and L. Meyer. 2013. 'Teens, Digital Media, and the Chicago Public Library: Research Report'. Chicago, IL: The University of Chicago Consortium for Chicago School Research. Available online at http://ccsr.uchicago.edu/sites/default/files/publications/YOUmedia%20Report%20-%20Final.pdf.

Shiels, M. 2008.'Online Time "Is Good for Teens"', *BBC News*, 21 November.

Sidhu, R. 2009. 'The "Brand Name" Research University Goes Global', *Higher Education*, 57(2): 125–40.

Suchman, L., R. Trigg and J. Blomberg. 2002. 'Working Artefacts: Ethnomethods of the Prototype', *The British Journal of Sociology* 53(2): 163–79.

Thomas, N. 1991. *Entangled Objects: Exchange, Material Culture and Colonialism in the Pacific*. Cambridge, MA: Harvard University Press.

Varenne, H. and R. McDermott. 1998. *Successful Failure: The School America Builds*. Boulder, CO: Westview.

Weiner, A. 1992. *Inalienable Possessions: The Paradox of Keeping-While Giving*. Berkeley, CA: University of California Press.

'YOUmedia at the Chicago Public Library'. Video uploaded by DigitalYouthNetwork, Uploaded by digitalyouthnetwork on 21 August 2009. Available online at https://www.youtube.com/watch?v=yRG2Bf-me6k.

'YOUmedia:Educate to Innovate'. Uploaded by macfound 16 September 2010. Available online at https://www.youtube.com/watch?v=NwPQzDsNVPU.

Chapter 9

ENTANGLEMENTS
Issues in Applied Research and Theoretical Scholarship

Tom O'Dell and Robert Willim

Ethnography can be understood as a mode of accumulating and producing knowledge by working closely with people in local settings beyond the academy. It implies continuous entanglements of fieldwork and theory. But how can we understand these entanglements in contexts of applied cultural research? The following chapter presents a series of empirical examples of our own cultural analytic work that highlight the manner in which diverse places and stakeholders are connected and entangled in the production and transformation of social and cultural theory. In the literature, scholars such as George Marcus (1998) often refer to the partners they have worked with as 'epistemic partners', and Marcus defines epistemic partners as those:

> who are not merely informing our research but who participate in shaping its theoretical agendas and its methodological exigencies. By treating our subjects as collaborators, as epistemic partners, our analytical interests and theirs can be pursued simultaneously, and we can share insights and thus develop a common analytical exchange. Crucially, we can pursue this kind of collaboration even if the ultimate aims of our analyses are different, if not radically opposed (Holmes and Marcus 2008: 3).

Epistemic partners are, in Marcus's thinking, closely linked to the phenomenon of para-ethnography, which is an ethnographic context in which scholars and their subjects share closely related analytical frames for understanding the world as well as the methodological disposition required to make sense of that world. Para-ethnography is predicated on relationships of complicity between epistemic partners (ibid.). However, these relationships are also ambiguous and seldom totally harmonious.

Our ambition in the following is to use descriptions of our work to help frame and illuminate the ways in which epistemic partnerships can take form. While Marcus's ambition is to even out the power field of relations at play between academics and their partners, we believe an empirically grounded consideration of what it means to work with 'epistemic partners' can help to reveal and problematize the nature of that partnership. In order to do this, this chapter will examine how theoretical models are being moved and launched in shifting contexts, arguing for a need to think of ethnographic work as more than a textual endeavour. This will be exemplified with the help of ethnographic material from a destination development project that took place in northern Sweden, as well as a number of art projects that problematize issues of locality and practices of representation in the world of museums. In the process the chapter will also illuminate the manner in which we can rethink epistemic partnerships in ways that are rather different to how anthropologists have framed them until now.

When Old Categories and Distinctions Don't Fit

A good deal of the work that we and other ethnologists have done in the borderlands of applied and academic research in Sweden has been oriented towards engagements with the public, relating it to what in the United States has been called public anthropology (Borofsky 2012). During the last decades, our own work, as it is described below, has often been conducted in conjunction with projects concerning regional development, destination management and the development of aspects of the cultural economy. At times this work has been inspired by academic scholarship, but at times the work we have done has been more explorative and experimental, inspired by the arts, particularly audio and video performance oriented presentations (O'Dell and Willim 2011a). In every instance, the work has always been multi-sited, pulling together intellectual strands from the university, and launching them in multiple locations with shifting audiences. The aims of these engagements have ranged from the desire of diverse epistemic partners to facilitate forms of debate and discussion about specific societal issues or local problems, to attempts to help local communities develop both socially and economically.

Most forms of applied cultural analysis are multi-sited to the extent that they mobilize ethnographers beyond academia, and usually require the engagement of multiple parties in a series of local settings. However, beyond this, this chapter will also argue for the need to reconceptualize our practices as not only multi-sited efforts to collect and process ethnographic materials, but also potentially as forms of what we shall describe below as multi-targeted ethnography. In arguing this point, we intend to demonstrate how applied cultural research not only moves to gather materials in multiple settings, but even tends to mobilize vernacular cultural theories in multiple sites. As we argue, this is part of a distributive process of developing new forms of both cultural awareness and cultural critique that help partners beyond the university system to meet the goals that they have (at least partially) defined and to create change.

While arguing for this augmented perceptual understanding of ethnography as multi-targeted, we will also advocate a continued need to proceed with caution when speaking about applied and academic work, avoiding the propensity to place the two in a dichotomous relationship where the one is practically oriented and the other is theoretically oriented. As others have pointed out, the vast amount of work being conducted in the name of 'pure' and 'applied' cultural analysis draws upon very similar (if not identical) epistemological fields of theory and methodological design (Partridge and Eddy 1987: 5), but there are still some who have argued that there remains an overriding perception that the factor most distinguishing 'pure' and 'applied' cultural analysis is the lack of theoretical development in the case of the former (see the discussion in Nolan 2003: 4, as well as the manner in which Grant McCracken enunciates similar concerns in Graffman and Söderström 2009: 6), almost as though applied cultural analysis were by and large atheoretical or theoretically impoverished. This is a view that we find to be both troubling and oversimplified. In other places we have focused on the methodological transformations that take place as ethnography is worked in contexts beyond the university (O'Dell and Willim 2011a, 2011b, 2013, 2014). In what follows, we want to problematize some of the theoretical transformations we have observed in our work beyond academia. This discussion will be used to highlight, in the second portion of this chapter, the methodological consequences that vernacular re-functionings of cultural theory can have for the distribution of applied research results over the course of a project. Central questions underlying the arguments presented here concern what it means to co-produce knowledge and share it with vastly different groups in society. How can the parameters of such shared knowledge production be understood?

Shifting Paradigms: From Products to Experiences and from Text to the Sensuous

The years around the new millennium constituted a watershed period for the expansion of applied cultural analysis in Sweden and larger portions of Scandinavia (O'Dell and Willim 2014). Whereas American anthropologists had already accumulated over a century's worth of experience with multiple forms of applied research (Partridge and Eddy 1987: 25), and the field had experienced a significant surge of interest in Great Britain from the early 1980s onwards (Wright 2006), the work of Swedish ethnologists and anthropologists had almost exclusively been based within academia, focusing upon research the results of which were primarily written up for the eyes of other scholars working within the university system. The issues and problems that these studies focused upon were at best presumed to be of importance for society, but the manner in which the problems were defined and investigated was always in the hands of the university-based scholar. An exception to this rule came in the 1970s in the form of action-based research, and a desire among a new politically critical young generation of socially engaged scholars who felt a need for their expertise to impact upon society and potentially change it (Arnstberg 1997; O'Dell and Willim 2015). But even here, the interest in engaged research was more strongly initialized from within academia by academics, than by explicit governmental directives or investments in action-based research, and even less by the appeal of local communities for the intervention of academic expertise on their behalf.

At the end of the 1990s a series of changes would make it possible for scholars interested in cultural analysis to potentially re-function their trade. Sweden's development from a rather poor agrarian society in the early twentieth century to a modern affluent industrial nation by the end of that century had been propelled by a strong engineering ethos, and belief in the power of science to transform the nation, economically, infrastructurally and socially (Frykman 1981). By the late 1990s an important avenue of focus for that engineering ethos was concentrated on rapidly developing forms of I.T., from computer and software products, to mobile telephony and internet-based services. Industry leaders diligently did their best to follow international trends, reading a new flora of high-tech industry-oriented literature branching out from more conservative sources of inspiration such as *The Financial Times* to more trendy and high-profile sources such as *Fast Company* and *Wired*. Where Swedish industry had once been able to concentrate its efforts on an engineering ethos of building the best machine possible, a growing cadre of business leaders, municipal officials and engineering/design schools were becoming aware that in order to succeed in the dot.com economy of the late 1990s it would be necessary to understand a new set of very ephemeral qualities that the work of the best engineers was going to have to relate to. Inspired by international trends, and the pressures of industrial competition that threatened some of Sweden's largest knowledge-based companies (Löfgren 2003; Willim 2002), a new vocabulary was mobilized that included such words as: experience, culture, identity, creativity, synergy and innovation. But how could you engineer an experience, design culture, or channel synergy? New groups of corporate, municipal and political leaders began to approach scholars in the humanities and social sciences in search of answers and insights.

Empirically Inspired Insights: Meetings with Pine and Gilmore

In the year 2000, The Knowledge Foundation (one of Sweden's larger research financiers since 1994) initiated a programme called 'Meeting Places for the Experience Economy' (Knowledge Foundation 2000), which focused on the creative industries and the establishment of 'meeting places' in which academics, and individuals working in the creative industries, could meet, share ideas and develop new experience-oriented services. This initiative led a few years later to the launching of the 'Aha-Academy'. In advance of the Aha-Academy's establishment, The Knowledge Foundation had identified eight sites spread throughout Sweden that would work as test cases for the development of new experience-based industries and destinations. Three of the sites were located in Sweden's largest cities, Stockholm, Gothenburg and Malmö. The remaining five (Hultsfred, Trollhättan, Piteå, Hällefors and Karlshamn) were located in remote sparsely populated areas of Sweden. To support the development of these rural sites, a group of municipal civil servants, private entrepreneurs and academics were assembled by The Knowledge Foundation and charged with the task of travelling to the five rural destinations, to participate in meetings at those sites that were geared toward facilitating the development of each site's specific experience-oriented profile. This implied collaboratively working with the leadership at each site to produce a clear actionable vision of the experience-oriented destination that was to be produced there, while simultaneously chiselling out the details of the processes through which that vision would be achieved in the coming years. The scholars who were invited to contribute to the Aha-Academy were identified on the basis of their academic records of working with and/or studying the creative industries. O'Dell was among the scholars chosen to participate in this project.

Each site was host to a two- to three-day-long meeting that usually included a presentation of the geographical area of the site, its history and the cultural context in which its experience profile was to be produced. Piteå, which lies in the far north of Sweden, was, for example, striving to establish itself as a destination along the themes of tourism, media and music. Participants in the Aha-Academy partook in presentations made by local actors active in these fields, many of which drew great inspiration from Joseph Pine and James Gilmore's book, *The Experience Economy: Work is Theater and Every Business a Stage* (1999). Indeed, the leadership of all five of the Knowledge Foundation sites were well-versed in such works as Mihaly Csikszentmihalyi's *Flow: The Psychology of Optimal Experience* (1990), Richard Florida's *The Rise of the Creative Class* (2003), and Pine and Gilmore's *The Experience Economy*. Consequently, similar types of texts were repeatedly referred to in presentations made at each site by the project leader at that site or by the local actors involved in the site's development. One difficulty that these individuals had seemed to be in moving from the theoretical contents of those texts to the specific situations that they experienced locally on an everyday basis. The problem was not that local actors lacked theoretical sophistication – they had used the texts they read to produce vernacular theories of the problems they faced and had developed some initial ideas on how to overcome those problems – but that there was a disjuncture here between theory and practice that they needed help in overcoming. This disjuncture was grounded in an uncertainty as to how to evaluate their own understanding of the theories they bore with them, and the solutions they tentatively approached. What O'Dell and the other members of the Aha-Academy brought to the table was a broader arsenal of theoretical understandings and past experiences that could be used to challenge, test and modify the vernacular models that local actors were assembling.

In light of this, it was perhaps not surprising to find very little of any of the five workshops' content to be text-based. Instead the Aha-Academy members were often broken up into smaller groups to engage in exercises anchored in problem-based learning pedagogy aimed at sharpening the site's profile and potential tourist offerings. Such exercises were always based on group discussions leading to the production of posters, pitches and PowerPoint images. In preparation for such activities, members were, in the case of Piteå for example, taken on a boat ride up Piteälven (the Piteå river) in the early evening of the first day of the workshop, offered a local specialty for dinner, which was then followed by an evening snow scooter safari through the forest of Norrland under the Northern Lights.

In one sense, the theme of 'the experience economy' had a presence in all of the five site meetings. The experience of the place dominated over the theorization of it. But the reason for this cannot be fully explained as a result of the experience theme of The Knowledge Foundation's work. In their study of the corporate boardroom and the cultural dynamics involved in corporate brainstorming meetings, Dawn Nafus and Ken Anderson have noted the significance of material culture as a catalyst to boardroom discussions (2010). Post-its, note cards and posters were all central artefacts required in the production of cultural insights among actors in the knowledge economy. In much the same way, snow scooters, boat tours and grilled local foods were used in Piteå to help pry open discussions anchored in hidden ways in the texts of Florida, Pine and Gilmore, and Csikszentmihalyi. The role of the cultural analyst was not simply to provide theoretical insight, but to provide a depth of field that linked the texts these actors had read with the experiences they knew so well corporeally (O'Dell and Willim 2011b). In this context, O'Dell found himself trying to understand how the people he was working with had understood what they had read. How was existing theory shaping perceptions of the local surroundings? This implied an initial stage in which the ethnographer followed the words of his partners, as well as the guided actions of those partners, as they led the ethnographer and the rest of the Aha-Academy members through the local setting. This being said, however, moving to the next stage of analysis, and the production of an actionable deliverable, required a transformation of those roles. The cultural analyst's role here became one of leading the work of linking empirical realities: the empirical materials that local actors had read in conjunction with their reading of the likes of Pine and Gilmore, and the empirical realities in which their lives were anchored in the local setting. This involved multiple discussions, and the creation of drawings on whiteboards, as well as short homemade digital presentations to provide new theoretical depth and understanding to the contexts which local actors had a very strong sense of, but which they were unable to understand in broader or more abstract ways. The cultural analyst's work was to a large degree a process of bringing different realms of theory and understanding together in non-text-based presentational forms to develop new cultural insights that were both slightly familiar to local actors as well as 'Aha-awakening' for them.

If We Are All Epistemic Partners, What Do They Need Us For?

All of this raises the question: What are the ends of theory? As we encounter actors beyond the university, we are often met with the presumption (on the part of these actors) that there is a fundamental difference between what academics do, and what non-academics do. This is a distinction that cultural analysts continuously question and distance themselves from. But if there is no distinction, then a very good question is, 'What do they need us for?' We seem to be quite sure that we need their input and participation in our work if it is to be of value. This is one of the reasons why cultural analysts have struggled with terms such as 'informants', 'collaborators' and 'epistemic partners'. If we are not to undervalue the significance of our knowledge and the effort we expend to hone our methodological and analytical skills, then there is perhaps a need for us to more fully problematize what it means to do cultural analysis, and perhaps what the limits are for such terms as 'epistemic partners'. As the case above illustrates, some concepts and theoretical frameworks move more easily than others. If O'Dell and the local actors he engaged with could share a common vocabulary around the experience economy, it did not necessarily stretch to discussions of non-representational theory, or the limits of Cartesian reason. But this being said, a cultural analysis that is incapable of understanding how cultural, social and managerial theories are converted into vernacular theories for modelling future actions is of limited or no use in applied contexts in which local agents are looking for actionable deliverables that make sense to them. In light of this, it becomes essential to continuously ask ourselves: What can we as researchers learn from the ways in which concepts are interpreted, used and applied? And how can we make the knowledge we produce more easily comprehensible (dare we say desirable?) for individuals not active in academia? Or phrased somewhat differently, it might be said that an important challenge here lies in rethinking how cultural analyses can be moved in directions that go beyond the text.

Empirically Inspired Insights: Concepts Beyond Theory

In our previous writings on rendering culture we wanted to take the discussion about cultural analysis, application, and theory beyond the linguistic realm (O'Dell and Willim 2015). One way to do this is through an understanding of the word 'concept' as a mutable entity, relating to both theory and practice. Theories can be seen as a meshwork of interrelated concepts that can be used to better understand the world. But concepts might work beyond words and theories as provisional entities enmeshed with concrete actions and including the evocation of feelings, perceptions, experiences and attitudes. Concepts are related to both the abstract world of ideas and to action, through concrete plans, intentions and approaches. This becomes especially evident when cultural analytic projects include outputs beyond academic writing and discussion.

In his practices entwining works of art with cultural analysis, Willim has often started out with the formulation of provisional concepts anchored in both theoretical arguments and concrete artistic renditions. In 2005, as part of his earlier examinations of the experience economy, cultural economy and place marketing (see Willim 2005a, 2005b), the art project 'Surreal Scania' took form. It was a collaboration between Willim and the video artist Anders Weberg and was based on six short site-specific films. At the core of the project was an interest from Willim's side in place marketing and the interplay between mediation and imagination when evoking aura around certain localities. The six films were all associated with specific geographical points in southern Sweden. The project played with the way places were pointed out within place marketing and tourism. It involved what were at that time novel media technologies like GPS and mobile video players, aligning it with what was called locative media art or locative art (see Hemment 2006; San Cornelio and Ardévol 2011). Along the way the concept was rendered into the six films, which were distributed through a website. One part of the concept was the opportunity for users to download the films, and through GPS find the specific sites where the raw material for the films was collected. At these sites various ways of visual representation and evocation could be compared. The surreal films played back on a media player could be related to the experience of being on-site. On the website (another spatial part of the project) so-called KML files could be downloaded. These files would open the Google Earth application (which was completely new at the time) and present another kind of visual approach to the site.

As the project evolved it received a great deal of international attention, and was presented and screened in several contexts from the Centre Pompidou in Paris to the Lincoln Center in New York as well as at festivals in Rio de Janeiro, Sydney, Tokyo and Barcelona, leading to exposure in newspapers, magazines, television and on various sites on the web. This became another dimension of the interplay between imagination and mediation, when films from the specific sites were screened in theatres and galleries around the world, evoking associations to distant points in southern Sweden. As the project developed, it also led to a smaller collaboration with Sony Ericsson's research centre and the company's experiments with locative media. At times Willim brought Surreal Scania back into academic contexts to challenge discussions on tourism, place marketing and how imaginary geographies are enmeshed with actual places. At one time in 2006 it was screened at a workshop on tourism and mobilities as part of the transnational Öforsk-financed project 'Two Nations for the Price of One: Tourism and Experience in the Öresund Region'. One hot summer evening the films were screened outdoors against a backdrop of the rural hills and fields of southern Skåne. Surreal Scania became entangled with paper presentations and discussions on theory, intentionally blurring the border between art and science, and between text and multi-media/multi-sensory presentation.

Surreal Scania was the start of a long collaboration between Weberg and Willim through which they developed several common works (like Elsewhereness, Sweden for Beginners, Domestic Safari, and Being There), all relating to Willim's work as a cultural analyst. While developing the artistic concepts of these works, theory played an intrinsic role and it also became part of international methodological and theoretical explorations of the way ethnography and anthropology are related to artistic practice. This is exemplified in several collaborations with the curator collective Ethnographic Terminalia in the United States and Canada (see Brodine et al. 2011; Errington 2012), which led to screenings of artworks, a residency and the inclusion in conferences, discussions and development of understandings of the ways in which art can be connected to ethnography.

The question of collaboration, the public, audiences and stakeholders becomes somewhat blurred when cultural analysis moves beyond the academic world and its preoccupation with producing texts. The concept of an artwork can, for example, be mirrored in the very process of creation in ways that seldom occur within academia. An example of this is the series of experimental films called Elsewhereness created by Willim and Weberg. Elsewhereness was based on audio and video material from cities that the creators never had visited. They chose to make filmic accounts of these places based on material from the internet, as well as their own preconceptions about the places. The work was a play with ethnographic presence, the multi-sited and possible significance of being at a site (for a long time) in order to represent it. Elsewhereness was an invocation of an imaginary geography as well as an exploration of the role of chance and distancing. When developing the conceptual framework for Elsewhereness, serendipity and the play between distance and proximity were integral to the workflow (Willim 2013). Willim and Weberg started by discussing the city they were about to approach. Then, isolated from each other, they collected images and sounds. Weberg composed the images, while Willim composed the sound. The first sketches of image and sound were made at a distance, and then some time into the project, image met sound. This method created surprising effects. The material of this process was used as the basis for the final composition, which was conceived as a kind of closed dialogue. Before deciding on the final rendition, they tried to retain as much as possible from the first, detached part of the process. This process accentuates the interplay between distance and proximity, alienation and intimacy.

Also, when delivering Elsewherenesss to the individuals who had commissioned the work, Willim and Weberg tried to keep some distance to highlight the core qualities of the concept. The first Elsewhereness piece was made for the Dislocate 08 festival in Yokohama. From the day the film was sent away to the organizers of the festival in Yokohama and published on the web, it was in a sense out of control. Throughout the lifespan of Elsewhereness and the production of its different parts, contact between artists and curators was mainly maintained through e-mail. While some overall suggestions on how to screen or exhibit the works was communicated, a distance was maintained. Willim and Weberg weren't concretely involved in any of the spatial, technological or aesthetic considerations that took place in the various art spaces and venues where the works were shown. The artists were elsewhere, at another site. It became an intentional stance to include a certain level of abandon in Elsewhereness, entangling the conceptual into the very process of working.

Along the way new works have been conceived. In 2015 Willim started a collaboration with the Museum of Ethnography in Stockholm and produced the live performance Possible Worlds. This work was based on ideas about ethnographic imagination, and how places and worlds are evoked in a museum setting. It started as a discussion between Willim and Lotten Gustafsson Reinius, head of the museum, at a conference about visual methods and digital culture. How could the concrete collections, rooms and archives of the museum be entwined with artistic exploration to problematize museum practices? The project became crucial for the museum in its efforts to create a programme examining notions of ethnography and museum representation through its work with commissioned artworks and the formation of an artist residency programme. In addition to this relationship with the museum, Possible Worlds has been included in forthcoming theoretical explorations, and iterations of the work have led to new collaborations both within and outside of academia.

This interplay between conceptual and theoretical dimensions and creative practices has characterized several of Willim's works. He has described the artworks as *art probes* that work as speculative instruments of evocation, and might possibly inspire or speak back to his research practices (Willim 2013). Art probes in this sense are launched with the intention of them (possibly) becoming active stimulants for discussion and changing forthcoming interactions, and as exploratory instruments aimed at processes generating knowledge. The notion of epistemic partners, as understood by George Marcus, could be broadened to include non-human objects such as Willim's art probes and the artefacts (clusters of Post-it notes, posters and scribblings on whiteboards, among other things) that were mobilized by O'Dell and the other Aha-Academy members. To the extent that epistemic partners, in Marcus's writings, are understood to inform theoretical agendas and understandings, while facilitating the development of analytical exchanges between the parties engaged in the ethnographic endeavour (Holmes and Marcus 2008: 3), the probes and material objects mobilized in the ethnographic places we have described here – such as exhibits, boardrooms and project meetings – have a similar capacity. In the case of artistic work and artworks, the epistemic partnership builds upon entwined practices of ethnography and cultural analysis, which are launched with the intention of challenging academic routines. They are in this sense methodological endeavours 'primarily attuned to the unpredictable nature of fact, thought and experience' (Parisi 2012). In order to fulfil the goal of challenging academic routines, launched probes require that the cultural analyst dares to relinquish control over her/his work and follow in the ripples of its effects, so that those effects can be observed, recollected and led in new directions of inquiry. The cultural analyst, in other words, assumes a position that is ever shifting between the role of the maker and that of observer, as well as between that of leader and follower.

Orientations of Cultural Analysis: From Multi-sited to Multi-targeted Ethnography

A central issue at play here is the question of the role and (dis)position of the ethnographer in the applied context. How do we understand the locations and orientations of cultural analytic practices and the direction in which they might be moved? Our engagements with stakeholders within the so-called Experience Economy and with different actors within art worlds are examples of how applied cultural analytic work can be understood as not only a multi-sited endeavour, but even one that is multi-targeted.

By invoking the concept of multi-targeted ethnography our intention is to focus attention more stringently upon aspects of the ethnographic process which George Marcus, before introducing ideas on para-ethnography, has pointed to in his writings on multi-sited ethnography, but which have yet to be more explicitly discussed and attended to at both the theoretical and methodological levels.

A central issue resonating through much of Marcus's work and his relation to the crisis of representation lie in a call for experimentation with ethnography. Among the experimentations he advocated was an expanded movement towards forms of non-rooted ethnographic praxis that strove to capture the complex interplay between the realms of macro- and micro-cultural processes. As he explained:

> (A) much less common mode of ethnographic research self-consciously embedded in a world system, now often associated with the wave of intellectual capital labeled postmodern, moves out from the single site and local situations of conventional ethnographic research designs to examine the circulation of cultural meanings, objects, and identities in diffuse time-space (Marcus 1998: 79)

This was the basis for multi-sited ethnography, which he argued needed to highlight connections where they had been overlooked or deemed to be beyond the realm of ethnography's potential for study. 'Strategies of quite literally following connections, associations, and putative relationships are thus at the very heart of designing multi-sited ethnographic research' (1998: 81). To these ends, he delineated six modes of engaging world systems through ethnographic practices that he described as: 1) follow the people; 2) follow the thing; 3) follow the metaphor; 4) follow the plot, story or allegory; 5) follow the life or biography; and 6) follow the conflict (ibid.).

A large ambition behind Marcus's appeal for the development of more mature forms of multi-sited ethnography lie in a desire to destabilize the static and bounded notions of culture as locked to a singular place, a field *site*, a *place* of fieldwork. And doing so by uprooting the ethnographer, and putting her in pursuit of that which was not bound to any one place – to 'follow' that which was not still. Ultimately, the decree '*to follow*' proved to be one of the most concrete, celebrated and *actionable* deliverables to come out of the postmodern anthropological critique of culture – a battle cry that has been, if not followed, at least heard and considered by a generation of anthropologists since the mid-1990s.

But this word to 'follow' has its own etymological implications, which after more than twenty years of use, are in need of reflexive acknowledgement. Etymologically, the word 'follow' comes from the Middle English term 'folwen', to 'move in the same direction as'. In this sense the ethnographer becomes a shadow figure, an entity on the coat-tails of a phenomenon. Beyond this, 'to follow' is a word whose cognates include 'Folgon' from Old Saxon and 'Fylgja' from Old Norse, both of which are derived from 'full-gan' or 'full going'. However, to move in the same direction as something is quite different from hunting it. 'Following' implies a somewhat more passive, withdrawn and distanced perspective than other terms that Marcus might have chosen, such as 'engaging with', 'confronting' or 'embracing' a cultural phenomenon. Indeed, in relation to words such as 'hunting', 'confronting' and 'embracing', following is an emotionally much cooler disposition of mobility. Those who choose a strategy of following also choose an ethical stance in relation to their work, in relation to what they study, and perhaps even unintentionally, in relation to the surrounding society in which they either partake, or merely observe. If we 'follow' Marcus a bit further, this becomes even more apparent:

> The most important form of local knowledge in which the multi-sited ethnographer is interested is that which parallels the ethnographer's own interest – in mapping itself. Sorting out the relationships of the local to the global is a salient and pervasive form of local knowledge that remains to be recognized and discovered in the embedded idioms and discourses of any contemporary site that can be defined by its relationship to the world system (1998: 97).

Following, for Marcus, is to 'parallel' something. It is to go along with phenomena that mirror the ethnographer's own interest. It implies a sorting out of relationships. But what does it mean to sort? What does it mean to untangle things? What does it mean to follow?

There is reason to be wary of the role that the ethnographer assigns him or herself in this context. To follow is, if we return to the etymology of the word, to be led. In our view, this brings unsettling questions to mind as to the role the ethnographer assigns herself/himself as an actor. What are the responsibilities of an actor who views herself/himself as a follower? To what extent is the empirical material that is gathered, or the processes that are studied, actants, or actionable entities, that the ethnographer chases after, or that s/he merely witnesses? To be led is not only the acceptance of a passive role, it is one that implies a preparedness to come 'just after' that which is observed, to be in the past of that which is happening.

There is a striking parallel here to the phenomena that Renato Rosaldo (1986) problematized in *Writing Culture*, of Evans-Pritchard observing what is happening around him from the door of his tent, passively sitting and noting what occurs. For those of us, ourselves included, who have practised, engaged with and striven to develop strategies for working with multi-sited ethnography, we wonder how many ethnographers have done more than swap the old canvas tent for a sparkling new camper, which has allowed us to enjoy both a degree of mobility, as well as a new door from which to sit and observe what is happening 'out there'.

Multi-sited ethnography has much to offer, and in raising questions about the manner in which the ethnographer is implicitly positioned in this practice, our intention is not to throw the baby out with the bathwater. Multi-sited ethnography offers ample opportunities to study and understand cultural processes that link the micro-, meso- and macroscales of cultural processes in ways that were never possible in single-sited endeavours. However, we do want to point out the degree to which multi-sited ethnography is (and has always been) framed as an *accumulative* practice, and a distanced one at that – a methodological mode through which materials are to be accumulated and brought together from different places and different times, and then combined with theory in order to present new compositions.

The accumulative process is part of the nature of most scholarly investigation and is an important means by which we create understanding, for ourselves at first, and then through our analyses even for others. We gather information and search for patterns, points of conflict, or taken-for-granted social constructions, and then work to explain them. But as we argue, there is a need to even more explicitly envision the ethnographic process as not only accumulative, but also as always distributive. The distributive aspect of ethnography is seldom addressed directly in methodology textbooks, but the knowledge we accumulate through ethnographic practices is of little value if it is not distributed. For most scholars, the distributive mode of ethnography focuses upon the production of the final analysis and the publication of the journal article or the ethnographic monograph (O'Dell and Willim 2015). But it is perhaps time to complement multi-sited ethnography with another mode of ethnographic endeavour, that of multi-targeted ethnography.

Conclusions

In the cases of the Aha-Academy and art probes such as Surreal Scania or Possible Worlds, the ethnographic endeavour was never intended to result in a single textual project (the journal article or the monograph). These were works that were either directed towards specific publics to help them meet their own goals and agendas (the Aha-Academy), or primarily directed at audiences beyond academic contexts as open-ended evocations (the art projects). The work we produced, stemming partly from our earlier ethnographic work, was in this sense handed over as tools to think or feel with. Herein lies an element of epistemic partnership. These were applied and public-oriented projects that built on the understanding that the partners we worked with (like workshop participants in Piteå, or fellow artists, curators and managers of art festivals and museums), were theoretically informed, and that they possessed empirically grounded understandings of the contexts in which they operated that we did not control. At the same time, this 'partnership' was underpinned by the understanding that our epistemic collaboration was never balanced or based on a relationship of absolute parity. In the context of the Aha-Academy, and in the context faced by most ethnographers working for clients beyond the academy, there is an understanding that the ethnographer is in possession of forms of knowledge and methodological competence that are not accessible to local actors and clients. This, we are arguing, is an important distinction to maintain and assert in applied contexts of multi-targeted ethnography (it is, after all, our skills, knowledge and experience that make us valuable as partners), even as we recognize and appreciate the degree to which our partners beyond the university are theoretically versed and informed. It is the recognition of this disparity, and the ability of the ethnographer to work with it, that is the basis for the mutual production of knowledge.

When working in the contexts we have described above where cultural analysis is combined with art, the researchers' knowledge was enmeshed with artistic creation, either through collaborations where the creative process was distributed between partners, or through a shift of roles, in which the cultural analyst abandoned the role of being a researcher for a while in order to work as an artist. Other partners, such as curators and organizers of arts and cultural institutions, were also given the lead at several times during the projects. The ethnographic concepts that Willim launched were allowed to move, be appropriated and transformed as part of the experimental process of challenging the parameters and limits of those concepts.

In this sense, working in a multi-targeted manner has implied taking the time to follow along with our partners until we reach the point at which it is necessary and expected that we take a leadership role. The need to take on such a role, and the ability to express the fact that we are capable of doing so, is an important asset that applied cultural analysts need to be able to communicate, even while remaining sensitive to the power relations that exist between all the parties involved in the ethnographic endeavour at hand. We are not arguing here for an attitude of academic elitism, but a need to emphasize the competencies we have honed through years of work (a position which may be undercommunicated if we unconditionally refer to those we work with as 'epistemic partners'). This requires us to recognize the theoretical models of the people we work with, but also to be able to help them push those models in new directions. To be successful, this has, for our part, included the need to let go of our own theoretical models as we have delivered them to our partners, allowing them to once again rework them into the languages that best allow them to meet their goals.

Part of a multi-targeted approach is a reflexivity towards our own theoretical preferences, preferred orientations and biases. As applied cultural analysts, we have to ask ourselves to what extent we as scholars might be 'led by theory', applying politically appropriate packages of theoretical detergent in order to wash out insights. What is the so-called critical scholar really following, and which roads are never taken? A multi-targeted approach puts us in situations in which we are challenged and forced into moments of reconsideration and doubt as well as into positions where we have to acknowledge that knowledge is somewhat ephemeral and context-dependent.

In the spirit of multi-targeted ethnography, we try to facilitate preconditions through which we might appreciate the different ways in which our 'epistemic offerings' are received and transformed. We also aim to steer them in new directions in the context of the project at hand, move them in new directions in other applied and public projects, or analyse the cultural processes we observe at work in these projects in academic writings directed to colleagues in other scholarly settings. Multi-targeted ethnography is always to some extent provisional, and always on its way to new forms of rendition.

Acknowledgements

The research which this chapter is based upon has received funding from Riksbankens Jubileumsfond for the project Runaway Methods: Ethnography and Its New Incarnations, and from the Swedish Center for Applied Social and Cultural Analysis (SCACA) at Halmstad University.

Tom O'Dell is a Professor of Ethnology at Lund University, Sweden. He is Guest Professor of Ethnology at Halmstad University, and Stockholm University, Sweden. Among his previous publications are *Spas: The Cultural Economy of Hospitality*, *Magic and the Senses*, and *Culture Unbound: Americanization and Everyday Life in Sweden*.

Robert Willim is Associate Professor of European Ethnology and Lecturer in Digital Cultures, at the Department of Arts and Cultural Sciences, Lund University, Sweden. He is Guest Researcher at Halmstad University, Sweden. He is also active as an artist.

References

Arnstberg, K.O. 1997. *Fältetnologi*. Stockholm: Carlssons.
Borofsky, R. 2012. *Why a Public Anthropology?* Honolulu, HI: Pacific University.
Brodine, M., C. Campbell, K. Hennessy, F.P. McDonald, T.L. Smith and S. Takaragawa. 2011. 'Ethnographic Terminalia: An Introduction', *Visual Anthropology Review* 27(1): 49–51.
Csikszentmihalyi, M. 1990. *Flow: The Psychology of Optimal Experience*. New York, NY: Harper and Row.
Errington, S. 2012. 'Ethnographic Terminalia: 2009–10–11. Exhibition Review Essay', *American Anthropologist* 114(3), pp. 538–542.
Florida, R. 2003. *The Rise of the Creative Class*. New York, NY: Basic Books.
Frykman, J. 1981. 'Pure and Rational. The Hygienic Vision: A Study of Cultural Transformation in the 1930's. The New Man', *Ethnologia Scandinvica* 11: 36–62.
Graffman, K. and J. Söderström. 2009. *Konsumentnära varumärkesutveckling – Effektivare varumärkesstrategi med kommersiell etnografi*. Stockholm: Liber.
Hemment, D. 2006. 'Locative Arts', *Leonardo* 39(4): 348–55.
Holmes, D.R. and G.E. Marcus. 2008. 'Para-Ethnography', in L. Given (ed.), *The SAGE Encyclopedia of Qualitative Research Methods*. Thousand Oaks, CA: Sage, pp. 596–598.
Knowledge Foundation, The. 2000. 'Meeting Places for the Experience Economy'. Available online at www.kk-stiftelsen.org/om/Lists/Publikationer/DispForm.aspx?ID=157.
Löfgren, O. 2003. 'The New Economy: A Cultural History', *Global Networks* 3(3): 239–54.
Marcus, G. 1998. *Ethnography through Thick and Thin*. Princeton, NJ: Princeton University Press.
McCracken, G. 2009. 'Foreword', in K. Graffman and J. Söderström, *Konsumentnära varumärkesutveckling*. Stockholm: Liber, pp. 6–9.
Nafus, D. and K. Anderson. 2010. 'Writing on the Walls: The Materiality of Social Memory in Corporate Research', in M. Cefkin (ed.), *Ethnography and the Corporate Encounter*. Oxford/New York: Berghahn Books, pp. 137–57.
Nolan, R. 2003. *Anthropology in Practice: Building a Career Outside the Academy*. Boulder, CO: Lynne Rienner Publishers Inc.
O'Dell, T. and R. Willim. 2011a. 'Composing Ethnography', *Ethnologia Europaea* 41(1): 26–39.
O'Dell, T. and R. Willim. 2011b. 'Irregular Ethnographies: An Introduction', *Ethnologia Europaea* 41(1): 4–13.
O'Dell, T. and R. Willim. 2013. 'Transcription and the Senses: Cultural Analysis When It Entails More than Words', *The Senses and Society* 8(3): 314–34.
O'Dell, T. and R. Willim. 2014. 'Applied Cultural Analysis: Ethnography as Compositional Practice', in R. Denny and P. Sunderland (eds), *Handbook of Anthropology in Business*. Walnut Creek, CA: Left Coast Press, pp. 787–800.
O'Dell, T. and R. Willim. 2015. 'Rendering Culture and Multi-Targeted Ethnography', *Ethnologia Scandinavica* 45:89–102.
Parisi, L. 2012. 'Speculation: A Method for The Unattainable', In C. Lury & N. Wakeford (eds), *Inventive Methods. The Happening of The Social*. Abingdon: Routledge, pp. 232–244.
Partridge, W.L. and E.M. Eddy. 1987. 'The Development of Applied Anthropology in America', in E. Eddy and W. Partridge (eds.), *Applied Anthropology in America*. New York: Colombia University Press, pp. 3–58.
Pine, J. and J. Gilmore. 1999. *The Experience Economy: Work Is Theatre and Every Business a Stage*. Boston, MA: Harvard Business School Press.

Rosaldo, R. 1986. 'From the Door of His Tent: The Fieldworker and the Inquisitor', in J. Clifford and G. Marcus (eds), *Writing Culture: The Poetics and Politics of Ethnography*. Berkeley, CA: University of California Press, pp. 77–97.

San Cornelio, G., and Ardévol, E. 2011. Practices of Place-Making Through Locative Media Artworks. *Communications* 36(3), pp. 313–333.

Willim, R. 2002. *Framtid.nu*. Eslöv: Symposion.

Willim, R. 2005a. 'It's in The Mix – Configuring Industrial Cool', in O. Löfgren and R. Willim (eds), *Magic, Culture and The New Economy*. Oxford: Berg, pp. 97–104.

Willim, R. 2005b. 'Looking with New Eyes at The Old Factory: On The Rise of Industrial Cool', in T. O'Dell and P. Billing (eds), *Experiencescapes: Tourism, Culture and The New Economy*. Köpenhamn: CBS Press, pp. 35–50.

Willim, R. 2013. 'Out of Hand – Reflections on Elsewhereness', in A. Schneider and C. Wright (eds), *Anthropology and Art Practice*. London: Bloomsbury: pp. 81–88.

Wright, S. 2006. 'Machetes into a Jungle? A History of Anthropology in Policy and Practice, 1981–2000', in S. Pink (ed.), *Applications of Anthropology: Professional Anthropology in the Twenty-first Century*. Oxford/New York: Berghahn Books, pp. 27–54.

Part V

Afterword

Afterword

THE DEEP DYNAMICS OF THE IN-BETWEEN

Paul Stoller

Several years ago I decided to travel to New York City to visit my West African merchant friends who have long sold their wares at the Malcolm Shabazz Harlem Market on 116th Street. After greeting my friends, we sat down on flimsy card chairs in front of one of their stalls and talked about a wide variety of topics – American politics, the economic and political conditions in West Africa, the latest movies and video games, as well as the mercurial rise and fall of the U.S. stock market. These discussions led to a late lunch – sumptuous West African fish and meat stews over rice – ordered from a local West African restaurant. When the food arrived, one friend turned over a milk crate, covered it with newspapers and placed our meal, which had been put in a large styrofoam container, on the 'table'. Armed with plastic spoons, we sat around the 'pot' and ate in silence. In West Africa eating is a serious activity that should not be disrupted by talk.

As we ate quietly, an African American man approached and greeted us. One of my friends asked him to join us. The African American man said that he'd already eaten. My friend said: 'But we have lots of food.' In most West African societies, if a person invites you to eat, you should accept. If you're not hungry, you should at least take a spoonful of food – a taste that demonstrates respect and bolsters social relations.

The man, however, preferred not to taste the food. Instead, he looked over our group and focused on me, the only white person there.

'Who's your friend?' he asked.

My friends said that that I was part of the group.

The man said: 'He doesn't look like one of you.'

Another friend ignored the African American man's comment and told him that I spoke his language and had spent many years in Africa. 'He's our brother,' he stated.

'Is that so?' the African American man asked me.

'My relationship to these men is complicated,' I said. 'We say we are "brothers" because I have lived in their world and they have lived in mine ... In West Africa the elders like to say: "Even if it floats in the river for one hundred years, a log never becomes a crocodile."'

My African friends laughed softly in appreciation of the oft-recited proverb.

The African American man wondered about its meaning.

'It means,' I said, 'that even though I've lived in Africa, speak an African language, and respect African customs, I'm not an African and will never become one. I am between Africa and America' (Stoller 2008: 4).

* * *

Like all human beings, scholars are always already between all sorts of things – between two continents like Africa and North America, between health and illness, between life and death, between mind and body, between past and present, between self and other, and, to focus this short afterword upon the present anthology, *Theoretical Scholarship and Applied Practice*, between theory and practice. Indeed, all of the chapters in this edited collection explore the murky and indeterminate spaces that extend between things, an arena of emergent discovery and unintended consequence. The publication of *Theoretical Scholarship and Applied Practice* is quite timely, for as Pink, O'Dell and Fors state in their introductory chapter, applied research will increasingly occupy the centre stage of current and future academic work. The idea of a 'pure' scholar practising 'untainted' research is quickly and inexorably giving way to collaborative multidisciplinary research projects on important subjects that have direct bearing on the quality of contemporary social life – climate change, racism, religious prejudice, terrorism and electoral politics. The complexity of these subjects requires that scholars build multidisciplinary links to publics beyond the boundary of academe. Put another way, applied research is the bridge that can connect theory to practice. And yet,

> what is glaringly lacking is a larger and extensive discussion of how forms of applied, public and practiced scholarship contribute to the development of cultural and social theory, and vice versa, how abstract theoretical insights

can provide concrete proposals, insights or solutions and understandings in concrete contexts of daily life and work (Pink, Odell and Fors, this volume).

The chapters in *Theoretical Scholarship and Applied Practice* demonstrate powerfully the dynamic interplay between the theory and practice of conversational analysis, place marketing and urban planning, science and technology studies and visual ethnography. They underscore the productive connection between concept and implementation in the study of audit culture, non-academic institutions, occupational safety and intellectual ethics. The contributors also discuss how the shift to a more public scholarship demands that scholars develop the capacity to communicate effectively to diverse audiences. Such public outreach, the contributors suggest in various ways, extends the reach and influence of academic insight.

One of the great strengths of *Theoretical Scholarship and Applied Practice* is that the authors skilfully navigate the turbulence that continuously disrupts the space between things. In so doing, they show us how to squeeze conceptual and methodological insights from collaborative practices that not only result in cutting-edge theories and innovative methods, but also recalibrate scholarly practice to the exigencies of twenty-first century social life. In this way, the contributors perceptively explore many important practical and conceptual dimensions that exist in the spaces between theory and practice.

The between, however, implicates other dimensions of human experience. The deep dynamics of the between compel us to confront profoundly existential issues. It is not easy to find yourself between health and illness or, for that matter, between theory and practice. It is not a simple matter to live in an ever-changing indeterminate state. It is much more convenient to remain mired on one side of the divide – on the side of theory or on the side of practice, in the village of the healthy or in the village of the sick. If you are in good health, you tend not to think about illness or death. If you are purely theoretical or purely practice-oriented, you can float peacefully on the calm waters of institutional tradition. The turbulent discomforts that criss-cross the space between theory and practice, however, can make innovative academic work exceedingly stressful. What are the personal and/or institutional rewards for stepping onto the bridge that links theory and practice?

Most scholars prefer to linger in the calm of institutional tranquility, which means they tend to avoid the institutional and existential turmoil of the between. The uncertain indeterminacy of the between can, after all, lead to lethargy, confusion and indecision. It can also lead to what Jean-Paul Sartre once called 'bad faith'. As I once put it: 'In bad faith our vision is so obscured by webs of self-contained illusion that shades of difference are shut out and the brightness of wonder is dimmed. In bad faith, we see, as David MacDougal (2006) has suggested, but don't look' (Stoller 2008: 4).

But if we struggle to draw strength from both sides of the divide, we can enter an extraordinary arena of imagination, power and creativity. In his brilliant book, *Imaginative Horizons*, Vincent Crapanzano suggests that the between is *barzakh* (the bridge) – a central concept in Moroccan mystical thinking. Citing the wisdom of his Moroccan mentor, Moulay Abedsalem, Crapanzano (2003: 57) wrote that:

> *barzakh* is what lies between things—between edges, borders, and events. He likened it to the silence between words and to dreams. 'The dream is between walking life and sleep,' he said, using the expression 'little death' for sleep to emphasize, I believe, the absence (*ghaib*) he, like other Moroccans, associated with sleep and dreaming.

Crapanzano demonstrates how the deep dynamics of the between are profoundly rooted in the classical Sufi thought of Ibn al-'Arabi (1165–1240), for whom the between is:

> something that separates ... two other things, while never going to one side ... as, for example, the line that separates shadow from sun light. God says, 'he let forth the two seas that meet together, between them a *barzakh* that they do not overpass' (Koran 55: 19); in other words one sea does not mix with the other ... Any two adjacent things are in need of *barzakh* which is neither the one nor the other but which possesses the power ... of both. The *barzakh* is something that separates a known from an unknown, an existent from a non-existent, a negated from an affirmed, an intelligible from a non-intelligible (Crapanzano 2003: 57–58).

In Ibn al-'Arabi's world, the between, which can be fearful and disruptive, is the pre-eminent space of creative illumination. Following Victor Turner and Arnold Van Gennep, Crapanzano underscores the parallels of classical Moroccan thought and liminality:

> The liminal has often been likened to the dream ... it suggests imaginative possibilities that are not necessarily available to us in everyday life. Through paradox, ambiguity, contradiction, bizarre, exaggerated, and at times grotesque symbols—masks, costumes, and figurines—and the evocation of transcendent realties, mystery and supernatural powers, the liminal offers us a view of the world to which we are normally blinded by the usual structures of social and cultural life (Crapanzano 2003: 58).

* * *

Lingering in the between, then, sharpens our sensibilities and awakens our creativity. It reinforces what John Keats once called 'negative capability', a capacity, as the philosopher John Dewey put it of 'being in uncertainties, mysteries, doubts, without any irritable reaching after fact or reason' which 'at its height cannot contain complete grasp and self-contained assurance. It must fall back upon imagination—upon the embodiment of ideas in emotionally charged sense' (Dewey 1934: 32–33).

I have long pondered the institutional difficulties and creative rewards you find in spaces between things. Too many of us, I'm afraid, spend much of our time following the path of the straight highway. Why not focus more on theory? Why not ignore theory and concentrate on practice? Isn't it safer to conduct our research or represent our research findings from within the safe confines of convention? Indeed, if 'we veer off the highway, we take many risks, for detours often lead us to distant, isolated places', places between things. 'And when we try to describe the wonders of these faraway places, many people don't want to listen. "Why did you go there?" "I've never heard of that place?" "Why did you wander so far off the path?"' (Stoller 1989: 156).

The contributors to *Theoretical Scholarship and Applied Practice* have walked along the indeterminate byways of the between. Having taken the institutional and personal risks of opening themselves to creative worlds of imagination, they have described a wide variety of collaborative multidisciplinary projects of broad public importance. On the bridge that links the known and the unknown they have innovatively calibrated their scholarship to the deep dynamics of the between. In so doing they implore us to join them on the *barzakh* so that we, too, can be inspired by the crosswinds that you can sometimes feel on the wings of the wind. In so doing they mark a path that leads to the future of academic thought and practice.

Paul Stoller is Professor of Anthropology at West Chester University and has been conducting anthropological research for more than thirty years in West Africa (Niger) and among African immigrants in New York City. This body of research has resulted in fourteen books, including ethnographies, memoirs, novels, a biography and collections of academic essays.

References

Crapanzano, V. 2003. *Imaginative Horizons: An Essay in Literary-Philosophical Anthropology.* Chicago, OH: The University of Chicago Press.
Dewey, J. [1934] 1980. *Art as Experience.* New York, NY: Perigee Books.
MacDougall, D. 2006. *The Corporeal Image: Film, Ethnography and the Senses.* Princeton, NJ: Princeton University Press.
Stoller, P. 1989. *The Taste of Ethnographic Things: The Senses in Anthropology.* Philadelphia, PA: University of Pennsylvania Press.
Stoller, P. 2008. *The Power of the Between: An Anthropological Odyssey.* Chicago, OH: The University of Chicago Press.

INDEX

A
Aboriginal art 200
Africa and America, being between 227–8
Aha-Academy 210, 211, 212, 217, 220, 221
Akama, Yoko 32, 43, 46
Amit, Vared 30–31
anthropology
    academic research in 4
    applied-theoretical anthropology, practice of 4–5
    applied/theoretical distinction in. evasion of 6
    cognate disciplines of, learning from 10
    distinctions between applied and theoretical anthropology 6
    public intellectuals, anthropologists as 6
    specificity in, tendency towards 10–11
Anthropology by the Wire project 45
applied cultural analysis, master's programme in (MACA) 8–9
applied practice, advance of 3, 16
applied practice and theoretical scholarship
    challenges and opportunities in bringing together 3–4
    ingrained division between 15
applied research, drive towards 15
applied research and theoretical scholarship, issues in 25, 206–22
    action-based research 209
    Aha-Academy 210, 211, 212, 217, 220, 221
    applied cultural analysis 207–8, 209, 217, 221
    Cartesian reason, limits of 213
    categories and distinctions, fitting in with 207–8
    collaboration 206, 214, 215, 216, 220–21
    cultural analysis
        art and 214–15, 221
        orientations of 217–20
        in Sweden, focus of 209–10
    empirically inspired insights 210–13
    concepts beyond theory 213–17
    epistemic collaboration, parity and 220–21
    epistemic offerings, reception and transformation of 221
    epistemic partners 206–7
        theory, epistemic partnership and ends of 212–13
    ethnography 206
        multi-targeted, from multi-sited ethnography to 217–20, 221–2
        university, ethnography beyond 208
    'experience economy' 211–12
    The Experience Economy: Work is Theater and Every Business

a Stage (Pine, J. and Gilmore, J.) 211–12
fieldwork and theory, entanglements of 206
Flow: The Psychology of Optimal Experience (Csikszentmihalyi, M.) 211
international attention 214–15
knowledge economy 212
Knowledge Foundation 210–11, 212
mediation and imagination, interplay between 214–15
multi-sited applied cultural analysis 207–8
multi-targeted ethnography 208, 217, 220, 221–2
non-representational theory 213
para-ethnography, phenomenon of 206–7
paradigm shifts 209–10
Possible Worlds 216, 220
power fields of academic relationships 207
problem definition, investigation and 209
products to experiences, paradigm shift of 209–10
public anthropology 207
reflexivity 220–21
The Rise of the Creative Class (Florida, R.) 211
Surreal Scania 214–15, 220
text to sensuousness, paradigm shift of 209–10
theory and practice, disjuncture between 211
Association of Internet Researchers (AOIR) 43–4

B
Bateson, Gregory 4
between-ness and the in-between 227–31
abstract theoretical insights, value of 228–9
Africa and America, being between 227–8
applied research, multidisciplinarity and 228
bad faith, Sartre's perspective on 229–30
being, belonging and 227–8
collaborative research 228–9
convention, safe confines of 231
creativity, awakening of 231
existential issues 229
Ibn al-'Arabi, classical Sufi thought of 230
Imaginative Horizons (Crapanzano, V.) 230
indeterminacy 229–30, 231
inspiration, crosswinds of 231
institutional tradition, tranquility of 229–30
liminality 230
scholarly practice, recalibration of 229
sensibilities, sharpening of 231
spaces between things, deep dynamics in 227–31
theory and practice
  applied research and bridge between 228–9
  dynamic interplay between 229
  turbulence of space between 229
West African society, traditions of 227–8
Beyond Behaviour Change (BBC) research programme 9, 170–71
Birth Project 22, 142, 144, 152–3, 154–6, 157–9, 163
  key impacts for 143
  use of film in, interdisciplinary issues 159–62
brokers, role of 15–16
Burrows, Roger 14

C

Center for Collective Intelligence (CCI) at MIT 62
Chicago Public Libraries 193, 195, 199
Clifford, James 31
collaboration in knowledge co-production 16–17, 20–21, 53–71
   academic-industry collaboration, organization of 54, 56–7
   activity and practice, differences and implications 62–4
   activity-based pedagogy 54
   applied cultural analytic research 55
   automagic 53
   automagical structures 60–62, 66
   Center for Collective Intelligence (CCI) at MIT 62
   co-productive potential 54
   co-productive workshop, conceptualization of 55
   collaborative knowledge production 53
   communities of practice 63
   coolness of creativity 58–9
   creative industries, organizational and discursive tendencies in 57–8
   creative workshops, handbooks on arrangements for 59
   To Do: Development of Cultural and Creative Industries in Practice (Linton, A. and Michanek, J.) 59
   idea-generating workshops, automagic of 56–8
   improvisation
      loss of 66–7
      process and 70
   innovation, creativity and 54, 70
   'innovation camp' 57–8, 60, 63–4, 65, 70–71
   innovation process, automagic and 60–62
   innovation support, handbooks on arrangements for 59
   learning by doing 62–3
   The New Production of Knowledge (Gibbons, M.C. et al.) 55
   practice, being out of 66, 68–9
   product-focused workshops, suggested alternative to 71
   'prototype lab' 57–8
   secret researchers, experiences of being 64–9
   situated interaction 63–4
   social dynamics, acknowledgment of 69–70
   social learning processes 59–60
   social level knowledge co-production 55
   social practice
      concept of 62
      development of 66
   working life, transformations of 58
   workshop methods 54
      development of 69–70
   workshops as sites for 'cool' encounters 58–60
collaborations with non-academic organizations, need for 15
Common Sense Media 192, 199, 202n5
Communities of Practice (Wenger, E.) 8
Complex, Clever and Cool (CCC) project 40–41
connections 15–17
conversation analysis 8
conversation analysis, CARM and 21, 73–92

best-practice interview
  protocols 79
'blue skies' *versus*
  'interventionist' research 77
caller to client studies 83–6
communication training 78–82
communicative encounters,
  training for and assessment
  of 79
conversation analysis
  application and 76–7
  basic aim of 74
  criticisms of 75, 76
  implications of 78–9
  theoretical underpinnings of
    73–4, 74–6
  traditional social science
    approach, rejection of
    75–6
Conversation Analytic Role-
  play Method (CARM) 74,
  81–2, 82–90, 91–2
  from caller to client 83–6
  interactional nudge 86–90
discussion, implications and
  91–2
domestic activities,
  reenactments of 77
ethnomethodological theory
  73
everyday talk 74
guidance 80, 81, 91
  for communication 81–2
  recommendations and 79
impartiality 84
institutional talk 74
interactional nudge 86–90
interview extracts 79–80, 80,
  84–5, 85–6, 87–8, 88–90
Justice Ministry (UK) 90
language, ethnomethodology
  and 75
mediation, procedural
  explanations of 86
oral communication
  competencies 79
parental involvement in
  decision making 81
qualitative analysis 75
simulations 73–4, 78, 81, 91–2
social interaction, systematicity
  in 77
social life as it happens 74–5
Superior Court Alternative
  Dispute Resolution Service
  (US) 90
tacit knowledge 79
talk, routinized and systematic
  nature of 77
Crapanzano, Vincent 230
cultural and social theory,
  scholarship on 5

D
Dewey, John 62–3, 231
Digital Media and Learning (DML)
  Community 190, 195–8, 200
Digital Youth Network 193, 194, 195
disciplinary boundaries, working
  across 11–12
*Doing Anthropology for Consumer
  Research* (Sutherland, P. and
  Denny, R.) 128

E
Economic and Social Research
  Council (ESRC) 13
Energy and Digital Living 124, 132,
  138
Energy and Digital Living website
  44–5
ethics 13–15, 17–18, 19–20, 29–47
  anonymity, visual research
    methods and 35
  Anthropology by the Wire
    project 45
  applied research 29
  approaches and ethics in
    42–5

design and digital mobility 31
Association of Internet Researchers (AOIR) 43–4
attribution scenarios 34
audit cultures 33–4
certainties, aim of creation of 36
Civil Contingencies 38
Complex, Clever and Cool (CCC) project 40–41
cross-disciplinary anticipation of 39–42
design practice, design anthropology interface and 37
digital research methods and 43–4
embodied experience and 35
empathetic understandings and 35
Energy and Digital Living website 44–5
ethical practice, institutions and governance of 29–30
ethics procedures, 'layering' in 39–40, 41–2
ethics review boards, interpretive discretion of 34–5
ethnographic filmmaking 32
ethnographic research locales and mobilities, shifts in 31
FabPod Futures research project 43
future-making processes 37
future-oriented applied research 38–9, 45–6
futures, imagination of 32–3
human geographers, work of 37–8
institutional anxieties 36
institutional ethical approval processes 34–5, 36–7
interdisciplinary projects, imagining the future in 32–3
International Visual Sociology Association 42
internet research and 43–4
Low Effort Energy Demand Reduction (LEEDR) 39–40, 41, 43, 44–5
National Centre for Research Methods 42
occupational safety and health (OSH) regulation 38, 41
open-ended collaborations, improvisation and 29
participants in research, responsibilities to 36
personas 37
processual ethics, potential for 45–7
researcher anxieties 36
sensory perception and 35
situated ethics, concept of 35, 41, 43
social relations, ethics in advance and 34
synchronic suspension in ethnographic present 31
technologies of the self 35–6
temporalities, issues of 32, 43
'truth,' uncertainty about question of 31–2
uncertainty and 30–33
visual disciplines, conceptualization of ethics across 42–3
Visual Research Collaboratory (University of Melbourne) 42
ethnographic ground-up working 14
ethnographic methodology 5
ethnographic-theoretical dialogue in applied anthropology 4–5, 10
European context 13
everyday life, complexity of 14

The Experience Economy: Work is Theater and Every Business a Stage (Pine, J. and Gilmore, J.) 211–12
expertise, location of 14

F
FabPod Futures research project 43
facilitators, role of 15–16
Ferguson, Annie 43
Flexit programme 12–13
Flow: The Psychology of Optimal Experience (Csikszentmihalyi, M.) 211
Fortun, Kim 131

G
Gilmore, James 211
grand theories 10

H
Hanging Out, Messing Around, and Geeking Out (HOMAGO) 24–5, 189–202
   Aboriginal art 200
   academia as regime of value 201–2
   applied research practice, undervaluation of 201
   Chicago Public Libraries 193, 195, 199
   collaborative research, importance of 189
   Common Sense Media 192, 199, 202n5
   Digital Media and Learning (DML) Community 190, 195–8, 200
   Digital Youth Network 193, 194, 195
   Digital Youth project 192–3
   engagement, importance of 202
   Entertainment Technology Center (Carnegie Mellon University) 193
   evidence-based theory of practice 200
   'experiential' and 'exploratory learning theory' 197
   'geeking out' 191, 194–5
   Hive Learning Networks 195–6, 197, 198, 200, 203n11
   impact agendas 189, 197–8
   innovative knowledge cultures 189–90
   interest-driven genres 191
   knowledge brokers and translators, role of 189–90
   MacArthur Foundation 190, 192, 193, 199, 202n3
   Mozilla Foundation 195–6
   MySpace to HipHop (Stanford University) 192, 202n3
   origin story 190–91
   participation, genres of 190, 194
   partnership agendas 189
   in practice 192–5
   practice-based settings 189, 192–5
   regimes of value in social life of 198–201, 201–2
   research 'for research's sake' 201
   Rethinking Mentorship (iRemix) 194
   social life of 189–202
   social networking 190, 191, 192, 203n9
   socialization 190–91
   space creation, importance of commitment to 196–7
   Teaching Tech-savvy Kids (Corwin Press) 192–3
   'tenure-clock' 199
   translations 192–3, 198, 199, 200
   value, regimes of 198–201
   Yollocalli Arts Reach 196–7

YOUmedia programme space 193–4, 194–5, 197–8, 199–201, 202–3n8
Higher Education Funding Council for England (HEFCE) 14
Hive Learning Networks 195–6, 197, 198, 200, 203n11
Hogan, Susan 9–10
Humanities, Arts and Social Science (HASS) disciplines 169, 171

I
Ibn al-'Arabi, classical Sufi thought of 230
Imaginative Horizons (Crapanzano, V.) 230
impact, drive for 6, 7, 12, 13–15
impact systems, critique of 14–15
innovative applied interventions, creation of 21–2, 97–115
    abstracted rules, gap between lived realities and 99–100
    anthropological commitments 113
    anthropological ethnography, development of 97–8
    anthropology of knowing 105–6
    applied organizational ethnography 108
    applied-theoretical scholarship, learning from 114–15
    article writing as probe of creatively between theory and ethnography 109
    communities of practice, notion of 111–12
    Construction Skills Certification Scheme (CSCS, UK) 105
    ethnographic materials, reporting on 112–13
    ethnographic-theoretical dialogue 98, 100, 101–2, 107–10, 112

flows, concept of 104–7
Health and Safety Executive (HSE, UK) 99
health care fieldwork 108
hygiene practices, ambiguities of 110
improvising towards safety, concept of 113
inevitability 113–14
Institution for Occupational Safety and Health (IOSH) 98, 105
interdisciplinary context 102–7
interventional ethnographic techniques 107–8
interventions, applied anthropology and crafting of 100
Knowing in Organisations (Nicolini, D. et al.) 104
knowledge flows, notion of 103, 107–8, 113
Labour Force Survey 99
material substances, use of 110
movement, concept of 106
Networked Systems of Production or Service Delivery 98, 101
occupational safety and health (OSH) 21, 98, 99–102, 104–7, 107–10, 111–14
    dominant perspectives in, challenges to 106–7
    ethnographic insights on learning about 111
    OSH knowledge 103–4
    rejection of the concept of OSH flow 108
    as research field 99–102
organization studies 98–9
participatory feedback 109
perception, concept of 106
phenomenological anthropology 105–6
place, concept of 106

practical problems, theoretical engagement with 102
re-enactment techniques 108
regulatory procedures, compliance with 100
relationality 113
representational work 108–9
research concepts, emergent findings in conversation with 108–9
research questions, critical interrogation of 102–3
Safety-I perspective 100–101
Safety-II perspective 100, 113–14
safety practice, tensions in 99
situated learning, notion of 111–12
technicalities and aesthetics of research writing 98–9
theory building, practice-based insights and 101
workarounds, notion of 113
working between disciplinary perspectives 111–14
institutional context 12–15
interdisciplinarity 7–12, 144–6
aspects for consideration 162–3
defining characteristics of 144–5, 146
interdisciplinary collaboration between social and technological sciences 136
interdisciplinary connections 121
interdisciplinary energy research project 122
interdisciplinary engagement, theoretical innovation and 135–6
revisionary argument about 135
sensory ethnography as route to 134–6
supradisciplinarity, interdisciplinarity or 150
see also sensory video ethnography research, interdisciplinarity in
interdisciplinary or multidisciplinary work 22–3, 142–63
agonistic antagonistic mode of interdisciplinary collaboration 151–2
art elicitation 142, 144, 152, 158–9, 160, 163
art making, ontological nature of 159
arts in research 143–4
artwork, kinaesthetic properties and 156–7
Birth Project 22, 142, 144, 152–3, 154–6, 157–9, 163
key impacts for 143
use of film in, interdisciplinary issues 159–62
changes over time, images and 155–6
crossdisciplinarity 149
disciplinary discourses 145
disciplinary norms, translation of 143
disciplines, exploration of synergies between 144
discourse, notion of 145
editing film 161
embodied knowledge, images and exploration of 156–7
empathetic understanding, images and 155
English literature 145
ethics 161
experiences, reconceptualising of 159
expert healer and patient, dichotomy between 142
exposition, modes of 144

film as research data, notion of use of 159–60
generalizability, images and 155
Higher Education Funding Council for England Research Excellence Framework (HEFCE REF) 161
image making, vitalization through 158–9
images
 comprehensibility of 156
 expressiveness of 153–4
 memorability of 155
ineffable ideas, pictures and exploration of 152
infographics 154
innovative ideas, images and attentiveness to 154–5
integration, notion of 146
interdisciplinarity 144–6
 aspects for consideration 162–3
 defining characteristics of 144–5, 146
interdisciplinary approaches
 classification of 151
 refreshment through 145–6
megadisciplinarity 150
methodological orientations 143
Mothers Make Art Group 159
multidisciplinarity 147–8
participants, protection of 160–61
participation 146
 participatory expression and aesthetic ideals, tensions between 144
permission forms 160–61
power and control, locus of 144
psychological expression 145
reframing of film material 161–2
social justice, images and actions for 156
supradisciplinarity, interdisciplinarity or 150
transdisciplinarity 148
visual methods
 benefits of 152–9
 conceptual divides and 145
 working across disciplines 143
 approaches to, Lattuca's views 151
 modes of 146–50
visual methods, discussion on use of 150–52
intervention, ethics of 17–18

K
Keats, John 231
Knowing in Organisations (Nicolini, D. et al.) 104
Knowledge Foundation 210–11, 212
Knowles, Caroline 14
Kozinets, Rob 8

L
Low Effort Energy Demand Reduction (LEEDR) 39–40, 41, 43, 44–5, 123, 124–5, 132, 133

M
MacArthur Foundation 190, 192, 193, 199, 202n3
Mead, Margaret 4
Miller, Daniel 13–14
Mitchell, Jon 13, 18
Mothers Make Art Group 159
MySpace to HipHop (Stanford University) 192, 202n3

N
national contexts 6, 12, 29
Netnography (Kozinets, R.) 8

Networked Systems of Production or Service Delivery 98, 101
The New Production of Knowledge (Gibbons, M.C. et al.) 55

O
occupational safety and health (OSH) 21, 98, 99–102, 104–7, 107–10, 111–14
    dominant perspectives in, challenges to 106–7
    ethics, regulation and 38, 41
    ethnographic insights on learning about 111
    Institution for Occupational Safety and Health (IOSH) 98, 105
    OSH knowledge 103–4
    rejection of the concept of OSH flow 108
    as research field 99–102
O'Dell, Tom 8

P
partnered research, gaining traction on positivist assumptions 23–4, 169–85
    bathing and laundering, quantification of 178–9
    benchmarking 175, 180
    Beyond Behaviour Change (BBC) research programme 170–71
    comparing something else 179–81
    comparison, benchmarking and 175
    compromise, challenging assumptions and 184–5
    control groups, preoccupation with 180
    counting (can't count-doesn't count) 175
    counting something different 177–9
    data, representativeness of 179
    data collection, quantification by 177–8
    risks in 178
    dataset comparison 180–81
    demographics 175
    difference, research and making 170
    embedded partnerships, development of 169
    energy demand, measurement of 178
    gaining traction 171
    strategies for 177–84
    Humanities, Arts and Social Science (HASS) disciplines 169, 171
    input-output assumptions 182
    interdependency and complexity 181–2
    intervention, challenging assumptions as 184–5
    knowledge, generation of 174
    knowledge brokers 185
    materials in everyday life, understanding role of 170–71
    neoliberal research environment 170
    partnership
        appeasement of partners 180
        outcomes of, agreement on 172–3
        partnering up 172–7
        uneven playing fields for 169–70
        working with partners 171
    people focus 176
    positivist assumptions 172, 174, 179
    positivist traditions and agendas, domination of 170
    practice perspective 173–4
    problems, reduction of 175

provocative personas,
  development of 182–4
qualitative methods 174
reality, knowledge of 176
research, positioning of 172
Resource Man 183–4
role in challenging
  assumptions,
  conceptualizations of 184–5
scaling up 176
Science, Technology,
  Engineering and
  Mathematics (STEM)
  disciplines 169, 171, 172
segmentation 176
showcasing complexity and
  interdependency through
  practice 181–2
social life studies,
  epistemological and
  methodological assumptions
  175–6
social practice, theories of 174
strategy of challenge to
  assumptions 184
subcontracted social data
  providers, social researchers
  as 169–70
theoretical orientation 173
transparency, importance of
  185
partnership
  appeasement of partners 180
  embedded partnerships,
    development of 169
  Hanging Out, Messing
    Around, and Geeking Out
    (HOMAGO) 189
  outcomes of, agreement on
    172–3
  partnering up 172–7
  uneven playing fields for
    169–70
  working with partners 171
Pels, Peter 34

People, Objects and Resources
  across Time and Space (PORTS)
  134
Pine, Joseph 211
Possible Worlds 216, 220
Prendiville, Alison 32

R
Rethinking Mentorship (iRemix) 194
The Rise of the Creative Class (Florida,
  R.) 211
Royal Institution 8

S
Sartre, Jean-Paul 229–30
Science, Technology, Engineering
  and Mathematics (STEM)
  disciplines 169, 171, 172
sensory video ethnography
  research, interdisciplinarity in 22,
  121–38
  analytic attention, (re)framing
    of 133–4
  analytically informed texts 131
  applied sensory ethnography
    124–7
  applied visual anthropology
    137
  bridging concepts 136
  coherence between theories
    121
  conceptual limits 122
  design data 125
  *Doing Anthropology for
    Consumer Research*
    (Sutherland, P. and Denny,
    R.) 128
  emplaced knowledge 127
  Energy and Digital Living 124,
    132, 138
  energy monitoring data
    psychological models and
    129
  relationship between video
    materials and 128

energy research project, interdisciplinarity in 122, 124–8
ethnographic fieldwork, design for 126
ethnographic-theoretical dialogue 122
ethnographic-theoretical relationships 131
everyday routines, re-enactment of 126
findings, communication of 133
flow, theme of 131, 132
home video tours 126
images to words, translation of 130
interdisciplinarity
  revisionary argument about 135
  sensory ethnography as route to 134–6
interdisciplinary collaboration between social and technological sciences 136
interdisciplinary connections 121
interdisciplinary energy research project 122
interdisciplinary engagement, theoretical innovation and 135–6
intuition 122
knowing, engagement with ways of 123
Low Effort Energy Demand Reduction (LEEDR) 123, 124–5, 132, 133
movement, theme of 131–2
multi-layered analysis 124
narrative portraits 130
non-verbal knowledge, video and 128
People, Objects and Resources across Time and Space (PORTS) 134
phenomenological detail 127
politics 123
post-energy monitoring 126–7
reflexivity, need for 122
relationalities and in-betweens of disciplines, interweaving of 137–8
Research Council (UK) 125
research materials 123
senses, attending to 123–4
sensory environments, experiences of 132–3
sensory-ethnographic practice 122–3
sensory ethnography approach
  characteristics of 129–30
  exploratory benefits of 137
serendipity 122
sharing sensory ethnography 127–33
sociocultural texture 128
time-stamping of audio-visual recordings 128
Transition Pathways 122
transparency of meaning 128
video-based sensory ethnography 124
video materials, characteristics of 129
Writing Culture (Clifford, J. and Marcus, G.) 131
Sinanan, Jolynna 13–14
Starn, Orin 14
Stokoe, Elizabeth 8
Strathern, Marilyn 34
Strengers, Yolande 9, 11–12, 17–8
Surreal Scania 214–15, 220
Swedish Foundation for Humanities and Social Sciences 12–13

T

Teaching Tech-savvy Kids (Corwin Press) 192–3

theoretical scholarship, relationship between applied practice and 3, 5–6
theory and practice
    applied research and bridge between 228–9
    disjuncture between 211
    dynamic interplay between 229
    evidence-based theory of practice 200
    theory building, practice-based insights and 101
    turbulence of space between 229
To Do: Development of Cultural and Creative Industries in Practice (Linton, A. and Michanek, J.) 59

W
Wenger, Etienne 8
Writing Culture (Clifford, J. and Marcus, G.) 131

Y
Yollocalli Arts Reach 196–7
YOUmedia programme space 193–4, 194–5, 197–8, 199–201, 202–3n8

www.ingramcontent.com/pod-product-compliance
Lightning Source LLC
Chambersburg PA
CBHW070920030426
42336CB00014BA/2468